# Getting A Winning Verdict In My Personal Life

## *A Trial Lawyer Finds His Soul*

# *J. Gary Gwilliam*

Pavior Publishing
Walnut Creek California

ISBN: 978-1-4243-4283-9


Library of Congress Cataloging-in-Publication Data

Gwilliam, J. Gary.
  Getting a winning verdict in my personal life : a trial lawyer finds his soul / J. Gary Gwilliam.
    p. cm.
  ISBN 978-1-4243-4283-9
  1. Gwilliam, J. Gary. 2. Lawyers--California--Biography. 3. Adult children of alcoholics--California--Biography. 4. Alcoholics--California--Biography. I. Title.
  CT275.G94A3 2007
  979.4'053092--dc22
  [B]
                                        2007022264



Pavior Publishing
Walnut Creek, California

If you are unable to order this book from your local bookseller you may order directly from our website www.pavior.com

# Dedication

To couragous, dedicated and caring trial lawyers everywhere and to all  those who support them.

And to my soul mate, Lilly, who gives me constant support, love and inspiration.

# PRAISE FOR
## "GETTING A WINNING VERDICT IN MY PERSONAL LIFE: A TRIAL LAWYER FINDS HIS SOUL"

"This book is a page-turning, passionate, life-affirming journey with one of America's most gifted trial lawyers. His rare combination of soul-baring humility and powerful competence enables him to share both the personally tragic and the publicly triumphant events of his life. Unlike most public figures, he doesn't need or want to be thought of as perfect—because he knows that none of us are. I feel more at peace for having read his book and blessed to call Gary my friend."
> *—Leo Boyle, past president of American Association for Justice*

"Gary Gwilliam is a man of many dimensions whom I have had the pleasure of knowing and admiring for many years. With the early days of his life sealed by his family life unraveling, alcohol abuse, and poor behavior, he was presented with a choice. He chose the right way but also the tough way. He truly deserves his place in the sunlight of success after his walk through the valley of death. He is one of the great trial lawyers in this country. Equally important, he has overcome the disease of alcoholism and carries that message wherever it will help. Gary has openly shared his life experiences in seminars where I was a panelist sharing my experiences with alcohol. This book is inspirational, enjoyable, and well written."
> *—Edwin Train Caldwell, founder of The Other Bar, past president of San Francisco Trial Lawyers Association and recipient of the Lifetime Achievement Award*

*"Winning Verdict* is a remarkably open and honest life story about a trial lawyer's journey through life, including his successful battle with alcoholism. This book will cause you to reflect on your own life. You will be astounded at the evolution and growth of this incredibly sensitive and thoughtful man who overcame adversity to become both a great trial lawyer and strong leader in the legal profession in a time of profound crisis."

—*David S. Casey, Jr., past president of American Association for Justice and Consumer Attorneys of California*

"This intensely personal book takes the reader on a spiritual journey with a very insightful view in the life of a real warrior for justice. This is the story of a lawyer who overcame alcohol abuse and other demons to become a strong and respected leader in the California legal profession. Gary shares the lessons he learned on his journey—lessons that are profound and insightful, lessons that provide a positive life roadmap."

—*Joseph W. Cotchett, nationally recognized trial lawyer from California*

"This book is a courageous and soul searching account of an amazing journey. I lived part of that journey with Gary and could not admire him more for it. It is unusual for someone to have both the journey and the ability to tell the story in such a page turning way. His message is important. It needs to be read."

—*Laurence E. Drivon, past president of the Consumer Attorneys of California*

"Gary Gwilliam does the unthinkable for a trial lawyer. Trained by his profession to hide weakness and attack the vulnerability of others in an effort to win, Gary violates this by exposing his weaknesses, limitations, and concerns to the entire world. By acknowledging his faults and flaws, he demonstrates his true wisdom and insight by leading us on a journey that is all too often ignored. He uses himself as the example, teaching how to embark on the journey that is necessary to undertake to achieve success in life."

— *Jeffrey M. Goldberg, past president of Public Justice Foundation*

"Gary Gwilliam has revealed new reasons for the affection and respect I feel for him as a trial lawyer and as a man. Never have I read a book so revealing about the personal and professional struggles of dealing with the demons and defeats, as well as the victories, of a long and successful life. *Winning Verdict* is Gary's greatest verdict and hopefully, it will be our greatest verdict as well. This book is a must read for everyone."

— *Browne Greene, past president of Consumer Attorneys of Los Angeles and Consumer Attorneys of California*

"In this remarkable book, Gary Gwilliam describes in elegant detail his hard-fought triumph over the sort of demons that plague many of us and his ultimate victory in emerging as a top-flight attorney. Gary shines as the quintessential trial lawyer, a man whose humanity bursts through while he works endlessly to obtain justice for those victimized by the misconduct and negligence of some of the country's most powerful interests. America desperately needs trial lawyers like Gary who hold wrongdoers accountable. This engrossing book will leave you inspired and amazed by the strength of the human spirit."

>    — *Jon Haber, CEO, American Association for Justice*

"Unlike most lawyers, who rarely talk or write about their courtroom defeats, Gary Gwilliam not only talks about them, but begins this book by describing one of his most crushing and disappointing losses at trial. He shares the lessons he learned from that and other professional experiences, but this is not just a book written by a lawyer for other lawyers. Instead, it is a no-holds-barred, intensely personal autobiography in which Gary discusses not just his legal work, but also reflects on all aspects of his life—from his Mormon upbringing and former gang affiliation to his rise as a prominent trial attorney while battling alcohol abuse and other personal demons. I highly recommend this immensely readable and enjoyable book, particularly to anyone who understands that life's pressures sometimes demand personal sacrifices."

>    — *The Honorable Thelton E. Henderson, Judge, United*
>    *States District Court, Northern District of California,*
>    *San Francisco*

"Gary demonstrates for all of us the one unassailable truth: To win in trial, as in life, one must face the unvarnished truth about oneself. I have had a ringside seat for the last thirty-five years. I can assure you that Gary doesn't have an inauthentic bone in his body. In this book, he has the courage to reveal his own personal journey without trying to look good in the process. I don't know too many trial lawyers who can say the same."

—*Eric Ivary, California mediator and long-time friend and law partner of Gary Gwilliam*

"Gary Gwilliam's story is a compelling tale of self-disclosure and personal growth. The simple sincerity of his friendly voice keeps you turning pages. He is a role model for what is good and right about lawyers. This book is filled with lessons for everyone, but especially for lawyers and their clients. If you need a champion, you can find a template of what to look for in this book!"

—*Stewart L. Levine, Esq. author of* Getting to Resolution: Turning Conflict Into Collaboration *and* The Book of Agreement: 10 Essential Elements for Getting the Results You Want

"What is at the core of a successful trial lawyer? Gary's journey reveals the truth and honesty that we can all bring to our lives and share with those around us. As a declaration of personal freedom, he turns all of his failures into successes. This book is a must read for any lawyer."

—*Maryanne Murphy, past president of the Santa Clara Trial Law yers Association*

"Gary Gwilliam shows that he has received a winning verdict, both inside and outside of the courtroom. Gary is an inspirational leader, a cagey lawyer, and most of all, a flawed but flourishing man. This book leads us on the journey of life step-by-step with Gary, providing

insight into the character of a complex man who also happens
to be a very successful trial attorney. The human element draws
the reader in as Gary provides a powerful tale of the successes he
garnered in his professional life which were equally matched by
the struggles he faced in his personal life. Gary has an astound-
ing amount of courage and humility to expose his innermost self
to the world through this book. The life lessons in this story are
relevant to everyone. Lawyer or not, we can all aspire to the deep
commitment Gary has made towards the principles of personal
growth and spirituality."

*—Peter Perlman, past president of the American Associa-*
*tion for Justice the Public Justice Foundation*

"All things happen for a reason, including this book. Gary Gwilliam gives a sobering account of his life journey in the pages of
this book. Poignant, insightful, and humorous, *Winning Verdict*
is filled with the kind of wisdom that only comes from experience. Gary tells his story with authenticity and integrity because
he is a man who truly is in touch with his inner self, indeed his
inner soul. We all are a product of our past, and Gary is no different. He examines his past and by doing so, he gains a deeper
understanding of himself and humanity, as do we. Gary's spiritual journey inspires us to let go of the fear in our own life and
reinforces the truth: Love is the answer."

*—Michael M. Reyna, Chief Executive Director, Consumer*
*Attorneys of California*

"There are few books that so explode with energy, emotion, insight, and deep feelings that they immediately impact the life of the reader. Gary Gwilliam's book is one of them. Somehow, this extraordinary advocate (and author) has grasped the true meaning of life and teaches us the lessons that he has learned in a way that enables us understand his feelings and desire for spiritual meaning in his life. Gary's book is fun, action-packed, and will jump-start every one of your emotions. *Winning Verdict* is the only book I have ever read where the author has me crying and laughing, all in the same paragraph."

  —*John F. Romano, past president of Academy of Florida Trial Lawyers*

"The stereotype of lawyers is that of implacable sharks, ever ready to slash all who get in their way, but Gary Gwilliam proves the falsity of this perception. In *Winning Verdict*, Gary takes the reader behind the scenes revealing the passion and dedication that motivate him and other advocates for justice. Gary's warmth and courage to expose his own personal struggles vividly illustrates why the law can be a profoundly noble calling."

  *Wesley J. Smith, co-author with Ralph Nader of No Contest: Corporate Lawyers and the Perversion of Justice in America*

"It is not unusual for successful lawyers to recount all of their court cases they have won by their brilliance. However, I do not ever remember any lawyers giving a lifelong account of their search for their soul. However, Gary Gwilliam has done just this in his book *Winning Verdict*, detailing his spiritual quest for us on paper. How someone can be both qualified to share what he learned on his spiritual journey as well as his wins in the courtroom will seem quite remarkable to you, as it did to me.

*—Frederick Sontag, Robert C. Denison Professor of Philosophy, Pomona College, California*

# FOREWORD

Gary Gwilliam has experienced life through many filters, from the view of a gang member, salesperson, and carefree frat boy, to a respected prosecutor, all of which give him a unique perspective. In this book, he bares his soul as he takes the reader through his painful losses and personal grief in growing from a reckless teen to an authoritative trial lawyer. How does a person change from an irresponsible youth, heavy drinker, and drug user, virtually written off by society, to someone who has achieved great success in his personal and professional life? Gary's book takes the reader through these stages in a memorable fashion.

Gary's exploits as a wild and reckless youth make entertaining reading. Stories about his early employment experiences picking fruit with migrant workers, washing windows, and delivering telegrams mesmerize the reader. His early work in sales taught him how to persuade a jury and become a successful trial lawyer.

Gary explains his radical shift from a staunch political conservative to a leader in progressive causes. He describes the metamorphosis of his social life, from a partying womanizer to someone who searched for and succeeded in finding his true soul mate. He gives inspiring accounts of some of the difficult legal battles he has won. He fought initiatives that would have unfairly limited the power of lawyers to exact justice through our judicial branch of government. His leadership within the California Trial Lawyers Association to fight tort reform sponsored by the insurance industry is an engaging example of his persistence in working toward goals that he believes in. In this battle, he and the association attained a win against great odds.

Reading this book has changed my perception of what it takes to be a good attorney and a successful trial lawyer. As a psychology professional, I find Gary Gwilliam's story fascinating on levels that go beyond his individual triumphs and setbacks. I am especially curious as to how early life experiences contribute to the making of a man.

How might his path have been different if Gary had a strong father figure in his life? Were Gary's gang and hard-partying fraternity memberships ways of gaining the male bonding that he craved?

The certainty of his mother's unconditional love gave Gary the feeling that, "I could do whatever I wanted" because she would love him regardless. Gary's story supports single mothers by demonstrating that the lack of a father figure may not necessarily be bad. The influence of women in Gary's life has led him to the vision of law that he holds today. Gary clearly embraces the fact that women are now entering the legal profession in progressively larger numbers. He sees them changing the way that we resolve conflicts—through mediation between non-adversaries rather than as combatants in costly court battles.

Stories about lawyers rarely include God. However, Gary persuasively points out that lawyers are not soulless machines but vulnerable human beings who often try difficult cases while they struggle with issues in their personal lives. Gary states that our personal battles are the ones that take the most out of us and, in the end, matter most.

Gary offers many insightful lessons learned during his

years of winning and losing: "We try to wrestle control over the little things, but the older you get, the more you realize that most of them didn't really matter. . . You do your best and turn the results over to a Higher Source." Gary's relinquishing of control has helped him to take a negative verdict less personally.

Gary's attitude is best summarized by his view that in life we all have to deal with the pain of losing. Since winning rarely permanently changes your life, neither should losses destroy it. While people, especially lawyers, rarely express this point, Gary's conviction is clear: "Real winners learn primarily from losing."

Gary relates the role of spirituality in his life. I was deeply moved by how his belief in a Higher Source has helped him through battles in both the courtroom and his personal life, and especially in his struggle against alcoholism. Gary shows the reader things most lawyers wouldn't mention: his search for his soul mate, experiences with past lives, and his belief in an afterlife.

In his chapter "Changes and Challenges" Gary relates his inspiring search for truth through spiritual understanding. Gary brings spirituality, love, and the presence of divine intervention into his personal encounters, while acknowledging that understanding these principles and trying to live them is not easy.

The legal profession is important to our democracy because it enables us to bring our disputes to court for settlement rather than to a battlefield. Courtrooms often appear to be battlefields with jury trials seen as fights between two combatants looking for a kill. This attitude puts enormous stress on the attorneys. Gary explains how he relieves this stress by viewing it in a new way—accepting what you can and cannot control. He reduces emotional stress by viewing a trial not as a win-lose battle between gladiators, but as a challenge in creative expression and communication. It is an impartial play where the lawyers and witnesses are the actors and the jury is the audience that decides whose play it likes best, that of the prosecution or the defense.

Gary has come to see lawsuits as more than just about money. It is equally important for the client to know that somebody cares. There needs to be a look at the whole person, which has prompted the rise of an organization of holistic lawyers of which Gary is a member.

These are just some of the themes and issues that Gary brings to light in this candid and inspirational book. Explore them with him, and you will never see a courtroom in the same light. You will gain an understanding of what it means to be a trial lawyer. You will become aware of how and where the spiritual dimension might operate in your own life—in particular, where you might least expect it.

Ernest F. Pecci, M.D.
May, 2007

I am a trial lawyer. I spent over forty years in courtrooms listening to witnesses swear to tell the truth under oath. Sometimes they have and sometimes they haven't.

Everything in this book is the truth, the whole truth, and nothing but the truth. I do so swear.

# TABLE OF CONTENTS

PRAISE.................................................................5

FORWARD ...........................................................13

TABLE OF CONTENTS .........................................19

**PART ONE:**

CHAPTER 1: THE VERDICT .....................................25

CHAPTER 2: MOM, THE MORMONS, AND THE

MATRIARCHS....................................................29

CHAPTER 3: WHAT'S A REAL FATHER?.................36

CHAPTER 4: FIRST EXPERIENCES..........................41

CHAPTER 5: TURKS ..............................................45

CHAPTER 6: MAN MOST LIKELY TO SUCCEED....59

CHAPTER 7: JELLY.................................................72

CHAPTER 8: SUPER SALESMAN .............................86

CHAPTER 9: HAVE YOU EVER THOUGHT OF

BEING A LAWYER? .............................88

CHAPTER 10: THE DRY WEDDING ........................92

CHAPTER 11: LOOK TO YOUR LEFT, LOOK TO

YOUR RIGHT ......................................95

CHAPTER 12: MR. DISTRICT ATTORNEY ..............99

CHAPTER 13: ALL FOUR OF THEM DIED ............104

CHAPTER 14: RABIES...........................................107

CHAPTER 15: BECOMING A TRIAL LAWYER......112

CHAPTER 16: LIZ..................................................118

**PART TWO:**

CHAPTER 17: GWILLIAM & IVARY........................126
CHAPTER 18: R-O-L-A-I-D-S...................................128
CHAPTER 19: BURNING OUT IN THE
                FAST LANE ........................................132
CHAPTER 20: INTERVENTION ..............................143
CHAPTER 21: THE ENVELOPE, PLEASE ..............149
CHAPTER 22: CHANGES AND CHALLENGES......159
CHAPTER 23: FIRST, LET'S KILL ALL THE
                LAWYERS..............................................168
CHAPTER 24: LESSONS FROM LOSING...............180
CHAPTER 25: LEAVING LIZ...................................192
CHAPTER 26: A PREDICTION COMES TRUE........205
CHAPTER 27: A COMMITMENT CEREMONY
                AND A BIRTHDAY WEDDING........221

**PART THREE:**

CHAPTER 28: SPEAKING ABOUT WHAT'S
                REAL....................................................231
CHAPTER 29: A MEN'S GROUP AND
                WOMEN'S ISSUES ............................244
CHAPTER 30: TRIAL: ART OR SPORT? ..................252
CHAPTER 31: BECOMING A HOLISTIC
                LAWYER...............................................260
CHAPTER 32: GOING IN A NEW DIRECTION.......264
CHAPTER 33: GRIEF, GRIEF, AND
                MORE GRIEF ....................................279

CHAPTER 34: FINDING MY TWO DADS...............291

CHAPTER 35: WHY ME?...........................302

CHAPTER 36: UNCONDITIONAL LOVE
                   IN THE COURTROOM....................311

CHAPTER 37: FIFTY YEARS LATER......................318

EPILOGUE:..................................................323

ACKNOWLEDGEMENTS AND
AUTHOR'S NOTE....................................326

BIBLIOGRAPHY:.......................................331

ASSOCIATIONS: .......................................333

ENDNOTES: ...........................................335

INDEX: ................................................342

# PART ONE

# CHAPTER 1: THE VERDICT

*The jury had reached a decision. My heart pounded like crazy. My emotions ran from excitement to fear to anxiety. What had they decided?*

*It had been the biggest and hardest fought case in my career. It was a trial against General Motors, at the time the biggest corporation in the world.*

*The gas tank in a pickup truck had exploded when a reckless driver crossed the road and hit it. The pickup driver had died. His wife, my client, had lost her eight-month-old fetus and had been burned beyond belief in the fire. Most of her fingers on her right hand had been burned off. She had sued for her injuries and her husband's death. It was a tragic case with huge damage potential.*

*I had been in practice for fifteen years. I was a plaintiffs' lawyer waiting for my biggest verdict. Although I had tried about a hundred jury trials to verdict, most of those were criminal or small-to-medium-sized personal injury cases.*

*The senior partners in my law firm had authorized me, a junior partner, to spend a huge amount of money on the case: $100,000, almost unheard of in 1976. All plaintiffs' lawyers wanted the big million-dollar verdict in those days. I was ready. I thought I had tried a great case.*

*The case had been a big challenge. The only help I had in preparing this case came from my hardworking secretary, Sandra Shaw. There had been no paralegals or associate attorneys working with me. We had settled the case with the driver for his minimal insurance policy but that hadn't done much to help my client, Sandy Staples. If we were going to get her any reasonable compensation for her terrible losses, we were going to have to prove a product liability case against the manufacturer of the 1973 pickup truck in which she had been a passenger.*

*I had sued General Motors contending that the truck's gas tank had been unsafely designed. We claimed that the gas tanks were improperly placed on the sides of the pickup. They hung over the frames in a saddlebag design, unprotected from a side impact. Only the thin aluminum panel on the side of the truck protected the tanks. We had design experts who showed that the pickup could and should have been better-designed to protect the gas tanks from exploding in a collision.*

*Our biggest problem had been the force of the crash. It had been immense. The other driver had been traveling approximately eighty miles per hour when he crossed the center line and hit the left side of the pickup. He, too, had been killed in the crash and both cars were incinerated. General Motors had contended that even a military tank could not have survived the collision. Additionally, they had vigorously disputed whether the gas tank could or should have been designed differently. It had been a battle of the experts. However, I thought I had an excellent chance of winning and I was in great anticipation when the jury finally reached their verdict. I was ready. Ready for my big verdict. Ready to be a hero to my client, my law firm, and the legal community that was watching the case.*

*The jury walked into the courtroom. There were only eleven of them. One of them had been kicked off at my request because she had gone to the library during jury deliberations. I had contended that she was guilty of juror misconduct because she was supposed to decide the case on only the evidence presented in the courtroom. She was a General Motors stockholder and I felt she had been against me. GM had fought hard to keep her on, but I had won that battle. The judge had excused her. The jury had now been deliberating for five days. They announced their decision:* **"We find in favor of the defendant, General Motors, and award the plaintiff nothing . . ."**

I was stunned. I felt as if someone had knocked the wind out of me. I looked over at my client as tears streamed down her sad, scarred face. I tried to be sincere when I congratulated the defense lawyer on his win. Then I tried to console my client. I spoke briefly with the jury foreman who had been one of two jurors who voted for us. He asked me why the judge had thrown out the best juror we had on the jury. I had been totally wrong about her. I had won the battle but lost the war.

I left the courtroom and got into my car. I wanted to die. I didn't want to call the office and tell them the verdict. I didn't want to go home and talk to my wife. What I really wanted to do was find a dark place, all alone, and get roaring drunk. I was full of shame. I felt worthless. I picked up a six-pack of beer and found a quiet spot to drink in my car. The verdict had shaken me to my core.

My first thoughts were about the trial. Where had I gone wrong? How did I misread that juror? What could I have done to win? Soon I began to wonder if anyone could have won that trial. I certainly had done the best I could. Had any jury ever held an automobile manufacturing company liable for an exploding gas tank?[1]

27

*My perspective broadened as I relaxed into my third and fourth beer. I still did not want to call the office. And I did not want to go home. I just wanted to be alone. I began to question who I was. What had led me to this dark, lonely, point in my career? I thought I was a successful young trial lawyer. What made me feel so shamed? I thought about my life. I thought about my ancestry, a long line of Mormons. I thought about my mother who was the dominant person in my life. I had been raised by a matriarchy and a weak stepfather. Was I still trying to prove my manhood by winning tough cases? Was I a weakling because I had lost?*

*Why was I drinking alone in my car? Did it have something to do with my wild youth? Being a tough kid and a gang member? Being part of a wild fraternity? Choosing this macho and difficult career as a trial lawyer? Or did it have to do with the role alcohol played in my family? All of the men in my family had been alcoholics. No, that couldn't be the reason. None of them were educated. I was. I was too smart to be an alcoholic. How wrong that was!*

*No, it was really about Mom. It had always been about her. I was the number one son. Even at forty years old, I still had to prove myself. I wanted to make her proud of me. My dark, shameful feelings came from my upbringing. My family. My ancestry.*

*I needed to dig deep into my life to understand these feelings.*

# CHAPTER 2: MOM, THE MORMONS, AND THE MATRIARCHS

*I sat in my car thinking and drinking. The shame of that courtroom loss had cut to my core. I became philosophical. Where did I come from? Why did I feel this way? What was my life about? What was the purpose of my life? I had to go back to my beginning.*

\* \* \*

I was born a white male to Mormon parents in Ogden, Utah. Each descended from pioneering families who had settled in Northern Utah. As with most Mormons, I have a detailed genealogy of my family history. On my father's side, there were the Gwilliams who came from Wales. They were sheep farmers who immigrated to America in 1836, decided to become Mormons and crossed the plains with Joseph Smith and Brigham Young. I was destined never to know them as well as I knew my mother's family. There was alcohol on that side of the family. A lot of it.

Actually, it was on both sides of my family. My father, my paternal grandfather, my uncle, my grandfather on my mother's side—all of the males in my family were alcoholics. After I later came to love and live with alcohol, I learned that, due to my genetic background, I was eleven times more likely to become an alcoholic. It was to be a lifetime issue for me.

On my mother's side were the matriarchs. They were strong women, ready and willing to get along without the help of men. The women in my life were to be a huge karmic issue that framed many of my life experiences. My mother was a strong, loving mother, the most dominant person in my life. My grandmother, a Mormon pioneer,[2] two strong aunts, four sisters and three daughters framed my life. Women! Women! Women! What did it all mean? I know that I always wanted to please them: my mother, my grandmother, my aunts, and all the other women who passed through my life. Had I failed them all by losing my case, my big case?

Then there was my Mormon ancestry. The most interesting was my great, great-grandfather, William Hickman, known as "Wild Bill" Hickman, one of Brigham Young's bodyguards. He was known to some as the Avenging Angel. He was rough and tough. He protected the Mormon leader and others. He killed and hurt people along the way. We have his diaries to prove it. He had ten wives and twenty-four children. Now that makes for a complicated family tree! An interesting book entitled *"Wild Bill" Hickman and the Mormon Frontier* recounts his unusual life. How was this ancestry to play out in my life? Was it a part of my later self-image as a tough, independent trial lawyer? These were some of the questions I needed to answer.

For me, my destiny was all about my mother. Marion Anderson was born in 1913, a pretty girl from Ogden, the first-born in her family. She was smart and independent. She completed high school as was typical then. She met my father, John "Jack" Gwilliam, a good-looking, intelligent guy who liked to party. So did my mom. Each wanted to escape the oppression of the Mormon community. They were not devout churchgoers and both were ready to break out. Of course, that included drinking. Although forbidden by the church, drinking was widespread among young people in those days.

Their relationship became serious and before long, they married. They still enjoyed partying and drinking. However, when Mom became pregnant, they agreed that they would not drink until the baby was born. Even then, people were concerned about the effect of alcohol on a baby during pregnancy. However, within a very short time, Jack broke their pact and routinely came home after drinking heavily. He was an alcoholic, even in his twenties. Although Mom enjoyed drinking, she stuck to her end of the bargain. However, Jack's alcohol abuse became a serious problem, even before I was born.

My birth went smoothly. I arrived at 12:45 p.m. on May 18, 1937 in Ogden, Utah. My mother oftentimes related how she sat under an apple tree shortly before I was born, thinking about me and how much she loved me. Even before I was born, I was loved. I was always loved. Perhaps loved too much. I knew Mom loved me, and more than anything else, an undying, an unconditional love from my mother permeated my life.

By the time I was two years old, Jack's drinking had increased to the point where it was intolerable. He had lost several jobs because of it. My parents lived in Eugene, Oregon. Mom wondered if she needed to leave the marriage.

One incident motivated Mom to leave Jack. Mom had to run some errands, so she left me at home in Jack's care. That was a mistake. When she returned, she found Jack in the bathroom trying to bathe me. In his drunken state, he was nearly drowning me. That was enough for her! She didn't need this kind of man.

She could make it on her own.

So one day my mother cooked dinner for Jack, left it on the table, and walked out the door with me. Jack tried desperately to win Mom back, but she refused. His rampant alcoholism was out of control. Mom needed to return to the matriarchy.

Thus, while I was still a baby, she returned to Ogden, Utah. For the next year or so, I was raised by my grandmother, my two strong-willed aunts, and a step-grandfather, a nice guy but really just a figurehead in the family. This was a matriarchy at its best. They would protect me. I was the number one son. I could do no wrong.

In Ogden, nobody mentioned my father. It was as if I didn't have a father. At two years old he was banished from my life. But I was happy. The matriarchy lavished attention on me. What did I need a father for? What was a father? When I was three years old, I found out when Mom brought a new man into her life.

My mother's brother, Vincent Anderson married and left Utah to live in Eugene, Oregon. Mom wanted to leave Utah so we moved to Oregon to live with my uncle, Vince.

One day in Eugene, Mom needed some laundry picked up, so she called the local drycleaner. To her surprise, she knew Wayne Ryan, the fellow who showed up to pick up the clothes. Mom and my father had lived in a duplex next door to Wayne and his wife. Now, both Mom and Wayne were divorced. After talking with her, Wayne suggested that they go have a beer together. That started what turned out to be a forty-seven year relationship. In my later years, I always wondered if they had an affair when they lived next door to each other. Both denied it and I think they were honest with me. Anyway, it really doesn't matter. What matters is that he came into my life. Wayne was a stranger to me. Another man was competing with me for my mother's attention. Even at three years of age, I was scared, confused, and afraid of being abandoned by Mom. These feelings were amplified in December 1940 when Mom and Wayne married.

I was three and a half years old. I have an early recollection of the marriage. A picture of me at the wedding ceremony shows a rather forlorn little boy with impetigo on his face. I look lost and miserable, and I was. I didn't want to share my mother. I didn't like the idea of a man moving in with us. Mom assured me it would be okay and I trusted her. She was a matriarch and I was her firstborn son. Wayne wasn't my father and she would ensure that she took charge of my upbringing.

Characteristically of a true matriarch, my mother made a deal with Wayne. She would marry him, but she would raise her son, not him. Wayne really didn't want children, so he easily agreed. I was a quiet, good boy. Wayne's role was to simply be a passive provider. Mom would take care of any discipline and would raise me as though she were a single parent. And that is the way it turned out.

Throughout Mom's life, Wayne and I competed for my mother's love, attention, and affection. A subtle, understated competition existed that was never spoken of, never openly recognized, but always there.

I knew from the earliest memories of my life, well before Mom met Wayne, that I was the number one son. My mother's love for me was unconditional. Nothing could bend it or break it.

But when Wayne moved in with Mom and they began sleeping together, I found myself a bit on the outs.

In the evening, the three of us would often sit in the front room with the radio on. Soon, Wayne would start to touch Mom. He would put his hand up her dress. She would giggle and laugh, and pretty soon the two of them would walk off into the bedroom and shut the door, leaving me alone. I was a good little three-year-old boy so I would sit there and listen to the radio or play a game until they came out. Sometimes, I would just go to bed. I didn't know what was going on, but I knew Wayne was doing something with Mom that left me out. I didn't like it.

I have a vivid recollection of the first time I saw Wayne naked. He slept without any clothes on and would frequently go into the bathroom in the nude. One day, he left the bathroom door open and I walked in and saw him standing there. I was three years old. I had never seen a naked man. I was stunned! Astonished! He had this huge thing hanging between his legs! It didn't seem at all like my little pee-pee. It looked ugly. I wondered if I'd have one of those things when I grew up. In any event, it was threatening.

I didn't understand my competition with and anger toward Wayne when I was young. It wasn't until years later that I took a psychology class and studied Freud's theory of the Oedipus complex, a son's competition with his father. The little boy and the older man competition started early for me and had a lasting effect on my life.

I had one thing to fall back on. I was the number one son. Mom loved me. The strong women in my life loved me. Wayne was an outsider to them. He couldn't displace me. Still,

I was a little boy and he was a full-grown man. Mom returned his affection and seemed to love him. I knew I would have to work awfully hard to keep her attention. I wanted her to be proud of me. I had no idea then how strong that motivation would be and how it would be with me for my lifetime.

Something important happened to me in those formative years. I learned that I could always make my mother happy. She told me that. I was three years old and I believed her. I was the perfect little man, always making Mom happy. Many years later I understood the importance of that conditioning. It was deep in my internal hard drive. I could make women happy. Any woman. Any time. If they weren't happy it wasn't my fault. Something must be wrong with them. Unfortunately, the women in my life turned out not to be as easy to please as Mom.

During those early years I was a classic good boy. I was always around adults and felt very comfortable with them. I didn't have many friends my age. When I was six years old, my mother gave birth to my half sister, Pat. This sister was just another person to take Mom's attention from her number one son, her perfect little man. At six or seven years old, I resented Pat. I wasn't very nice to her in those early years.

\* \* \*

*I sat in my car reflecting on my early childhood. What did these years mean? Why did I feel like I wanted to die just because I had lost a jury trial? I popped open another beer and continued my reflection.*

# CHAPTER 3: WHAT'S A REAL FATHER?

In the early forties, kindergarten wasn't mandatory in Eugene, Oregon. My mother registered me for the first grade under the name of Gary Ryan. That was my name as far as I knew. Wayne hadn't legally adopted me, but Jack was long gone and everybody referred to me as Gary Ryan. Jack never supported me and had virtually no contact with my mother those early years. So what did it matter if I used the name Ryan? Legalities weren't important. The matriarchy would take care of me.

One day everything changed. I was eight years old. Jack Gwilliam had changed. He had reformed. He had stopped drinking, remarried, and started another family. He and five others founded Alcoholics Anonymous in the state of Utah. Now Jack wanted to acknowledge his son. Not to support him, just acknowledge him.

So Mom needed to talk with me. I will **never** forget that discussion. She took me quietly aside. Her face was serious.

"There is something I want to tell you, Gary," Mom said.

"Okay," I replied.

"I need to talk to you about Wayne." *Oh, him.*

"Okay."

"Well, Gary," she continued, "I want to tell you that he is not your real father." *What???*

"What do you mean?" I asked.

"Well," Mom explained, "You have another father who is

your real father and Wayne is what we call your stepfather."

I looked at her, confused, and asked, "What's a real father?" *Pretty good question, I thought. Tough for her to answer.*

"Well, he is the one who brought you into this world," she replied.

I didn't quite get that. Sex education wasn't taught in the second grade. But if Mom said it, then it had to be true.

"So," I asked, "Wayne isn't my real father?"

"No," she replied.

"Good," I said. I wasn't sure what all this meant but I wasn't real happy about this Wayne guy. I never had called him Dad. He was always just Wayne. Then Mom dropped the bomb:

"Your real father wants to meet with you." *Wow, what does that mean?*

"Okay," I responded.

It's hard to remember exactly how I felt, but I know I felt more indifferent than curious. I really didn't want another father. Wayne was problem enough. But soon the meeting was to occur.

We returned to Utah for a typical summer vacation. Jack lived in Ogden. When we arrived we set up a meeting in his office. At the time, he sold insurance and had an office in a downtown building. Mom and I went there to meet with him. I didn't exactly feel fear; I just felt weird. My "real father" had to be better than Wayne. But what did all this mean? It turns out that it didn't mean an awful lot. I met with him in his office and we had one of these stilted conversations that adults have with children. He opened up with:

"Well, hi, Gary, how are you doing?"

"I'm doing okay," I answered.

"Do you like school?" he asked.

"Yeah," I replied.

He continued, "What else do you like?"

"Not much."

And so the conversation went. Very superficial. Very uncomfortable. Very forgettable. I don't know whether it was to answer his curiosity, or whether he was busy with other things in his life, but I only saw him three more times before I turned eighteen.

We returned to Eugene and my life resumed. I attended Condon Grade School through sixth grade. Mom suggested that I needed to change my surname to Gwilliam. What a weird name. Like William with a G in front of it. Ryan was a lot easier. Even though I didn't like Wayne, I didn't want to change my name. I was Gary Ryan. But Mom gently persisted. Finally, by the time I entered the seventh grade, we changed my school records to my real name, John Gary Gwilliam. I hadn't even known I had a different first name. I had always gone by Gary. I guess the matriarchy had wanted to banish Jack's real name, John. I hated the name John. I wanted to stay Gary. So we decided I would go by the name Gary Gwilliam.[3] At least I kept one familiar name. So I went by this new name of my real father, whom I didn't know, but perhaps it was better than the name of my stepfather, whom I did know.

* * *

In the 1940s we lived in Eugene, Oregon near Hayward Field, the football stadium for the University of Oregon. Wayne wasn't making much money working as a drycleaner. He worked for his uncle, Clyde Smith who was a terrible skinflint. At one time, Wayne earned a $100 a month, but after some years, he finally made $100 a week. Even that didn't really support a wife and two kids. By the time my sister entered school and I was about twelve, Mom had one of those life-changing events. She put on what was known as a Stanley Party.

Stanley Home Products were similar to those sold by the Fuller Brush Company, but Stanley sold their products at home parties, much like the later Tupperware Parties. Stanley Parties were a big deal in the Northwest. When a hostess put on a party, she received a gift. Mom held a successful party and earned a nice new lamp. It seemed like an awfully good deal. She enjoyed it and someone suggested that she become a Stanley dealer. Now that her kids were both in school, she thought she would give it a try.

She was an overnight success, booking three parties a day, one on the morning, one in the afternoon, and one in the evening. She kept about one-third of what she sold. So, if Mom sold $100 at a party, she kept about $30 in profit. In those days, $30 bought food for two weeks for a family of four. Twenty-five cents got you into a movie theater and a dime bought a good size candy bar or large popcorn. Another nickel got you a drink.

In no time, Mom was making much more money than

Wayne. So Wayne decided to give up dry-cleaning and join Stanley. He also became a dealer. Both were successful in the late 1940s and early 1950s.

I also helped out with the business. Mom and Wayne would go to a party, sell the products, and come back with order sheets from each person at the party. We would send them in to the company which would send us the products like hairbrushes, mops, cleaning solutions, personal items, etc. It was a pretty good line of products and probably better than in most stores. When the products arrived a couple of weeks later, I would put them together in bags for each person and then we would put the bags into separate boxes for each party. On Saturdays, we would go out and deliver them. I helped Mom do that. I got to know the products well and enjoyed being part of our newfound success. Before long, Stanley promoted Mom to unit manager and we moved to the River Road area, on the outskirts of Eugene. We had new cars and a much nicer house. There wasn't the concern about budgets or money. We had moved out of a rental house and into our own house in suburbia.

* * *

*Those were pretty happy times. As a teenager, I never realized how complicated life can get and how ego involved I could get in my work. Drinking alone in my car after a big loss? But here I was.*

# CHAPTER 4: FIRST EXPERIENCES

I entered Colin Kelly Junior High School and met new friends. I was a teenager' and ready to party. I had a new name. With my new name and new neighborhood came a new me. I was leaving the good little boy behind. I was ready to grow up.

I distinctly remember my first experience with alcohol. The older brother of a friend of mine threw a party while his folks were out. He served alcohol and I tried beer. The moment the alcohol entered my system, I felt good. I felt warm. I felt high. I loved the feeling. I wanted more. If one beer was good, two had to be better. And then three. And then four. Little did I know I was beginning a long and difficult path of loving something that didn't love me back.

I was still a pretty good kid. My friends and I were a little bit on the wild side but not out of the norm. Cars fascinated us. The River Road area in Eugene wasn't terribly developed. There were a lot of gravel roads near where we lived. If we could borrow someone's car, we would cruise around the back roads, learning how to drive and doing a little hot-rodding.

One day I had an unforgettable experience. A buddy of one of my friends drove an old Ford Phaeton convertible. We decided to go out riding on a Sunday afternoon. Two guys sat in the front seat and two friends and I sat in the backseat. We sat up on the trunk area with our feet hanging down inside where we should have been sitting. I sat on the left, behind the driver and we made a lot of noise and yelled as we sped down a gravel road.

We came into an S-curve at a pretty high speed. The three of us in back braced to the right, but were unprepared for the curve back to the left. When the driver whipped the car around the curve, my torso flew out of the car and I fell face first down by the left rear wheel. My right leg went up in the air. Fortunately the friend next to me fell onto my left leg and grabbed me so that I did not completely fall out of the car. But I was dangling helplessly facing the hubcap. Everybody was yelling, but the driver had no idea of my plight and continued to speed along. My hands hung over my head and I could feel the gravel from the road kicking up and hitting them. Twelve inches separated my head from the roadway. The hubcap spun inches from my nose. My life flashed in front of me. *Was I going to die at the age of fifteen?* I half-braced for the fall, but I had no idea what would happen if I fell out of a car traveling so fast. The car sped on down the gravel road for what seemed like an eternity, the longest minute of my life.

At last the driver realized that I was outside the car and finally pulled to a stop. I dropped to the ground and was fortunate that the flying gravel cut only the palms of my hands.

That scare has always stayed with me. As teenagers, we think we are invulnerable. Immortal. I faced my mortality and it scared the hell out of me. However, I escaped with only minor cuts, and maybe that added to my risk-taking attitude. Maybe I was living a charmed life.

It didn't take me long to become seriously interested in girls. I'd been raised around women. I loved them and they loved me. I was a typical horny teenage kid, ready for something more than the so-called "self-pleasuring."

Doesn't everyone remember their first sexual experience? I certainly remember mine. I worked as a busboy in a restaurant. A cute girl, a year older than me, worked as a waitress there. She flirted with me. The problem? Her boyfriend, the star quarterback at the high school and much older and bigger than me. I had to be careful. She seemed ready to take the experience further than flirting in the restaurant. Hormones always get the better of good judgment, especially with teenagers. I was ready to take the risk.

She asked me to come by her house one night after her folks had gone to bed. She said she would sneak out the window. *Great!*

With my folks off at a convention and my sister, sound asleep, I slipped out of my house. I drove to the waitress's house. My heart beat like crazy. With excitement or fear. I didn't know which. Before long, she climbed out the window. We got into my car and drove back to my house. We sneaked into the house and kept the lights off. That was good. We sat on the couch and started necking. Before long, it was obvious that she had more experience than I did. Nevertheless, what I lacked in experience, I made up for in enthusiasm. Anyway, we "went all the way" as we said in those days. It was one of those hard-to-describe, first-time-ever, never-to-be-repeated experiences. In fact, I probably fumbled through the whole thing as first-timers are prone to do. But that didn't matter. I was a man! No longer a virgin. No longer a kid.

When I returned to school the next day, everything seemed different. None of my friends had gone all the way. They were still kids. I was a man and ready for more. I was ready to roll. I liked women and I was sure they liked me. Unfortunately, I didn't realize that, like alcohol, too much can get you in trouble.

In the meantime, my mom was promoted to branch manager of the entire Northwest division. That necessitated our family moving to Seattle, Washington. By then, I was ready to leave small town Eugene and move on to the big city.

\* \* \*

*I continued to sit in my car, licking my wounds and feeling the pain of the jury's verdict. I felt the influence of the alcohol now. Frequently when I drank, I thought back on those teenage years. My wild years.*

# CHAPTER 5: THE TURKS

We moved to Seattle in 1953 and I entered a new high school, Roosevelt High School in northeast Seattle. I didn't know anyone. But I liked to party and I liked to drink, so I wanted to find kids who enjoyed the same. I gravitated towards the kids who smoked and drank and hung out in a couple of little cafés near the school. Some of the kids were dropouts. I met new people and ran around and partied. By then I had a car and little money. Mom and Wayne had their own parties and attended conventions. There was always a lot of drinking around the house. I had a lot of freedom.

My mother loved me deeply. We had a great relationship. Mom almost never disciplined me. In sales she learned about sales techniques and success slogans. *The Power of Positive Thinking*, a book written by Norman Vincent Peale in the 1940s, influenced her. Peale strongly advocated the belief that you can be whatever you want to be and do whatever you want to do. Mom grabbed on to that idea and applied it to herself and to her sales techniques. It worked well for her.

She also repeated to me again and again, "Gary, you can be whatever you want to be." I believed her. If I really wanted to, I could become a millionaire, or president, or anything. Oddly enough, as I moved into my teens, I began to apply the corollary of that thinking to my behavior: "You can get away with whatever you want." That wasn't quite what Mom had in mind, but that was the way I began to think.

I had always been such a good kid that Mom simply let me go. Over the next couple of years I had very little supervision.

I changed from a partying kid into someone quite different. I ran around with rougher and rougher guys. Many of them were not in school. We experimented with hard liquor and drugs. I went to wild parties with runaway kids. Before long, we decided that a group of us were the tough kids in Northeast Seattle. We formed a gang called the Turks.

Why the Turks? The leader of our gang, a fellow named Lloyd Horn, had seen a picture of the Turkish flag on an Arm & Hammer® Baking Soda box. The Turks seems like tough guys. They had huge, curved knives. We didn't know anything about Turks, but the name sounded good. So we decided that would be our name. Now we needed to show everyone we were a gang. About that time, we had heard about a gang in East Los Angeles called the Pachucos. They were infamous on the West Coast. They put a tattoo on the web of their left hand that consisted of a cross with three little lines radiating from the top of the cross. That was their gang mark.

A gang mark seemed like a great idea, so we wanted one. Ours was a half moon with a star and three little lines radiating from it. The Turkish Flag ⌣ We were the Turks. Tough guys. Gang members.

Anybody who didn't tattoo their hand was not a legitimate member. These were homemade tattoos. I had no idea how to put on a tattoo, but it was pretty simple. First draw the half moon, star, and three lines with a pen or marker on the web of the left hand between the index finger and the thumb. Then take a pencil with a new eraser and a needle. Jam the back end of the needle into the eraser so that the sharp end shows. That gives you some control. Then wrap the tip of the needle with black thread, leaving the point exposed. Next, get some India ink. Dip the needle and thread into the ink and prick little dots along the penned outline. The needle hits into the hand like a tattoo parlor machine. Quick little painful pokes drive the India ink under the skin. It's painful, but that's part of being a macho gang member. It was a real tattoo and it was permanent.

My mother noticed the tattoo shortly after I did it and asked me about it.

"I just put it on my hand for fun," I lied.

"Well, wash the darn thing off," she replied.

I mumbled something about it being a tattoo. I don't think she understood. A week or two later she insisted I remove that thing from my hand. In those days, only sailors, prisoners, and gang members sported tattoos. I told her that a tattoo would not come off. She didn't believe me. She dragged me into the bathroom, grabbed the washrag with soap, and began vigorously rubbing my hand. Of course it didn't come off. Then she broke down in tears. Her once good-boy son had tattooed himself.

What next? I felt bad, but there was nothing I could do. The tattoo was an important symbol of me being a tough guy—a gang member.

* * *

I had something special that helped me be successful with the girls I dated. It was a car. It wasn't a pretty car. It was a six year old pea-green 1947 Plymouth, a four-door sedan. My mother and grandmother had helped buy it for me on my sixteenth birthday for $700. The car didn't have a lot of power, but it had something special: A big bench back seat. It also had a bench front seat and a trunk big enough to sneak somebody into the drive-in along with a case of beer. It was a slow car made for fast women. I took every advantage.

I didn't maintain my car very well and it began to leak brake fluid. The brake pedal would almost always go all the way to the floor. Sometimes I couldn't tell the difference between the clutch and the brake. Every time I got gas, I poured in a little brake fluid. I simply didn't have the time or money to fix the brakes.

One night we decided to go to the drive-in out on Aurora Boulevard, a fair distance from where we lived. The brakes were just about shot. I tried to stop by pulling on the emergency brake but that brake was also shot. I could only stop the car by jamming it into reverse. That was not good for the transmission, but I really didn't care. That night my buddy and I had hot dates and a case of beer, and we needed to get to that drive-in theater. So I limped along at about fifteen or twenty miles an hour on the side roads until I got to the drive-in. By the time I was there, my brakes were totally gone, but I wasn't thinking about brakes. I was a heck of a lot more interested in the young lady next to me and visualized a hot necking session at the drive-in theater.

So I drove to a good spot at the drive-in and pulled up onto a little berm or hill ready to plug in the speaker. I stepped on the brakes but the pedal went to the floor. Suddenly, the car rolled downhill and before I knew it, BANG! I rear-ended the car in front of me. Well, I have seen some surprised people, but the look on the faces of the two old folks who were minding their own business when I rear-ended their car was one for the books.

They exited their car, rubbing their necks, cursing, angry, and stunned. I made lots of excuses then I backed the car up, jammed it in forward to stop it, and proceeded to drink beer, neck, and watch very little of the movie. I think the folks in front of us were probably even more irritated about the fact that our car kept rocking back and forth with laughter as we visualized them suffering a whiplash after being rear-ended in the drive-in. Such was my life.

*  *  *

I began carrying a switchblade knife and pegged my pants (tapering the legs to a narrow opening at the cuff.) I grew my hair long and combed the sides to the back of my head, parting my hair with a downward stroke of the comb into what was called a ducktail. I was a hood. I didn't attend any high school functions. No football games, no social parties, or dances. I wasn't involved in high school stuff. Instead, I partied downtown on First Street and grew up fast. Although my drug of choice was always alcohol, I did take heroin and marijuana whenever we could get it. We stole a few cars, primarily for joy rides. I became quite isolated from the mainstream in high school. We hung out in Snow White's, a little café around the corner from the school. No good girl would go near the place. The Turks owned that joint. High school guys steered clear of it unless they needed some dope. Not that we had a lot of connections, but we could get some bennies and dexies (Benzedrine™ and Dexedrine™) from time to time, and sometimes stronger stuff.

Seattle is a long way from Mexico, where most of the marijuana came from. It wasn't homegrown in those days and it was hard to get. This was the fifties — it was only 1954. But somebody saw that the marijuana we had, which was full of seeds and stems, looked a bit like catnip. It even smelled a little like it. Wasn't catnip some kind of "loco weed?" We had a plan.

There are two wealthy areas around Roosevelt High School and the rich kids came to us from time to time to buy joints. We decided to see if we could sell them a substitute: catnip joints. We charged them a dollar a joint. What a deal! High profit margin. We sold big, fat joints of the stuff. The only problem was that we had to smoke it with them to show that it was real. I've smoked more catnip than anybody alive. We would sit in the car and smoke the stuff. It killed our throats but we had to pretend to get high. Our customers would get a contact high. We didn't have many repeat customers, but we did laugh a lot and we made a few bucks to buy the real stuff.

I had a great time. I was a tough guy. A gang member. A party boy. Wild women came to our parties. I had a lot of one-night stands. I was proud of my conquests. I kept a little list in my wallet of the girls that I made love to. I hasten to say it was all consensual. I never forced myself on anybody, but I wanted to prove to myself that all women loved me just like Mom. Right? So I learned to be very persuasive. I made love to eleven different women in the eleventh grade. That was the advantage of being a gang member.

Then there was the music, the beginnings of rock and roll. Elvis Presley was born in January 1935, two years before me.

By 1955, his music took off. His appearance on the Ed Sullivan show caused a huge uproar with his gyrating, "disgusting" hip movements. Elvis's energy woke things up during what would later be called "the sleepy fifties." We didn't want the Big Band music of our folks. We were ready for the new rhythm and blues era, the name used before the term "rock and roll" became popular. Bill Haley & His Comets started it with "Rock Around the Clock." Then came Fats Domino, Chubby Checker, The Drifters, and The Platters. There were some great songs like "Earth Angel (Will You Be Mine)" by the Penguins, "Young Blood" by The Coasters and, of course, Jerry Lee Lewis and his own "shocking" piano routines with a "Whole Lotta Shakin' Goin' On." We were searching for music that defined our own generation and we found it. African-American music. There were some great concerts. A guy named "Big Jay" McNeeley, a sax player, put one on that was a blast.

Seattle's blue laws meant that no one could buy booze after midnight on Saturday because alcohol could not be sold on Sundays. So what were we to do if we were out partying late on Saturday night, as we always were? Find an after-hours club, of course, particularly one that played rhythm and blues music. We found a great place, the China Pheasant in south Seattle. Although it was quite a distance from where we lived, it was worth the trip. There was only one little problem. We were seventeen-year-old white kids and this was an all-African-American club. What would happen if we went out there? We heard that they were friendly so we decided to give it a try. Fortunately, the regulars tolerated us pretty well. They accepted us as an oddity, really just a bunch of kids who loved listening to the music and dancing to it. However, they made one rule: Don't take their women out of the place. We went out there from time to time and had a great deal of fun, although it was a bit scary in some ways.

There was one night that I vividly remember. I stayed the night at my friend, Danny Roth's house. But we planned to slip out as soon as his folks went to bed. We headed for the China Pheasant. How to get there? For some reason, my car wasn't available so we decided to "borrow" his dad's brand new 1954 Chevrolet. Danny could take the keys and we could push the car quietly out of the garage. We would be back before dawn. No one would ever know. So, off we went!

Unfortunately, that was the night we broke the rule. After too many drinks and too many dances, a big, sexy, laughing Black woman named Willie said she wanted us to drive her home. We were horny. We forgot the rule. There were three of us seventeen-year-old kids full of booze in an African-American nightclub. Danny and I got Willie into the Chevy. Fortunately, our friend, Lloyd Horn, followed us in his car. I was in the backseat with Willie doing God knows what when Danny turned around and watched us instead of the road. He drifted off, sideswiped a telephone pole, and totaled his dad's new car. There we were: four o'clock in the morning, stuck on the roadway, scared shitless, with Willie who was taller than any of us. What were we going to do now? Thank God Lloyd came along and picked us up. We took Willie home and Lloyd drove us to Danny's house just in time. We returned the keys and got in bed with our clothes on.

Time to get up!  Now, Danny's dad wondered what happened to his car. Obviously, it was stolen. Later it was found wrecked in south Seattle. We wondered who did that. I think he always suspected us, but he couldn't prove it. A close call.

I really didn't date many high school girls. They called me a "hood," a label that I proudly wore. The good girls didn't want to date me. I didn't want to date them either. I wanted to date the wild girls. They were ready to hang out with gang members and the kids who had lost their way. It was a place where morals didn't matter anymore.

I wore my long, dark black hair combed back into a big ducktail. That alone set me aside as hood. But I also had pegged pants worn low, but not so low where the crack showed. We hadn't quite gotten there yet! I wore blue suede shoes, a bright pink shirt to match my vivid blue sport coat. My high school senior-year picture hints as to who I was. I carried a switchblade knife in my front pants pocket. I didn't use the knife and I never intended to. The knife symbolized who I was. It gave me a sense of power, perhaps it was even a phallic symbol. The women who passed me in the halls at school looked at me with some fear, loathing, and even a bit of interest. I was different and kind of scary. I liked that image. I was wild and out of control. I liked drinking and partying all the time.

Frequently, we would go down on to First Avenue in Seattle, which was a pretty rough area at the time. There were bars, tattoo parlors, and a number of burlesque houses. The burlesques were hot! We liked to go in them and watch the girls dance. I don't exactly remember how I met her, but I did get introduced to a young dancer who was a friend of a friend. She probably wasn't any older than I was, about seventeen. One night we got together after her "performance." I told her that I would drive her home and she slipped on a sweater. When we arrived at her house, we began to neck. Suddenly, something was very wrong. When I pulled her close to me, I felt a painful sensation where her soft breasts should have been. I felt like I had been stabbed.

"What was that?!" I exclaimed.

"Pasties," she replied.

"Pasties?" I asked.

"Yes, those are the little things that you put on your nipples so that you are not completely undressed while dancing. They are hard to get off."

"Yeah," I replied, "They're also hard to neck with."

The date was short lived. But I learned something about burlesque dancing: pasties . . .

I was wild. Out of control. The good boy no more. But I was getting fearful. My lifestyle was too dangerous.

But what about Mom? Didn't she know what was going on? My mother had to know that I wasn't doing very well, but I don't think she had any idea about how wild my life really was. She was either out late at her Stanley parties, or held drinking parties downstairs in our house, or just wasn't home. I was pretty much on my own. No one checked the time I came home. Usually I came home quite late.

I was able to get through high school simply because there was an hour-long study hall every day. That was time enough for me to complete basic homework. I did almost none at home. I got through with the help of my "uppers:" my bennies and my dexies, now known as "speed" or amphetamines. They buzzed me up and kept me going. I could stay out all night with those darn things. But I was slowly running down. I felt stuck.

I was drifting deeper and deeper into trouble. My friends were more like minor criminals than high school kids. I knew that I really wanted to get out of there. I had some ambition. I didn't want to spend the rest of my life with the Turks. I didn't want to get hurt or go to jail.

I was nearly thrown out of school for smoking on the high school steps on my eighteenth birthday (May 18th.) Mom had to come down and bail me out of trouble with the principal. My grades were barely passable but luckily, I would still get a diploma.

Then Mom left to attend a convention back East with Wayne and Pat, leaving me home alone. They trusted me. I had always been a good boy. They were gone for over a week. Things spiraled out of control. My friends found out that I had an empty house and people started partying there even when I was gone. I was working part-time as a bus boy in a local restaurant. I couldn't control the parties. The neighbors finally called the cops. When Mom, Wayne, and Pat came home, the shit hit the fan.

I had done everything I could to clean the house up, but I wasn't very successful. The party room downstairs had a juke box and an old one-armed bandit slot machine. A big old-fashioned bear rug hung on the wall with the bear's teeth showing. Mom checked out the house. She ordered me downstairs to look at something. The room didn't look bad until

I saw the bear. One of my buddies had thought it would be pretty funny to put a beer can in the bear's mouth. It was still there. The evidence was clear.

Before anyone spoke, we heard my sister shouting and yelling. Some of her clothes had been stolen. Even worse, my mother called me into her bedroom. Her face was white and Wayne was visibly angry.

"Look at this!" Mom shouted as she pointed to the bed.

She pulled back the bed covers. My friends had left obvious signs of sexual activity, including pubic hairs and semen. I was humiliated and embarrassed.

Another incident soon after also shocked and scared me. My drug of choice was always alcohol, but I did occasionally get into heavier drugs when they were available. I smoked a little pot now and then. On a few occasions I injected heroin and Demerol. One of our Turks was becoming a serious addict. I don't remember Jay's last name, but I vividly remember him as the little guy constantly into needles and looking for drugs.

One day Jay called me and told me to come to the motel where he hung out. He had long since been kicked out of his house. He said he had some great stuff. I knocked back a few drinks and went along with the idea. I thought I would inject Demerol or something like it and get a great high. Jay was very enthusiastic as he got out the needle. As soon as the stuff hit my vein I knew something was very wrong. I suddenly felt flushed and hot. In a matter of minutes, my entire body itched and burned. I felt like I was on fire.

Jay began to laugh.

"Guess what?" he said, "That was penicillin! I thought it would be pretty funny to give you some to make you healthy."

But it wasn't funny to me. I thought I was going to die. I remember going outside in the cold Seattle winter and lying on the ground simply trying to cool off. Going to the hospital was out of the question. What was I going to tell them? It took several hours for that stuff to wear off. Of course I was angry at the damn fool for almost killing me. But more importantly, I really did feel my life being threatened and I began to seriously question my lifestyle. But I couldn't find a way out.

By the time I graduated from high school, my outlook for success wasn't very good, to say the least. I didn't have the grades for a four-year college. I wasn't sure what I wanted to do, but I knew I did want to get the hell out of Seattle. Out of the twenty kids in our gang, only three of us graduated from high school. Of those three, one later went to prison. The other committed suicide. I didn't want to go the route of the other guys. One Turk became a bricklayer, an honorable profession. He is still a friend of mine, even after all these years: Lloyd Horn, the tough guy who protected me. We never really got into many fights, at least I didn't. That wasn't the purpose of the gang. It was to have fun. It is a different sort of gang than the kind we see nowadays. But it had all gone too far. Most of my friends were addicts, thieves, and lazy bums. I wanted to change. Who would help me?

\* \* \*

*I thought again about the words on the jury verdict form: "We find in favor of the Defendant and award the Plaintiff nothing. . . ." Why would those words cause me such horrible pain? When I looked back on my wild and failed years in high school, I thought that I had come a long ways, even to be able to be a lawyer. Yet, I had failed my mother in those years. I vowed not to do it again. But had I failed her by losing the biggest case in my career? Why all this terrible shame?*

# CHAPTER 6: MAN MOST LIKELY TO SUCCEED

Help was soon on the way. My mother reported my situation to my grandmother and the matriarchy went into action. My grandmother hopped on the train (her husband, my grandfather, was a railroad man so she had free passes) and came to Seattle to rescue her number one grandson. They decided Jack Gwilliam should step in and do something to help his son. It was 1955 and he had long since quit drinking. He had married a wonderful woman named Helen, had three young daughters, and lived a successful life in Glendora, California, a city a few miles east of Los Angeles. He participated as a leader in Alcoholics Anonymous and had returned to the Mormon Church. He worked as a real estate agent, and bought a new Cadillac every year, whether he needed it or not. After abandoning me for so long, Mom and Grandma were convinced that he should take me in. After he and Mom divorced, I had only seen him three times. He had never given my mother a dime of child support. The matriarchy decreed that it was time for a change. My grandmother took charge. She phoned the former son-in-law whom she hadn't seen in years. Her words reportedly were:

"Jack, this is Oveda Sturm. I'm here in Seattle. Your son is in trouble. You've got to get your ass up here and help him. You haven't done a damn thing for him all these years and it's time for you to start acting like a father."

I'm not sure of Jack's exact response, but he couldn't deny my grandmother's demands. He agreed to take me in, move me to Southern California, and send me to college.

That was great with me. I needed to get out of Seattle

before I went to jail or was killed. In the summer of 1955, Jack arrived in Seattle driving his new Cadillac. I piled in some clothes and off we drove to Glendora. Me and Jack, a man I barely knew, and a family that I didn't know at all.

The plan was to get me a job and then get me into college. It sounded fine to me. My grades weren't good enough to get into a four-year school, mostly Cs and a few Bs. I could start at the junior college, two-year colleges they were called, near where Jack lived. Citrus Junior College in Azusa, California, was to be my place of redemption.

Jack, Helen, and my three half-sisters lived in a modest house on Foothill Boulevard in Glendora. Fortunately, I could stay in the guest house, a renovated chicken coop. Jack and Helen had done a nice job turning it into a three-room cottage with a bathroom, small front area, and a bedroom. It was perfect for the new resident. *I was going to college!* Nobody in my family had ever graduated from college and I certainly was ready to give it a try.

When I moved in with Jack, he was ready to help me get started in college. But he had a couple of conditions. First, I had to cut my long hair and unpeg my pants. Those were easy. He also wanted me to remove the tattoo. It didn't look good for a college student to have a tattoo on his hand. By now, I felt different about my old gang. I had escaped and really wasn't a Turk any longer. So, I decided to go along with my father.

Jack said he knew a good doctor who could help. It turns out that the doctor was nothing more than a general practitioner with a small office in Azusa. He did not have the slightest idea about how to remove a tattoo, but he had a simple solution. He simply lifted the skin in the web of my hand, cut it off, then sewed the edges together. I was too dumb to realize that this presented serious complications. But I learned what those were right after the operation. Not only was the wound painful as hell, but shortly thereafter, I developed an infection — a bad one.

My hand swelled up like a huge balloon and a blue line formed up the vein on the inside of my arm. A serious infection. Fortunately, a massive dose of antibiotics controlled the infection, but by the time the swelling went down I was left with an ugly scar. Not the "hairline" scar that the doctor had predicted. For a long time, it bothered me, but as I grew older I began to realize that it was a part of my life. It became a badge of honor, proof that I was once a gang member who had survived.

Another condition of my moving to Southern California was that I would start work. I agreed. I had been working outside the home most of my life. When I was a teenager, I started working part-time and then full-time during the summers. A strong work ethic was part of my family culture. As with most young men, my early work involved manual labor.

At fifteen years old, I got my first summer job in the fields outside of Eugene. There wasn't much work for a young kid at that time, so I started right out with the field workers. We picked green string beans in the fields on a local farm. We were paid three cents a pound. If you worked hard all day you could pick one-hundred pounds of beans. $3.00 per day. It was incredibly hard work. I started early in the morning when the dew was still wet on the beans. String beans have large, sticky leaves and with the morning dew they become especially irritating to the skin. As the day heats up, we tried to hide behind the bean poles for a little shade. We sat on a bucket pulling the beans and putting them in a sack. Then we'd drag the sack to the end of the row to be weighed. I was competing against experienced field workers, mostly families of Mexicans who traveled from farm to farm doing the picking. I didn't stick with the job very long, but I learned something important: This was not something I wanted to do for a living. But I was ready to try pretty much anything near my new home in Southern California.

My first job in Glendora was at the Rosemead Nursery. I carried heavy five-gallon plants around a very large nursery. It was hard physical work. I couldn't compete very well with the young Hispanic kids who made up most of the work force. I didn't last there very long.

Next I tried commercial window washing. The detergents ate into my hands and tore them up. That disgusting and difficult job lasted only a short time. So I looked around for a job more suited to my talents.

I soon found a perfect job. I went to work for Western Union delivering telegrams all over eastern Los Angeles County. A number of us worked out of the office in Azusa. We would deliver telegrams over a fifty-square-mile area that included Glendora, Azusa, Covina, West Covina, Baldwin Park, and Irwindale. I hit the job full of enthusiasm. We stood around until we had a bunch of telegrams, maybe about ten or twelve, then we planned the route, and drove our own car to deliver them throughout the area. We were paid by the hour with no expenses for gas or car maintenance.

We had maps, but before long I knew every single street and cross street in that fifty-mile area. I was able to deliver the

A TRIAL LAWYER FINDS HIS SOUL

telegrams quickly and return for a new batch within a couple of hours.

After about three or four days on the job, a couple of the old-timers took me aside for a talk. They told me the rules:

"Look kid, you are delivering the telegrams too fast," one said.

"Yes," I responded, "Isn't that what I am supposed to do?"

"No," he answered. "Think about it. The faster you deliver the telegrams, the more miles you put on your car. You are not doing anybody any good by delivering six or eight telegrams per hour. We have a rule here. Three telegrams per hour. That's what you deliver. If you have some extra time, go do what you want to do with it. You are making us all look bad, so wise up, kid."

That was the union talking. Well, I wasn't about to buck the system. So I found that I could actually deliver eight to ten telegrams every hour while checking into the office on the basis of three per hour. I had lots of extra time. I studied during my off time. However, the best deal was that the office closed at 10:00 p.m. If we checked out a bunch of telegrams around 9:00 p.m., we simply signed our own time slips when we finished. Another friend of mine also worked for the company, and we partied together. We would combine our telegrams, take one car, deliver them all in an hour or so, come back in, and sign in a time three hours in the future. By the time we were officially "done working" we were long gone and out having fun. It was a heck of a job while it lasted.

My job at Western Union did have one drawback: dogs.

Most of the telegrams we delivered were known as "duns." They were retail and credit card companies threatening people with lawsuits because of unpaid bills. People did not want these telegrams. Many of the other telegrams were about people dying. Again, not very good news. Of course, some were happy telegrams, such as birthday wishes and the like. Most of the people didn't know we were coming. Many of the telegrams that were delivered at night were to homes with dogs. Big dogs. Dogs that didn't like strange men coming up to their doors.

I had always liked dogs. I had a wonderful dog in high school named Nipper, a cute, little dog that I loved dearly. Most dogs are territorial. Many times when I delivered telegrams, I walked to the front door and would hear a growl and see some animal glaring at me from the front porch. This was especially frightening after dark. So I would simply walk backwards off to my car and tell the office that they would have to deliver the telegram by mail. We were told we didn't have to fight with the dogs. That was good.

My most frightening dog encounter was delivering a telegram to the famous burlesque dancer Sally Rand. She danced with feathers and moved them so as to partially reveal her naked body. She was a very well-known figure who lived in a lovely house on the outskirts of Glendora. I drove up her small circular driveway and looked around. I didn't see anything so I got out of my car and walked about thirty feet to her front door. I rang the bell, but no one answered, so I left the telegram in the door. Then I turned around to go back to my car. Suddenly I encountered a huge, ugly creature.

I had never seen a mastiff. I didn't know what it was. I didn't even know dogs grew that big. This thing was huge and he was standing between me and my car. He didn't bark. He just stared at me. I stared at him. *Oh, shit! My life is over. How am I going to get around this dog?* I had visions of racing to my car, trying to leap to the top of it, with him dragging me back by my leg. Sweat began to pour down my back and forehead. So I decided to talk to him:

"Nice dog. I won't hurt you and you don't hurt me. Okay?"

He didn't respond. He just looked at me.

I had been frozen to the spot but I decided that I needed to do something, so I very carefully took a step.

He stayed where he was.

Another step.

Backing slowly away.

Not appearing threatening.

Moving around him gently.

He remained in one place, staring me down. Menacing. He didn't bark. He just looked at me.

It seemed as if it took me an hour to cross the thirty feet to my car. I slowly wound around the front and slipped into the passenger side door.

The dog stood where he was, never taking his eyes off of me.

I was shaking so badly that I could barely drive. But I was safe and continued to deliver more telegrams.

Another dog experience took place at night. I was in the dregs of Azusa, in a very poor neighborhood with railroad tracks. The street was exceptionally dark with small, cracker box houses. There were no street lights. I pulled up to the house where the telegram was to be delivered. I could see light through the windows in the front door. As I stepped from the car, I heard very loud barking and growling coming from the back of the house. I remained where I was. I could hear this vicious beast growling and pulling at a chain. If he was chained up, I thought I would be safe.

I walked the short distance across the street to the front porch and rang the doorbell. I gave the lady her telegram and turned to head back to my car. The dog was still barking but suddenly the sound changed. I heard a rattling of chains and the barking became louder. I turned around and saw a huge dog racing around the corner of the small house dragging a long chain and a stake. He had pulled the pole out of the ground and he was headed directly for me! He was big and moving fast. I froze in my tracks. He jumped and landed about three feet in front of me. I jumped back about five feet. He jumped forward. I jumped back. He hadn't quite gotten to me yet.

Suddenly, the door opened.

"Now, Fido," a woman said, "Come here. Be a good dog."

The dog turned around and began wagging his tail as he quietly walked to her door.

The woman looked at me and I looked at her. I am sure I was white as a sheet. She smiled at me. I didn't know what to say.

"Does he bite?" I asked.

She simply shut the door and collapsed on the floor,

rolling with laughter. It wasn't that funny to me. But I escaped death once again. So much for my experiences with dogs.

I was working hard and going to school, but I still enjoyed partying, drinking, and especially girls. With my short hair (the ducktail was long gone) and socially-acceptable clothes I started a more normal dating pattern. I dated an interesting young woman named Terri Black,* a high school senior. Naturally, we met at a party.

This girl liked to drink and party. She especially liked to drink. So did I. Country Club Malt Liquor was our beverage of choice. We would get a six-pack and head off to a drive-in or simply find a quiet place so that we could neck in my car. She was a popular high school girl. She was quite prim and proper, that is, until about the third malt liquor, at which time she would change from Dr. Jekyll into Mrs. Hyde. She would suddenly become wildly passionate and ready to make love. No problem for me. But the car was kind of cramped so we needed to find a better place.

The usual way I entered the cottage I lived in was to walk down the driveway that was located next to the main house. But I found a way to sneak in the back through a neighbor's yard. That is how Terri and I slipped in. I parked my car on the street and we snuck quietly into my little cottage. No lights. Just the two of us and a bed. It was quite idyllic until I found myself getting Terri home later and later. Eventually, her folks laid down the law. She couldn't date "that boy" anymore. He was a bad influence. *Was I?* I am not sure who was influencing whom, but it was a short, happy, and passionate experience.

---

*Pseudonym

At the same time something more serious was taking place within me. I was determined to do well in school and to make Mom proud of me. In high school I had embarrassed her and let her down. Pleasing Mom had always been the most important thing in my life. It was time to be the good boy again.

I began to study seriously. A few Korean War vets attended my college under the GI Bill. They worked very hard and were role models for me. By the time the first semester was over, I had earned the best grades I ever had: All Bs and an A or two. Within two years, my grades were straight-As. I still liked to party, but I was in control. I was redeeming myself.

The two years between 1955 and 1957 were formative years for me. I was doing well in school, and in every aspect of my life. I was dating, drinking, and partying, but I was in the mainstream. I earned good grades and Mom was proud. I was physically active, studying hard, and working well in my job. I was more productive than I had ever been. My gang years seemed long behind me. I was becoming a new man.

* * *

The auditorium was crowded and noisy with voices twittering and chattering. Most of the din came from nervous and excited twenty-year old kids like me. We were about to graduate with our Associate of Arts degrees from Citrus Junior College. The parents were smiling and proud. Their kids had made it on beyond college. Even though it was only a two year degree, for most of us it was a significant achievement. It was a Saturday in late May, 1957. Although the exact date is a little unclear in my mind, the event is not. This was a big day.

My stepmother, Helen, was there with my half-sisters, but my father, Jack, was not. He had recently had an affair with a woman he had met at an A.A. meeting and had moved out of the family home. Once again my relationship with him was estranged. But I really didn't care. He had never been much of a father to me and, I felt he wasn't important in my life. The most important person in my life was there.

My mother had flown down from Seattle and sat next to me in a little folding chair. She kept reaching over to squeeze my hand as she beamed with pride and excitement. I gently but firmly pulled out of her grasp. Holding one's mother's hand was not cool for a twenty-year-old guy about to graduate. Albeit it was a junior college, it was still a college degree.

However, something else added to the excitement for me. It was a special award. Five of us were in the running. Each of us had been selected by the faculty and then the student body had voted on who was to receive it. Today the results of the votes would be announced for "The Man Most Likely to Succeed,"[4] the most prestigious Citrus Junior College graduation award.

As our names were called, each of us marched proudly to the stage, to receive our parchment scrolled degrees. The audience cheered and clapped for each of us. Soon it was time for the important announcement.

The faculty dean stepped to the podium.

"Now it's time to tell you the winner of our special award," he announced.

My heard pounded like crazy.

Mom was squeezing my hand and I couldn't get her to let go.

I knew I had a decent chance of winning, but I didn't believe that I could really win.

"The award goes to Gary Gwilliam."

*Oh my God!* I was excited beyond belief.

Tears streamed down my mother's face as she looked at me with love and pride in her eyes. I walked up to the stage to receive my award, a beautiful new Whitenauer wrist watch. Engraved on the back of the watch was "Man Most Likely to Succeed, Gary Gwilliam, CJC 1957."

That moment is seared in my memory. I was almost numb with excitement as the faculty and my fellow students cheered for me. As I returned to my chair and sat next to my mother, my mind flooded with thoughts. My wild lost years in high school seemed like a dim memory. My tattoo was gone. I was a Turk no more. I was not only a student with a degree, but I was the Man Most Likely to Succeed. I had redeemed myself in the eyes of the person most important to me in the world, my dear mother.

Mother had never been more proud of me. I had proved her right. I could do anything I wanted to do and probably be anyone I wanted to be. But that corollary hung on: I could also get away with whatever I wanted. I was doing great on the surface, but a streak of wildness and a love of drink lingered in me. I felt that odd dichotomy so common in young men, a sense of growing personal male responsibility while still needing to "sow my wild oats." It was a dichotomy I would live with for years.

* * *

*I thought about how far I had come in those few years. Now after the Staples v. General Motors trial I am sitting in my car feeling sorry and shameful after losing my big case. I can barely remember the happiness I felt in May 1957. I could feeling nothing but the burning words: "We find in favor of the Defendant. . ." Nothing else seemed to matter.*

# CHAPTER 7: JELLY

After I got my Associates of Arts degree from Citrus Junior College, I wanted to go on to a four-year school. I hoped to stay in the area, so I applied nearby to Pomona College in Claremont, California. At the time I didn't realize how good a school it really was. I wanted to stay near the friends that I had made at Citrus, particularly the girls. Fortunately, I was accepted and entered Pomona College as a transfer student in the fall of 1957. Most of the students lived on campus in dormitories, but they were full. So I was placed in a dormitory at Harvey Mudd College, a new Claremont college that was being built. Before long, an opening came in a Pomona dorm so I transferred to Norton Hall. Oddly enough, this was to be a life-altering event for me.

I was put on the floor where many of the athletes resided. Most of them belonged to an infamous local fraternity known as the Kappa Deltas or KDs. The KDs were the dominant and wild fraternity on campus. They were the athletes, the party boys, and the hard drinkers. I fit right in! I was not an athlete, but I had a sense of humor and got along well with the others. When it came pledge time, I assured them that I had something to offer the fraternity: party girls. My female friends from Citrus Junior College would love nothing more than to come up to the big college campus and meet some fraternity boys. After a crazy initiation ritual, the fraternity admitted me. My two years at Pomona College turned out to be some of the best of my life.

Our fraternity was quite small. There were only about fourteen kids in our pledge class and about eight in the class behind us. The KDs didn't pledge you until you were halfway through your sophomore year, so the kids got to know each other pretty well before they joined. The KDs were very selective.

Once you joined, you had to have a nickname. Mine became Jelly. Why? Well there are two stories. One is that I became the keeper of the jelly jar at the dining hall table where the KDs always ate. The second is that I was prone to have a bit of a beer belly and so I was called "Jelly Belly." It didn't matter. I loved my new name. It signified that I was once again accepted as part of a select group. Just like in my old gang, the Turks. My KD friends were Turkey, Grab, Booger, Nobby, Big Fella, Humper, Rastus, and Kritter, among others. These were nicknames that stuck with us forever. It was male bonding at its best.

We did everything together. Not too much studying. Mostly partying. Always looking forward to the weekend. Always trying to top each other with wild stories and stunts. The KD parties were notorious. Most of the young girls who entered Pomona College were studious by nature. They had to have good grades and were kind of naive, particularly when it came to hard party guys like the KDs. The girls were not used to profanity and vulgarity which shocked them, much to the delight of the KDs. We often dropped our drawers and displayed a "BA"—a bare ass, later known as mooning. Our fraternity may have invented that form of indecent exposure. If not, we were certainly one of the early proponents. Early and often. We particularly loved to drive by the women's dorms honking the horn with a couple of "BAs" hanging out the window. Needless to say, the dormitory advisors for the young girls started the school year with a lecture about KDs and how to avoid them. But some women were tempted. They were curious. They came to our parties. Usually, they came only once.

Saturday night was a big night for the KDs with either a major or a minor party going somewhere. We had several great party places. One of them was our cabin on nearby Mount Baldy, donated to us by a benevolent alumnus some years before. A long, winding road led to the cabin perched on the mountain above Claremont. The cabin was simple and small, but the kitchen worked, with a place to keep the beer cold, and enough electricity to keep the party going. It was a great place to take our dates, because they couldn't escape from the party. It was a long way down and dangerous as hell, particularly after we were all roaring drunk. Fortunately, no one in my class ever died, although a couple of serious accidents happened going down the hill. We had the same attitude of many young men. We felt immortal and didn't really care about personal danger.

Another placed we partied was an old dance hall in Chino a few miles from Claremont. We would hire a band, rent the hall, and then take the girls down there for a wild dance party.

But the biggest party of the year was the luau, held at a beach near Laguna Nigel. First we would gather up some grain alcohol. Usually the guys in pre-med or chemistry could get it. Grain alcohol is one-hundred percent alcohol, not just 100-proof. It is twice as strong as the most potent hard liquor on the market and very raw tasting. However, if mixed with good fruit juice, it made what we called our "Luau Mai-Tais." After one of those, you were really buzzed and after two you were well on your way to glorious drunkenness. The girls never knew what quite what hit them.

We would also bring along some wonderful steaks. Somebody bought them at a special market. They were always big and thick. No fat on them. One hitch: They were horsemeat. They looked great and didn't smell bad, but they tasted like leather. We thought it was funnier than hell to see somebody served the steak, take a bite of it, and chew the thing for three or more minutes before they finally swallowed a big lump, or spit it out. But if you were drunk enough, it really didn't matter.

Again, it was tough for the girls to escape from the party at the remote beach location. We always seemed to set the party up near the railroad track that ran alongside the beach. Every time the train would come along, the KDs would give the train a BA. But our parties had one thing in common. The guys tended to leave their dates alone and just hang around together. Unless someone was dating someone special, the guys just roamed around, getting drunk, and acting stupid. There wasn't any sex at the parties, but there was a lot of vulgarity and numerous attempts to shock the innocent young coeds. We did a great job of it.

Looking back now, I think it was typical, disgusting frat house behavior,[5] but at the time we loved it. Every Monday night the KDs would meet in our fraternity room. It was a special room downstairs under Clark Hall that was reserved for our ritualistic meetings. The main order of business on Mondays was the Man's Award, a special award given to the woman who was the "shittiest date at the Saturday night party." The so-called "award" was in the shape of a toilet. The shittiest date got flushed down the toilet. Unfortunately, the brother who brought the date had to then immediately call her and tell her that she had received the Man's Award. Somehow or another, we would make a flushing sound and tell her that she was the worst date at the party. Pretty humiliating sometimes for the guy, let alone the woman. I don't know why we all thought it was so funny. Now it seems juvenile, chauvinistic, and totally insensitive, but that was the mentality of the fraternity. That was 1959. Boys were boys and KDs were KDs. I can now understand why the female advisors warned the girls so vociferously about staying away from us. Only a few suffered through our parties on a regular basis. Lots of one-time dates. But we were having the time of our lives. Once again, I was wild and out of control.

My background was quite different than most of my fraternity brothers. Claremont College is a private school that compares well academically with Stanford University and the East Coast ivy-league schools. Most of the guys in our fraternity came from educated, well-to-do families. Many of them had attended private prep schools instead of public high schools. They dressed accordingly. Very casual, cool, and preppy. In Southern California, that meant t-shirts and jeans with loafers or tennis shoes, and not much more. Although I had been a student at Citrus for a couple of years, I still hadn't adjusted to the dress style. I still wore some of my high school wardrobe. I wanted to dress more like Elvis Presley, Billy Eckstein, or some of the rock and rollers. That meant blue suede shoes, pegged pants, and a flashy shirt and jacket. Colorful stuff.

It didn't take long for our dress styles to clash. Early on, my new friends began to rib me about my clothes. I responded in kind by telling them they looked like The Beach Boys. But I was outnumbered. The joking became more serious. They wanted me to conform. I had one particular jacket that was especially irritating to them. It was a long-sleeve, blousy, casual jacket with wild colored stripes. The KDs referred to it as my "jelly jacket." Of course, I loved the jacket and wore it often, sometimes just to flaunt them. But one day, some of the brothers decided to take matters into their own hands. Turkey took the lead.

Pomona College required that most of the students live on campus. However, there was some overcrowding, so Turkey, Nobby Orens, and I had rented a house on Central Avenue in Montclair, only a few miles from the campus. The place was built in 1920 and became a party house. It wasn't unusual for me to come home to find my friends there having a few beers and fun.

I remember one Friday night in particular. I came home from campus and saw a bunch of the guys hanging out there in front, as usual. I especially remember Turkey, who was having a big laugh, as he saw me driving into our small circular driveway. However, this time, something was different. They had built a bonfire. Why did they have a bonfire in the middle of the afternoon?

I soon found out. *They were burning my clothes!!!* Especially the jelly jacket. I was too late to save it. Fortunately, I was able to fight them off and keep some of my wardrobe intact. They had won the battle, but not the war. I felt (and still feel to this day) that I'm a better dresser than most of them, but the burning of Jelly's wardrobe remains one of those fraternity legends.

I was nearing the end of my senior year in college. Turkey and I had lived together for almost a year and had become best friends. We loved nothing more than to go out, drink, and party together. One night, after a hard night of drinking, we came home to our house in Montclair. We were sitting in the front room and Turkey noticed something that had bothered him for a long time: the big, bright street light across the way. It was a huge, florescent lamp nearly thirty feet high that shone directly into our house. He felt it was too bright. I agreed.

"So what can we do about it?" I asked.

One of us (it might have been me) came up with a bright idea: "Let's shoot the thing out!"

Turkey had a .22 rifle and it seemed like one easy, quick shot could take care of the problem. No one would even know who did it. These were the thoughts of a drunk, or worse yet, two of them.

So Turkey got out his trusted .22 rifle and quietly opened the front door. He took aim and fired.

Ping! The bullet hit the light cover and broke some glass, but missed the filament.

He quickly fired off another round. Same result.

Now this thing was becoming a challenge!

After his third shot, I took over and said I could do a better job than him. I fired off a couple of more rounds, hit the filament and the light finally went out.

We then sat down on the couch. We were pretty proud of ourselves so we decided to have another beer before we went to bed. *The damn light was finally out!*

The street was now covered in broken glass, but fortunately traffic was light. However, some our neighbors must have heard the gun shots. Duh!

A few minutes later there was a knock at the door. We peered out the window. *A police car!* We tried to pull ourselves together and look sober. Turkey cracked the door open:

"Yes, officer, can I help you?" he asked.

"I'm Officer Smith from the Montclair Police Department. We've had reports of gunshots fired from this house. Do you own a gun?"

Turkey was a terrible liar. As a matter of fact, he couldn't lie at all.

"Why yes," he responded, "I own a .22."

It didn't take long for the officer to step in, examine the gun, and arrest us both. Down to the police station we went. We were booked for discharging a firearm in a residential area, disturbing the peace, and I don't know what all. Suddenly, our prank wasn't funny anymore. I had been thinking about going on to graduate school and the last thing I needed was an arrest on my record. Turkey didn't care about grad school and already had a couple of high school arrests on his record, so criminal charges weren't important to him. We got together and struck a deal. He would admit to the whole thing and say that he was the only person who fired the gun. Then, assuming he did not receive any jail time, I would agree to pay the fine and make restitution. So that's the way it went down. I avoided a criminal record and my friend took the rap.

Looking back on this event, I now realize how stupid and dangerous the shooting really was. But at the time, as seen through the eyes of a twenty-one-year-old wild, drunk, college kid, it seemed like just another prank and a great story to tell my fellow KDs. I still had not really learned to take responsibility for my actions. It was another example of Mom's corollary: I could get away with whatever I wanted to do.

I have kept most of my KD friends all these years. They are like the brothers I never had. It is amazing what a strong bond we formed and how it has lasted for almost fifty years. This was a very different group than the Turks. I lost touch with almost all of those guys. Although the KDs were wild, most of them ended up successful and responsible. Several of them became doctors, although I am the only lawyer from our pledge class.

There was my dear friend "Rastus," who is now known as Dr. Robert I. White. He was a lifeguard and would get exceptionally brown over the summer, hence the politically incorrect nickname. He went on to graduate number one from his medical class at Baylor University and was recently honored there as alumnus of the year. He was the best man at my first wedding. We are still great friends and his success is exceptional.

There was Ward "Big Fella" Jones. He became an anesthesiologist and had a long and successful career in Thousand Oaks, California. He was an athlete and played rugby, even until he was in his sixties. He was also a hero in Vietnam, although he would disdain that label.

Then there was "Grab" Kobayashi. Now he is Dr. Steven Kobayashi, one of the most respected physicians in Bishop, California. He is a great general surgeon and probably one of the few doctors that I would ever consider allowing to cut me. His is an interesting story of a Japanese-American who has done exceptionally well. He was also in my first wedding and has remained one of my dearest friends.

Then there was "Humper," now known as Dr. James Harper, who turned into an excellent cardiovascular surgeon and practiced in Long Beach for many years. He retired and lives in Wyoming. We still stay in close contact.

There are a couple of others who deserve mention. One is Nobby Orens. I don't think he ever needed a nickname. He was just Nobby. He was the wildest and craziest of us all. He was probably the best athlete, but he was a man who seemed to have an absolute disregard for the safety of his body. He was football player who would not hesitate to tackle someone three times his size. He ran headlong into everyone he could, becoming a KD legend in later years. He had a cool new red Oldsmobile convertible and had little trouble finding dates. He also was notorious for his motorcycle, which he would occasionally ride around on in the nude. That was quite a sight! In our senior year, he and I lived together along with someone who turned out to be my closest friend. That was "Turkey".

Mr. James Montgomery Ross, known as Monty and to the KDs as Turkey, was six feet five inches tall, weighed 170 pounds, had a protruding Adam's apple, and a sharp beak-like nose. He looked like a turkey. It was a perfect nickname for him. We loved to drink together and had a lot of crazy experiences. As I mentioned earlier, he took the rap for me on a criminal charge. However, like my other wild KD brothers, he is also exceptionally talented, a true genius, and an inventor and businessman. I was the best man at his wedding and he was also in my three weddings. It was an even tradeoff—one for three. I am known to his kids as "Uncle Jelly." I have to say that nearly fifty years after first meeting him and drinking hard with him all those times, he is still my best friend. It's a bond that can never be broken.

Another KD brother who deserves special mention is "Kritter," known to the world as Kris Kristofferson. He was in the class of '58 and is an amazing guy. He was a hard drinker and a great party guy, but also a great athlete. He seemed to have a Midas touch. He had many talents and did exceptionally well at all of them. He majored in English and was a terrific writer. When he was a senior in college, he submitted five short stories to the *Atlantic Monthly* for a contest. A classmate's aunt was on the selection committee and she told us that they judged the stories blind, meaning that the committee did not know who wrote what story. As it turned out, Kritter received the first five awards. Because it wouldn't be fair to give all the prizes to one person, the committee had to modify the awards. They ended up giving Kritter a first place, a third place, and an honorable mention. I remember reading his stories at the time. They were brilliant, and he certainly could have had a great future as an author.

However, Kritter loved music and often composed dirty songs for our fraternity, such as the ditty "In Bulhonkis, Tennessee . . ." What a great song that was! When Kritter strummed his guitar, he brought something special to our fraternity.

He was also a boxer and an athlete. He entered the Golden Gloves competition but ended up with a concussion. We were all gravely concerned because he insisted on continuing to box, even after doctors told him that he could suffer irreversible brain damage. He also wanted to continue with his football career. In fact, one of the short stories he wrote was about these kinds of decisions that an athlete may have to make. I thought that story was great and certainly very relevant to all of us at that point in our lives.

Kritter had come from a military family, so he eventually went up to Fort Lewis, Washington to complete his officer candidate training. Once there, they tested his athletic skills, as they did for all of trainees. He excelled at all levels and set some athletic records there that weren't broken for years. He was a good looking guy, a brilliant scholar, a great musician, and surprisingly modest. He also became a Rhodes Scholar, one of the few in the country and studied at Oxford University. With his military background, he received a teaching appointment at the United States Military Academy at West Point.

It was at that stage that he decided to throw in the towel and do what he really wanted to do: be a musician. So he went to Nashville, Tennessee and worked as a janitor just to make living, hoping to sell one of his songs to the right person. He eventually found that person: Johnny Cash. Kritter's first song became one of Johnny Cash's best hits: "Sunday Morning Coming Down." The song was terrific. Janis Joplin later recorded another of his songs, "Me and Bobby McGee." This became an all-time great rock music hit. Kritter's acting career took off as well, and he became a movie star, playing a memorable lead role in the movie *Alice Doesn't Live Here Anymore*. Kritter is a legend in his own time. He is writing his memoirs as I write mine and I will be most interested to see his book. He is a good friend who has had a wonderful and varied career. Perhaps most importantly, his success has never gone to his head. He has always remained modest and never abandoned his KD buddies.

I recently went to visit him at his home in Hawaii. I took him a 45-rpm record that he and one of our KD brothers, Tony "Furry" Lynds, had cut. That was in 1958, long before he became famous. He had lost his copy along the way and appreciated me keeping it for all of these years. Kris was recently inducted into the Country Music Hall of Fame and received a lot of exposure over his good friend Johnny Cash's recent death. Kris remains a KD to this day.

As I said over the years, I have remained friends not only with my current classmates, but with anyone else who was a KD. We have a common bond. There are a couple of lawyers in our area that I have become exceptionally friendly with, even though I was several years ahead of them in college. There is Jon "Porker" York, a successful insurance defense lawyer and tough trial lawyer. To call him a character is an understatement. He is a good friend and an excellent trial lawyer. There is Stephen (Steve) "Nipper" McNichols, Jr. who is a successful lawyer in Pleasanton, California. Steve is a brilliant attorney who has many other talents. Our KD bond has enabled us to maintain a close friendship. He practiced law for several years with Robert (Bob) "Crab" Randick, another KD. We get together for dinner every so often and reminisce about our common experiences as KDs back in the fifties and sixties.

* * *

In looking back at these college experiences, I am tempted to wonder what they mean. I certainly needed male bonding and found it with the KDs. It was a much healthier outlet than my Turk gang in high school. Yet I was still trying to prove my manhood and make up for my lack of a male role model in my life.

* * *

*The anguish of losing my case diminished as the alcohol anesthetized my pain. I popped open another beer as I thought about why I had even become a lawyer. By my senior year in college, I had no idea what I really wanted to be. I assumed that I would do something in sales.*

## CHAPTER 8: SUPER SALESMAN

After my junior year in college, I went home to Seattle for the summer. Mom suggested that I could help by selling Stanley Home Products. That sounded like fun. I had worked with Mom and helped her distribute the products for years so I knew the line well. I had heard all the training about how to sell, so it was easy to get me up to speed. Stanley Home Products was a big, national company and every summer they had a sales contest for all college students. Mom signed me up and lined me up with a whole bunch of parties to start the summer. You can put on three parties a day. They take about two hours each and you could make pretty good money if you could sell, and I certainly did well. By the end of the summer, I had done well enough to place second nationally in the contest and received a small award, a scholarship worth a couple of hundred dollars.

Of course, that wasn't good enough. Being second never is. So the next summer, I really loaded up. By that time, I had experience and repeat customers that I could call on to put on parties for me. It was a whirlwind of one party after another. I made several thousand dollars. This time I placed number one for the scholarship. Once again, I made my mother proud. I felt that I'd atoned for those difficult days at Roosevelt High School when I put that mark on my hand. The Stanley parties usually had about a dozen women, give or take a few, who listened to me sell them products. So, standing up in a front of a jury of twelve strangers and selling my case came quite naturally.

There was also a big fringe benefit to this whole summer sales work. All of my customers were women. Every size, shape, age, and marital status you would ever want. I was a young, good-looking college student entering into their midst with my sales case in hand and a glib presentation to make. Most of the women were a bit older than me, but that didn't make any difference. I thought I had enough experience to handle it, and I guess I did. I worked with many women Stanley dealers. Some were married, some were not. Some didn't care. But I had a heck of a lot of fun during those two summers. I think Mom knew a little bit about what was going on, but as always she tolerated it and thought it was good fun. She did nothing except tease me a bit.

\* \* \*

*I thought I could sell pretty much anything to anyone. My sales experience had given me confidence and I talked myself out of a lot of tough situations with my persuasive sales ability.*

*But I wasn't meant to be a traditional salesperson. No, I was going into a different kind of sales. One that would be a lot harder. One that might lead to expectations and losses. One that led me to be depressed, let down, and sitting half-drunk in my car.*

# CHAPTER 9: HAVE YOU EVER THOUGHT OF BEING A LAWYER?

In the fall of 1958, I was a college senior and having a great time as a KD. Our fraternity and the administration were constantly battling. Fortunately, we had a great friend and advocate on our side, Fred Sontag, a premier philosophy professor at Pomona. He was the relatively new KD advisor and he was always there for us. Fred is an intellectual and a deep thinker. We wondered why he tolerated or wanted to be around a bunch of wild kids like the KDs. But he seemed to enjoy it and stood up for us, time and time again. Additionally he advised us individually.

None of my family had gone to college and I didn't have a very clear idea about where I wanted to go in life. I had done some sales work and was successful in that. Everybody in those days was getting an MBA. I didn't want to think beyond college since I was having so much fun. I really didn't want to go out into the real world. Then Fred gave me a message that changed my life.

One day Fred took me aside and asked me what I wanted to do. I told him that I didn't know, maybe I'd get an MBA somewhere. He looked me in the eye and said something I will never forget:

"Have you ever thought of being a lawyer?" he asked.

A lawyer, I thought. *What does he do? I'd never met a lawyer. I'd never seen a lawyer.*

I paused.

"That's interesting," I said.

"You know," he responded, "You could be a great lawyer. You have a good mind, the gift of gab and you get along well with people. You are able to think on your feet. You should give it a try."

A light bulb went off in my head. It was a gestalt moment. *He was right. It sounded like fun!*

So I sent off applications to several law schools, including Harvard University, Yale University, the University of Chicago, and Boalt Hall at the University of California at Berkeley, among others. Other than Yale, all of the law schools accepted me. I had to decide whether to go to Harvard or Boalt Hall. Boalt was closer and I was dating and in love with a girl. So I decided to stay in California.

\* \* \*

I had met her in the spring of 1959. We were both seniors at Pomona College. I met her in my psychology class. Her name was Georgia Laflin. Georgia was a local girl—her family lived in Claremont. We studied together. Before long, we went on a date. If I was going to date her seriously, I had to be careful about the KD parties. She wasn't against to drinking, but our wild KD antics would obviously be too much for her. I guess that would be true of any sensible girl.

There were problems with Georgia's and my relationship from the very beginning, but I couldn't see them. I was too wrapped up in my own perception of what a woman should be— strong like the matriarchy. Georgia struggled with issues related to a previous boyfriend. She said that he had been involved in some covert government activity, like spying. That seemed crazy to me, but I didn't think she'd lie about it. Georgia was clearly disturbed. She needed to be rescued. And I was the guy to do it. I had always made women happy, just like Mom and the matriarchs, so I was sure I could do the same with Georgia.

I thought I could rescue Georgia and I thought that she would be just like Mom. I thought Georgia would appreciate me, just as Mom always did. I could always make Mom and my aunts happy, so why shouldn't the same be true of Georgia? I thought I was in love with her. However, my love was confused with a deep obligation: I could rescue her and make her live happily ever after, especially if we married.

Georgia's neediness appealed to me. Maybe it went back to the time Mom was getting her divorce from Jack. Mom needed her little man. I was her little man and could always make her happy. Why should Georgia be any different?

Georgia and I enjoyed our psychology studies together and had some pretty good dates. Things got heavier between us and pretty soon neither of us was dating anyone else. We became engaged. I really thought I loved her.

\* \* \*

*It was starting to get dark but I wasn't ready to go home. I couldn't face my partners, I couldn't face my peers, and I couldn't face my wife. I felt I was a failure for losing my case.*

*Sure, I'd redeemed myself from my wild high school years by going to a first-rate college and making some lasting friends, but what did that mean now? I knew I was still trying to please Mom, but was I still looking for my missing Dad? Why didn't I want to talk to my wife? What did she have to do with my feelings of shame and guilt?*

# CHAPTER 10: THE DRY WEDDING

It wasn't long before Georgia and I graduated in June 1959. The bloom was still on the rose. I was off to law school while she worked on her teaching credential. I lived in Seattle for part of the summer and corresponded vigorously with her. When the fall came, I moved to Berkeley and we kept up our long distance correspondence. There is much to say for the old adage "absence makes the heart grow fonder." Sometimes it is easier to keep the flame and passion burning while people are apart.

By the time I finished my first semester of law school, Georgia moved to Berkeley and started teaching. Even though we were intimate at the time, we did not live together. She moved into a little studio apartment with a roommate. What a disaster. She and the roommate didn't get along. That conflict made our dates and times together very difficult. But I was committed and we planned our marriage for the summer of 1960.

There were serious signs of a deteriorating relationship long before we exchanged our vows. Problems began with the wedding planning. Georgia was an only child. Her mother was also an only child. Between her mother, her grandmother, and Georgia, the wedding planning became obsessive-compulsive, to say the least. The Laflins were conservative Republicans. Her mother and grandmother particularly considered themselves blue bloods, even though they didn't have money. They wanted to emulate the DAR (Daughters of the American Revolution.) Everything had to be just right. They read Emily Post time and again. They began to argue about every little teeny thing, from the colors of the napkins to the style of the glasses.

In the days leading up the wedding, Georgia and I had a number of arguments. The bloom was definitely off the rose, but I was trapped. I simply could not get out of the wedding. Furthermore, I really thought that I loved her. I did like her parents, especially her father, George. I worked with him during that summer. His company, the White Van Battery Company, sold wholesale batteries to service stations and auto supply stores all over Southern California. George was the largest independent dealer west of the Mississippi.

I had a good time working with George and found that job very interesting. I drove a little battery truck all over Southern California. George and I always enjoyed each other's company. He was a guy who liked a couple of big martinis before dinner and that certainly suited me. I relished drinking with him and we had a great relationship. I think my reluctance to see the problems with Georgia was because I loved her dad so much. He was like the father I never had.

Big issues with the wedding plans caused more problems. The first was when they suggested that I should not invite my Grandmother Sturm. They were afraid she wouldn't have the right manners because she was a "pioneer woman." I blew up and we had a huge argument which led them to reluctantly agree that we could send her an invitation.

The second was almost as bad. They were afraid that my friends would ruin the wedding. Those wild KDs—they were going to get drunk and be rowdy at our wedding. Georgia's family decided to solve this problem by holding the wedding in the hills of Claremont, which at the time was a dry town. This meant that alcohol could not  be served.  I wasn't in favor of having the wedding there, but they insisted.  Guess what?  We were going to have a dry wedding.  No alcohol.  What a drag that would be.  But they were insistent so I acquiesced.

My friends who came to the wedding didn't stay very long.  They wanted to find somewhere where they could have some fun.  There was one bit of poetic justice in this dry event.  The reception was held outdoors at the college chapel and they planned to serve some ugly, green, lime punch.  The wedding was on July 23, 1960, an exceedingly hot day.  The large punch bowl and ladle were outside on the table in the sun.  After the wedding ceremony, they prepared to serve punch.  When they poured the ice-cold punch into the sun-heated,  glass punch bowl, the bowl broke in half, spilling the vile, green liquid all over the table.  *Good!*  Served them right.

* * *

*As my mind rambled on reviewing important events of the past, I paused to think a little more about that wedding. My mood was already sour from the shame of the verdict and remembering my anger over that dry wedding didn't help matters. So I popped open another beer just for good measure.*

# CHAPTER 11: LOOK TO YOUR LEFT, LOOK TO YOUR RIGHT

I graduated from college just short of Phi Beta Kappa but law school was different. My law school classmates were the most competitive, hardworking, anxious bunch of guys I had ever been around. The tone of the school was set by Dean Prosser, author of a book on torts and one of the best known law professors in the country. My first year class comprised of about 270 students. On our first day of orientation, we received a rude shock. We sat nervously waiting for Dean Prosser's orientation speech:

> "Gentlemen. (There were only three women in our class that year.) The law is a jealous mistress. If you are going to succeed here at Boalt Hall, you are going to have to work harder than you ever worked in your life. Some of you will make it, but a lot of you won't. So I want you to do this. Look to your left and look to your right at the people sitting next to you. By the end of the first semester, one of the three of you will be gone. That's right. One third of this class is going to flunk out. Will you be one who succeeds or one who fails?"

That speech didn't set my mind at ease. Furthermore, as I came to know my classmates, I found they were the most intelligent and ambitious group of people I'd ever known. Most had been at the top of their class at one good school or another, so the competition for number one was fierce. Who was going to be in the top ten? Who is going to make Order of the Coif, the honorary academic legal society?

I dove in and worked hard, but I must say I had no idea at the end of the first semester whether I would flunk out or be near the top of my class. I certainly didn't expect to be at the very top and that turned out to be true. At semester's end, our grades were posted and we were ranked. That's right. Number one down to the bottom of the class. Ranking was posted for all three years of law school, when about 147 of us finally graduated. At one time, I think I was number fifty. The ranking convinced me that I was a bit smarter than fifty-one but not quite as smart as forty-nine.

Law school grades were everything. After the first semester, many of the students who spoke up a lot in class and who seemed so smart were gone. Others who said very little and quietly sat through class turned out to be at the very top. Much to our chagrin, one of the three women, Kay Mickle, turned out to be our number one student.

*What?! A woman at the top of the class?! We men had never seen that happen before.* We were shamed. Was there a smart male who could unseat her? *No.* She remained at the top of the class, I believe for a couple of years, before she moved to Washington, D.C. (much to the relief of some of us.)

However, she later returned to California and did extremely well. She eventually married and now her name is Kathryn M. Werdegar. She is currently a Justice on the California Supreme Court and is one of the great successes of our class. I feel very differently about women in the law now than I did back then. I am proud to have been her classmate, but that didn't change how we felt in law school.

I formed many good friendships in law school. I sat next to a fellow named Armand Habiby whose father had been on the Supreme Court of Palestine. He was the only Arab in our class. About one-third of our class was Jewish. It was interesting how they argued back and forth, but maintained a deep-seated respect for each other, regardless of their politics. I also became very good friends with Stewart C. Adams, Jr. and Richard (Dick) A. Regnier, both of whom are excellent attorneys and good friends.

I still liked to drink and attend parties, so I soon joined a legal fraternity called Phi Delta Phi. It was a hard-drinking, legal fraternity and we had some great parties. Every Saturday night we'd go somewhere like the Berkeley Marina and blow off some steam. But party time was limited. We had too much studying to do to go out during the week. I was studying harder than I had ever had. Georgia was teaching and we lived on her salary and my summer work income.

While in law school, I developed an intense interest in politics. But unlike most of my law school peers, I came from a very different direction. I learned my politics from Georgia's parents. They were staunch right-wing Republicans and fed me a lot of rightwing literature. I read articles by William F. Buckley, whose views I came to respect. I joined the Young Republicans. There were only eight of us. One of them, Pete Wilson, later became governor of the State of California.

I strongly supported the death penalty, unlike almost everyone else in my class. I defended the actions of the House of Un-American Activities Committee, which drove some of my classmates absolutely nuts. I was right and they were left. I was a staunch conservative and supporter of Barry Goldwater. Ronald Regan was just coming on the political scene. I strongly agreed with his politics. Once again, I felt different from the majority, since a great majority of the students were leftwing liberals. However, I got along well with most of them, particularly on the social end.

I graduated from law school in June of 1962. Mom attended the graduation and was so proud of her number one son. I had become the success she always thought I would be. I had come a long way from that kid in high school. But now I had to find a job. And Georgia and I were trying to have a family.

\* \* \*

*Here I was crying in my beer after losing my big case. Even though law school was difficult, I had never doubted my choice of career. My feelings about the loss of the case didn't include regrets about becoming a lawyer.*

# CHAPTER 12: MR. DISTRICT ATTORNEY

By the time I graduated from law school, I knew I wanted to be a trial lawyer. I liked public speaking and enjoyed thinking on my feet. It dovetailed with my previous sales experience.

When I graduated from law school, I was interested in being a prosecutor. One of the top offices in California was the Ventura County District Attorney's Office. Ventura County, just north of Los Angeles, was the fastest growing county in the state. The district attorney, Woodruff "Woody" Deem, traveled around the state visiting the top law schools and recruiting candidates, just like the big law firms. One of my good friends from law school, Dick Regnier, had signed up already. I wasn't quite certain that I wanted to move to Ventura, but Dick encouraged me to come on down. Fortunately, Woody Deem hired me.

Woody had an ulterior motive in recruiting me. He was a staunch Mormon. He was a stake president, a high position in the church. It was easy to see from my résumé that I was born in Ogden, Utah: Mormon country. No sooner did I settle in my little apartment in Ventura, than there was knock on the door. Mormon missionaries. They were there to visit "Brother Gwilliam." I had not grown up in the Mormon Church and had long since "escaped" from them. I didn't want to offend my boss, so I had to feign some interest and leave the missionaries hoping that they could bring me back into the fold. But it wasn't going to happen. In the meantime, I became a successful prosecutor. Woody kept me on and promoted me regularly until I left four years later.

I felt comfortable in the courtroom and enjoyed the work when I started trying cases in the Ventura County D.A.'s office. In my experience in home party sales, I had to go into strangers' houses, put them at ease and talk to people I didn't know usually about a dozen of them. I had to convince them to believe in the products. The same skills worked in the courtroom.

In the courtroom I was selling my case. I was selling the fact that the D.A. was right and that the defendant was guilty. I had learned to speak extemporaneously. Talking to a jury came naturally. I related well with juries.

After four years as a prosecutor, I had tried about forty jury trials, including some of the first child abuse cases ever tried in the state. The law had just been changed to give immunity to doctors, hospital staff, and other health care providers for reporting child abuse. The district attorneys around the state began to look at child abuse as a crime. However, only a few cases had actually been criminally prosecuted.

The most important case I tried was in 1964 when I prosecuted a woman named Karen Jackson. She was a young, white nineteen-year-old totally unprepared to be a mother and unfit to be a parent. She had a five year-old child, another who was about three, and she delivered a third referred to as Baby Jackson. Karen and her boyfriend lived in a hovel and didn't really feed the kids. The second child had been "dropped" and had a serious head injury. There were other instances of what appeared to be abuse of these children.

Baby Jackson was born normal at just under five pounds and gained a little weight before she took him home. Five weeks later, he was dead. His weight had actually decreased. His little body looked like a skeleton or one of those horrible Holocaust pictures of the starving Jews. The county coroner reported the cause of death as starvation. In addition, the little infant had eleven broken ribs and a broken collar bone! The testimony at the trial was that Karen had beaten the baby and starved it to death. Ultimately, her boyfriend took a plea bargain and testified that Karen ignored the infant's plaintive calls for food because she didn't really want the child and hoped it would die. She got her wish.

The trial was widely covered in the local media. I was a young attorney with only about three years in practice. But I was fired up for this case. Here my wife and I wanted so badly to have children and this miserable creature who called herself a mother had abused her children and had actually even killed one. We went for first degree murder.

I'll never forget the testimony of one of our key witnesses, an inmate in the county jail with Karen Jackson. She was the last witness I called. I had already proved a strong case through the testimony of a pediatric radiologist, the pathologist, and other witnesses. Although I cannot remember the name of the witness, I will never forget her. She was a huge woman who weighed close to three hundred pounds. She was quite a sight as she waddled her way to the witness stand and plopped herself into the seat. Her testimony was short. I asked her to state her name and to say whether she knew Karen Jackson. She said that she knew Karen and that they were both in the same complex at the county jail. I then established that the witness was not being paid to testify.

Then I asked her if she remembered when Karen Jackson

was released from jail so that she could attend Baby Jackson's funeral. The witness said that she remembered the day well. I asked her if she had spoken with Karen after she had come back from the funeral.

"Yes," the witness answered.

"Please tell us about the conversation," I urged.

To this day, I will never forget her response.

"She walked in from the funeral with a little white rose in her hand. She turned to me and said 'Here's a flower from the little bastard's funeral' as she tossed the rose in my lap."

"No further questions," I said and sat down.

You could hear a pin drop in the courtroom. In all of my years of trying cases, I have never seen jurors who were angrier. If they could have, I think that they would have climbed out of the jury box and choked the defendant. In any event, the jury convicted her of second degree murder. It was a good victory at the time considering how little was known about child abuse then. People in that era really did not believe that mothers would do such things to their own children.

A final postscript to this case: The judge was a pretty softhearted fellow and did not want to send a mother to jail. Instead of issuing a jail sentence, he gave Karen Jackson probation, much to the chagrin of the entire D.A.'s office. However, to prevent this from happening again, he did something that is now illegal, but served an important purpose. As a condition of her probation, he insisted that she be sterilized so that she could never again become pregnant and have other children. She complied with the condition of this probation. I'm glad. I don't know what ever happened to her, but I do know that she never had any more children.

* * *

*I thought I was pretty hot stuff as a young D.A. I had once won twenty cases in a row. Sure, I had lost a few, but I really had not learned much about how to handle the loss of a big case.*

*I didn't know how to handle it now. Here I was, sitting alone in my car, drinking beer, afraid to talk to anyone, and full of frustration and anger. Getting off to a great start in my young career had not prepared me for this.*

## CHAPTER 13: ALL FOUR OF THEM DIED

A thick glass window separated me from him. I could barely hear his faint, raspy breathing. I could see his little chest heaving back and forth as his immature lungs attempted to take in oxygen. He was in a strange-looking, clear plastic box. I think they called it an isolet. He was tiny and helpless. He only weighed one pound, thirteen ounces. He was my son. He was my son and he was going to die.

I was exhausted. I had been up all night during the birth. My little son's three sisters had just died. They had each weighed only one pound, nine ounces, or one pound, ten ounces at birth. They were premature and there was no chance of their survival. I felt drained and devoid of emotion. The whole experience had seemed so unreal. I had never felt so tired, numb and totally helpless. Georgia was still in the maternity room. There was nothing more to be said with her. I wanted to go home. I wanted to drink. I wanted to go back to work. I took one last look at him and slowly walked out of the hospital.

Georgia and I had begun trying to have children shortly after we were married. That's what you did when you first got married in those days. Nothing much was happening, so we decided to go to a fertility specialist. The best people in the area were at the University of California at Los Angeles (U.C.L.A.), at a place called the Tyler Medical Clinic.

There appeared to be two causes of our infertility. Georgia had a tipped uterus and, more importantly, I had a very low sperm count. It had nothing to do with performance; it simply was the quality of those little fellows. They weren't getting the job done. So Georgia began to take an experimental hormone that would release more than one egg at a time, in the hopes that it would increase her chances of conceiving. They also began to collect my sperm (an embarrassing process to say the least) and inject it directly into her uterus, instead of having us use the old-fashioned method.

Then, in the fall of 1964, Georgia became pregnant. We were ecstatic! But before long, we learned that this was not a normal pregnancy. It was going to be a multiple birth. In those days, the doctors took x-rays of the uterus. They didn't yet have the sonogram technology that developed later. The doctors counted four little heads. That's right. *Quadruplets!* I was stunned. What were we going to do with four babies?

However, no sooner did we get the news about the quadruplets than the problems started. Georgia began to bleed and go into premature labor. Although we had good obstetrical care, having quadruplets was rare. As it turns out, ours were the first set ever to be born in Ventura County. They would also be the first set to die in Ventura County.

The babies were born in January of 1965, when I was twenty-eight years old. The birth was not a joyous occasion because we knew the babies could not survive. Georgia was only seven months along, the babies' lungs were not sufficiently developed, and they could not breathe. They did not even have a faint hope of surviving. We waited so long to have children and now we were only to have a funeral. We never gave the babies names. It seemed so pointless. They simply were born, died, put into small coffins, and buried. They weren't really births. They were deaths.

Watching those infants die, especially the last little boy, was the worst experience of my life. I didn't know how to deal with it. No one suggested a counselor to give us any help. That wasn't done much at that time. So I did what I had always done when I was confronted with a serious problem: I worked and I drank. I worked harder and drank more, and that seemed to ease the pain, at least for the time being. But after this trauma, our marriage, which wasn't the strongest in the first place, was never the same. We were beginning a downhill spiral and were heading for disaster. Although we continued to try to have children while we were living in Ventura, it never happened. Instead, we experienced more frustration and had an abnormal sex life.

\* \* \*

*Pain begets pain. My mental journey back through my life caused by the intense pain of the loss in the Staples v. General Motors case made me pause at this point. Nothing in my life had ever been more painful than the loss of our quadruplets. Certainly the loss of a legal case could not compare. Or could it? Had I become so ego-involved in my profession that the loss of a case was on equal par with the loss of a life? Maybe that's why I was drinking to anesthetize the pain and shame of even thinking about comparing those experiences.*

# CHAPTER 14: RABIES

Another incident occurred that caused a further separation between Georgia and me. Georgia was always nuts about cats. I wasn't. I tolerated them for her sake. It was one of those little resentments that begin to grow bigger over time. Then something happened that really accelerated it.

Georgia and I were still struggling with our infertility and driving sixty miles to the Tyler Clinic at U.C.L.A. for treatment. One afternoon, we headed down Highway 101 towards Los Angeles. A large median area covered with ice plants separated the north and southbound lanes. Soon, Georgia spotted a little kitty stuck in the ice plants in the median divider. She wanted to help it. She insisted that we turn around and go back and rescue the poor creature. I was against the idea but, under pressure, I agreed to turn around, drive a mile or so back, and cross the freeway to see if we could help the kitten. Running across a couple of lanes of a busy freeway is no picnic, but off I went to bring home the little kitty. Georgia instructed me to carefully pick the kitten up by the scruff of the neck like the mother cat would do so that it couldn't hurt me. I wasn't experienced in that methodology. Neither did I want to be.

In any event, when I got to the kitten, it turned out to be a half-grown cat that was angry, frightened, and not one bit happy to see me approaching in the ice plants. I tried to position myself behind it and reach around to get its neck. I wasn't successful. Instead, the cat turned around, bit me hard on my hand and for good measure, severely scratched my arm. *That's it!* I ran back to the car and wrapped my bleeding hand in a handkerchief. My comment to Georgia was blunt and to the point:

"Fuck that cat! I don't care if it dies or not."

She pleaded with me to make another try.

"No way! We are going to our doctor's appointment."

The next day, Georgia suggested that we call our local doctor about the cat bite. It looked pretty severe and threatened to become infected. My doctor told me to come to his office so he could talk to me. It wasn't the infection he was worried about. It was something else. After the examination he looked at me and asked,

"Do you know anything about this wild cat?"

I didn't.

Well, you know, a wild animal like that might have rabies, " he continued.

*Rabies?!* I hadn't even thought of such a thing.

"So what should we do?" I wondered.

He instructed me to see if we could find out anything about the cat. Maybe someone had found it and if so, they could test for rabies. If not, I would have to consider taking some treatment. The doctor said that we had something like three to five days to find the cat before we needed to start "the treatment." We tried to find the cat by advertising in the paper and checked with the local S.P.C.A. and various animal shelters. No luck.

I went back to the doctor a couple of days later. We had a more serious discussion:

"Well, Gary," he began, "We need to talk about rabies."

I replied that I didn't know anything about it and listened to him intently.

"The chances of you getting rabies are pretty slim. Not more than five percent, possibly even as low as one percent. But I want to tell you something. If you do have rabies, you will die the most horrible, unimaginable death possible. There is no cure for rabies once you contract the disease."

I was in a state of shock.

"So what do you suggest?" I asked.

He went on to tell me that there was a known cure for rabies, but it involved a painful and extensive series of shots of duck embryo. This was a surefire cure for any possible case of rabies, but I would need to start receiving the shots as soon as possible. I had a choice: Go through a very painful procedure or take the chance that I would die a horrible, excruciating death. The answer was pretty clear.

"I'll take the shots."

The series of rabies injections turned out to be the most irritating, uncomfortable, painful medical procedure that I had ever undergone. The doctor had to inject a large amount of duck embryo into my body every day for fourteen consecutive days. This required a huge needle to be injected into my groin or buttocks area, an uncomfortable and painful procedure. But even worse, my body would react with a huge, painful, and itchy welt much like a large skin hive. My doctor couldn't give the shots in the same place because the skin would be irritated and swollen so he had to move them around my body. He started at one buttock, went to the other buttock, then on to the groin area on the left, and then another shot on the groin area on the right. By then, we'd start again on the fifth day on the same area.

These huge, irritating hives lasted for several days. By the time one was just about settled down he would blast it with another huge injection of duck embryo. They hives were alternatively painful and then would itch like crazy. Fourteen consecutive days. Three and a half times around the circumference of my body. I was constantly scratching and moving around to the point that someone would have thought I had Saint Vitus Dance. After each shot, I got a little more angry at Georgia. *Her and her goddamned cats!* That nasty experience didn't add to our marital harmony. As if I thought our marital discord would somehow disappear on its own, I continued drinking and focused on my work.

When we moved to Ventura, Georgia made it clear that she always wanted to return to the Bay Area to live. That was okay with me. I loved the whole San Francisco Bay Area. So after about four years in the D.A.'s office it became time to move back. Now, strangely enough, Georgia began to hesitate. Maybe we should stay in Ventura. I think that her feelings were tied to the loss of the quadruplets. This drove me nuts. We still weren't getting along that well anyway and this switch in attitude was just another reason for me to be angry with her. I began to feel that I really didn't love her anymore.

*Why wasn't she like Mom? Why couldn't I make her happy?* I had done everything I could, but she wasn't responding right. *Was it just her? It couldn't be me, could it???* The myth that I could make all women happy was busting wide open, yet I could still rationalize that the problem wasn't on my end, in part, perhaps, because my career in the D.A.'s office was quite successful.

I tried a number of other interesting cases and eventually became the chief trial deputy in the office. I trained a young man who later became the D.A. I think it was clear that I could have been the Ventura County District Attorney at quite a young age, if I had so desired. It was a constantly expanding office and was growing faster than Orange County, which later became the fastest growing county in the state. However, Georgia wanted to return to the San Francisco Bay Area. I agreed.

I began looking for a job in the Bay Area and was fortunate to find one in very short order. On May 1, 1966, I was pleased to join a plaintiffs' trial firm. I wanted to continue my trial work which I really enjoyed. I was going to become a plaintiffs' lawyer. I started working at a law firm called Nichols, Williams, Morgan & Digardi. I was ready for a change in direction and I got it big time.

\* \* \*

*I was definitely feeling the alcohol now. It wasn't that the pain of the loss went away. It was just that I really didn't care so much any more. I didn't care when I went home. I didn't care if people were worried about me. Nobody could find me (no cell phones or car phones in those days.) I'd get home when I was good and ready. It would probably be late. So what.*

*I was a plaintiffs' lawyer now. And I thought I'd been a pretty good one until that verdict came in. I still distinctly remember how my career as a plaintiffs' trial lawyer started.*

# CHAPTER 15: BECOMING A TRIAL LAWYER

When I joined the Nichols law firm in May, 1966, it was by far the best known plaintiffs' firm in the East Bay. Jesse Nichols was one of the most famous trial lawyers in Northern California. He started trying plaintiffs' cases in the early 1930s and won the first $100,000 verdict in the area in 1948. At that time, a verdict like that was unheard of. His reputation was stellar. He was also generous, warm and friendly. He was to become my mentor in the firm and the father figure I needed to fill the gap from my lack of a "real father."

During my time at the Ventura County D.A.'s office, I had advanced to the position of Chief Trial Deputy. I was the number three man in the office in good part due to the tremendous growth and turnover in that office. I had tried forty jury trials to verdict, including several felonies. I'd been involved in death penalty cases and tried some of the early child abuse cases in the state, including getting that second degree murder verdict against the mother who starved her five-month-old child to death. I'd accumulated a lot of experience for only being in practice four years. However, I had no civil law experience.

I distinctly remember my interview with Jesse Nichols and his partners in early 1966. I expected to have to take a salary drop since I was earning the hefty sum of $1,100 a month. (I had started at $450 a month shortly before I passed the Bar.) When they asked me about salary, I told them I felt I would be willing to take a pay cut down to a $1,000 a month. To my great surprise, they actually offered me $1,200 a month. I was ecstatic, ready to get into a new phase of my life. So Georgia and I returned to the Bay Area. Although Ventura had been a good place for me, it was tainted by the death of our quadruplets. I hoped that my relationship with Georgia would improve once we came north.

We found a lovely little apartment on Benvenue Avenue near Alcatraz Avenue on the Oakland/Berkeley border. It was a wonderful little one bedroom apartment in a beautiful building that was designed by the famous architect Bernard Maybeck.

On the job, I rolled up my sleeves and was ready to go. I didn't know much about plaintiff's work, but it seemed to me that it was fairly simple. As a prosecutor, I was carrying the burden of proof and going after the bad guys. The same seemed to be true with being a plaintiffs' attorney. But it turned out not to be that simple.

I had little formal training at the firm. I guess it was just assumed that I could try the plaintiff's side of the case because I had gained success as a prosecutor. But being a plaintiffs' lawyer was much harder. I now had something called a client. I wasn't used to that. My client in the D.A.'s office had been the people of the State of California. There was nobody to nag you or anyone for you to worry about. You started ahead of the game, particularly in a conservative county like Ventura. I had won twenty cases in a row as a prosecutor, and thought I was pretty hot stuff. Yet, I soon learned that being a plaintiffs' attorney wasn't going to be easy.

I was given a caseload and began to try cases. But it was a struggle. They were tough little cases and I was up against some pretty good insurance defense lawyers. I launched ahead the best I could. Success was hard to find. I lost the first five jury trials and began to seriously doubt myself. *Maybe I wasn't cut out to be a plaintiffs' lawyer. Being a D.A. was a lot easier.*

But there wasn't time to pause. I had trials calendared almost every week. One right after another. Before long, I began winning some cases and felt a little better about myself and my work. One of my early successes involved an African-American client who had been involved in a classic intersection accident at a small, blind intersection in East Oakland. It was a tough case since the defendant came from his right and in those days we had pure contributory negligence. That meant that if my client at fault in any way at all, he lost the entire case.

But he was a very nice, humble Black man, as were so many of our clients in Oakland. This client had an ongoing medical condition that caused him to need to urinate frequently. Immediately after the accident, my client needed to urinate and actually ran across the street, knocked on the door of a nearby resident's house, and asked to use the bathroom. I tried to prove that this problem was related to the accident. The defense hired one of the top urologists in the area who said that my client had some kind of a bug and that with a little medicine, he could recover completely. He testified that the accident played no part in my client's urinary problems. My case looked bleak.

Our trial was held in the courtroom right across the hall from a major criminal prosecution against the notorious Black Panther Huey Newton. The defense attorney in my case carefully kicked off all of the African-Americans, which was routinely done in those days. (Today, that practice is illegal.) So I had an all-white jury. But I had a very nice client. His background and demeanor were so opposite to the perceived violence of the Black Panthers that I think my jury wanted to give him a break. The jury awarded my client $5,000 and the defense attorney was livid. His settlement offer was around $750. In those days, this was a big win. I had learned something important from this case: Good plaintiffs make for good results. The same is true today.

I remember another funny little case that I tried early on in my career. Our client was the plaintiff and the wife of a very well known prosecutor. We took the case as a favor to the local D.A.'s office and because I was the new lawyer in the office, I got stuck trying it. It was an interesting little accident that occurred in an outlying suburb called Pleasanton. The Pleasanton Fire Department was having a fire drill in a new housing development. The firefighters hooked up their truck to the hydrant. However, instead of attaching the hose to the truck, for some reason they just let the water from the hydrant shoot directly on to the street.

Along came my client, Beverly V., minding her own business, just driving down the street with her car window open. Although several firefighters claimed they tried to stop her, she drove directly into the stream of blasting water and got soaked. She also had a whiplash. When I inherited the case, she had a list of about fifty items that had been "ruined" by the clean water from the fire hydrant. These items included her garter belt and all of her hosiery. Fortunately, I was able to talk her out of those claims, but we still had to go to trial. They offered me $250. I demanded $500 and stood by my demand. We tried the case in a little municipal court out in Newark, a suburban town in southern Alameda County.

This was a case that I probably shouldn't have won, but I did because the defense made a fatal error. After each of the firefighters testified, they came back in the courtroom and huddled together, joking with each other and laughing at us. Poor little Beverly V. just sat there quietly at the counsel table. It was just her and me against all of those firefighters and the defense attorneys. We became the underdog. The jury didn't like them so I won a plaintiff's verdict of $1,500.

In one of my old files, I still have the defense counsel's motion for a new trial based solely upon the "excessive damages" that the jury awarded. My $1,500 was too high, they indignantly claimed. Fortunately, the judge denied the motion so the defendants had to pay the whole darn thing off plus costs, which finally totaled around $1,700. Nobody tries cases like that anymore. They were a lot of fun.

But with each little trial, my reputation grew. I was a budding young trial lawyer. With no formal training, I was learning by trial and error (to use an old pun) and having a great time. My cohort in the firm was Bill Gibbs. He and I spent twelve years together in that firm and became best friends. We were the young associates, since all of the partners were about twenty years older than us. Jesse Nichols was actually forty years older and the driving force of the law firm. Behind him was Ed Digardi, who continued to practice law until his death in 2005, when he was well into his eighties. Gene Morgan was another partner with a deep voice and friendly manner that endeared him to all. Jack Williams, an honest and decent man, rounded out the foursome of the senior partners.

Plaintiffs' work was a lot easier in those days. There was no tort reform, although soft tissue injuries were hard to prove. The term whiplash had long lost its magic appeal and had been turned back on us. Whiplash became synonymous with an exaggerated neck injury. Juries were suspicious of neck and back injuries. Of course, in all of those cases, the defense always hired doctors who said that my client was either exaggerating the injury or was a total malingerer. In those early years, I continued trying case after case.

In 1970, the plaintiffs' lawyers in the area decided to reactivate our local trial lawyer chapter and elected me treasurer. This was the start of my long leadership career with various trial lawyer organizations. It was exciting. These were good times for me at work. I loved my job and it sustained me through the difficult times that I was experiencing at home.

\* \* \*

*Yes, success came to me again. I started winning more cases and perhaps my confidence turned to cockiness. I thought I could win any case. I expected to win every case. I ignored the possibility of a loss. So my ego got bigger and by the time I started the biggest case of my career, I was ripe for a big dose of humility. I got it big time with the jury verdict in the Staples v. General Motors case.*

*The verdict has caused me to review my life and to try and make some sense of this almost unbearable shame. Only alcohol seemed to numb the pain. I popped open the last beer.*

# CHAPTER 16: LIZ

My relationship with Georgia continued to deteriorate. The loss of the quadruplets had greatly stressed our marriage. We continued to see fertility specialists, but it seemed pretty hopeless. Georgia wanted a baby. She was adopted and was adamant that we not adopt. She wanted her own pregnancy and her own baby. Eventually donor insemination was suggested and I consented to that procedure. I quit seeing the doctors but Georgia continued to go on her own.

One day in 1968, when our marriage was totally on the rocks, my wife bounced in happily to tell me that she was pregnant. I was stunned. We hadn't had sex in over a year. I hadn't given any thought to the artificial insemination that she was undergoing. I was ambivalent. On the one hand, Georgia and I had wanted a child for so long and the pregnancy was a wonderful blessing. On the other hand, I knew in my heart that our marriage was a failure. Even before Georgia became pregnant, we were seriously discussing divorce. I really didn't believe that a child could save the marriage, but I was determined to at least give it a try. And I am very glad that I did. My wonderful daughter Catherine was born in March of 1969 and she is very dear to me. However, it soon became quite obvious that our marriage could not be saved.

By now, I had been working at the Nichols firm for four years. At that time, lawyers had their own private secretaries. In those days, we didn't have computers and only lousy lawyers did their own typing. One day a new temporary secretary was assigned to me. She was a Kelly Girl (the once common yet sexist term used to describe a woman who worked for Kelly Services, a temporary employment agency.) As soon as she walked into my office, I knew I wanted to hire her. She had great skills, seemed very professional, and had terrific legs. Those were the days of miniskirts and they suited some women better than others. They suited her to a T. Her name was Liz Cornell and I hired her on the spot.

Our relationship began professionally. She was very efficient and we worked well together. Soon we got to know each other and found that we shared some interesting similarities in our lives. Her mother's family was from Brigham City came in northern Utah, just a few miles north of Ogden where I was from. Given Utah's polygamous past, we were probably related as seventh or eighth cousins, which was common for people living in Utah. We also shared something else — fertility problems. Liz had been married for several years and was going through the same difficult problems that I was. However, Liz's attitude towards adoption was the opposite of Georgia's. That drew me to Liz.

Liz and I maintained a cordial relationship but it became increasingly clear that we were attracted to each other. One day in early 1970, I took the first step. I invited her out for a drink after work. It started out innocently enough. We talked about a lot of things we had in common, including my work. One evening out led to another and before long we fell in love. She was having trouble with her marriage and Georgia and I were constantly bickering. Liz was quite moral and insistent that we not have an affair or sexual relationship until we married. So we each made the difficult decision to leave our spouses and find separate places to live.

I moved out of my house on my birthday, May 18, 1970. Liz had already separated from her husband and was living with her mother in San Francisco. I got an apartment in San Francisco and both Liz and I instituted divorce proceedings. We made every effort to finalize them quickly so that we could get married as soon as possible.

We tied the knot on October 16, 1971. For our honeymoon, we sailed to Hawaii on the old *S.S. Monterey*. I had never been to Hawaii, but Liz was born and raised there. It was a beautiful trip and was the beginning of many wonderful trips to Hawaii with her.

Liz and I vowed to adopt in the near future. That worked out beautifully. Our first daughter Lisa was born on March 15, 1973 and our second daughter Jennifer was born on October 21, 1975. We got them both as infants and raised them as loving parents. They were healthy and happy kids. They turned out great and I always did my best to be a good father. Liz and I had great times in those early years. She had a sense of humor, as did I. We shared many laughs, traveled together, and enjoyed many remarkable trips. My success at the firm continued, and aside from the difficulties of my bitter divorce from Georgia, life was very good.

By the early seventies, Bill Gibbs and I were both partners in the law firm. Other lawyers joined us, including Mike Brown in 1969 and Joe Campbell in 1975. I loved being a trial lawyer. All of my friends were trial lawyers just like me. They worked hard and played hard. In those days, after the trial was over, you and your opponent would go out for a drink. Often it turned into a whole evening of drinking. I felt accepted again. I was one of the boys, just like my gang days in high school and my fraternity days in college. But this was different. I was doing good work helping people. I was trying exciting and interesting cases. I was working like crazy.

About the time Mike Brown came to the firm, I was handling 180 personal injury cases by myself with just one secretary to help me. At that time, we really didn't have as much discovery or pre-trial work as there is nowadays. When Mike came onboard, I was able to give him sixty of my cases. I felt as light as a feather. I was only handling 120 personal injury cases! Nowadays, a load like that would be almost impossible to handle, particularly when you have to try case after case. At that time, I had a different trial set almost every week.

In 1976, I was invited to join a prestigious trial lawyer organization, the American Board of Trial Advocates (ABOTA.) It was an invitation-only group of plaintiff and defense attorneys who were the most experienced and deemed the best in their profession. To join, you had to certify that you tried a certain number of trials. By then, I had been practicing law for fourteen years. I sat down and listed all of the cases I tried at the D.A.'s office and then counted all of the cases I tried at the firm. I had tried another sixty cases as a plaintiffs' attorney. I had tried one-hundred jury trials to verdict. The ABOTA lawyers were mostly a bunch of hard drinking lawyers just like me. I felt like I belonged. My work sustained me. As a matter of fact, my work was consuming me.

It was about this time that I finally got my big opportunity. I had won a lot of good medium-sized verdicts, but I really wanted the big one. A huge case came into the office. It involved a woman who had lost her husband in a car accident. She had also been badly injured. The simple part of the case involved the responsibility of the other driver who had crossed the center line and caused the accident. That part of the claim was easily settled. However, I wanted a chance to prove myself. I was ready to take on a much tougher part of the case. I strongly urged my partners to let me take on the other part of the case. Sure, it would cost a lot of money, but I was hot. I was on a roll and I knew I could win it. They agreed. Soon I was on my own with, by far, the biggest case I ever tried.

So I took the case of Staples v. General Motors and was ready to prove that the exploding gas tank was the real cause of my client's injuries and her husband's death. I was confident and self-assured, perhaps even a little cocky. Little did I know what was in store for me.

\* \* \*

*It was totally dark now. I'd just finished the last beer, so I guess it was time to go home. Time to face the music. The conclusion was becoming clear even in my alcoholic haze. Something was wrong. I was burning out. I was working too hard and drinking too much. I had two wonderful young daughters at home and a marriage that started out great. Now it was slipping.*

*I knew I needed to cut back on my drinking. Not quit, mind you, just cut back. The idea of quitting was repulsive.*

*All of my friends drank and every enjoyable experience I had revolved around drinking. I was a big Oakland Raiders fan and I couldn't imagine going to a football game without some beers, let alone having fun on Saturday night.*

*But this drinking alone in the car wasn't fun drinking. This was stress drinking. This was drinking to anesthetize the pain of my loss.*

*So I started the car and headed for home. I knew my wife would accept me and sympathize with my loss. My kids would still love me, and so would my dog. My partners would sympathize with me and understand, although I felt that my image as the rising star of the firm was tarnished.*

*And I knew what I would do. I would go back to work. I'd try more cases. I'd continue to be the fun-loving, hard-drinking trial lawyer. That's the way it was and I didn't want to change. Not yet. I was a trial lawyer and that's the way we were.*

# PART TWO

# CHAPTER 17: GWILLIAM & IVARY

In early 1978, there was a massive, sudden change in the old firm. Jesse Nichols had retired several years before, as had another partner, Jack Williams. Now Gene Morgan decided to retire even though he hadn't yet turned sixty. To add to our problems, Bill Gibbs decided to go to Texas and try his hand selling real estate with an old friend. Mike Brown started a practice in the Pleasanton area where he had lived for many years. That left Ed Digardi and me with all of the cases.

Ed was a bit of a father figure to me, a little like my stepfather, Wayne. But Ed sensed my weakness. He was concerned with my drinking. Ed wanted to have his own firm so he chose Joe Campbell, a young associate, over me to join his new firm. I felt rejected. As it turned out, that was the right thing for Joe, who still remains a friend, and, in the long run, for me as well.

So, the firm officially broke up and I started my own firm. Fortunately, I was able to get help from an old friend who I had known since about the time Liz and I were married. His name was Eric Ivary. He and his wife Mary had become good friends with Liz and me. Our kids were the same age. The four of us played bridge and our families vacationed together. I distinctly remember our great trips to the mountains at Lake Tahoe and to the ocean at Sea Ranch.

Eric worked for another lawyer who had been with the Nichols firm back in the fifties, so Eric was also an experienced plaintiffs' lawyer. However, he was ready for a change. Eric agreed to leave his firm and the two of us struck out on our own

126

on September 1, 1978, forming the law firm of Gwilliam & Ivary. Shortly after that, we brought on a man I had known for quite some time. Jim Chiosso worked as an insurance adjuster for many years before becoming in-house counsel for Traveler's Insurance Company. Jim joined our firm in January of 1979. Before long, we added another partner, Steve Cavalli, who had worked for us as a law clerk in 1979. Once Steve finished law school and passed the Bar, he joined our firm in 1981. We all shared office space with Ed Digardi and Joe Campbell. Even though we were in competition for the same clients, we worked very well together in the same office space.

On the surface the firm was doing fine. There was a new sense of excitement in our work. However, I was feeling the pressure. I was now the senior partner and had to carry the firm. I had some nagging doubts. *Could I win the big one? Would we really succeed?* We were in a tough and competitive business and I continued to drink, but never at work. Although I would occasionally have a drink at lunch, I was always very careful if I did, since that often led to the loss of a whole afternoon. I never drank if I was in trial. Even so, my drinking worried me.

I don't want to imply that the late seventies and early eighties were bad years. I formed deep and lasting friendships with my law partners and we shared some enjoyable times. I loved my work as always and it sustained me.

## CHAPTER 18: R-O-L-A-I-D-S

A bunch of us guys always went over to San Francisco during the Christmas season to shop for gifts for our wives. The group included Bill Gibbs, Joe Campbell, Jim Chiosso, Eric Ivary, and sometimes others. We typically had lunch and couple of drinks and then we would shop for a while in the afternoon.

A week or so before Christmas in 1980, we stood in front of the I. Magnin department store across the street from Union Square in downtown San Francisco. I had a little buzz on from lunch when Joe Campbell approached.

"Hey," he said to me, "There's a guy who wants to talk to you about a Rolaids® commercial."

The fellow approached me holding a small tape recorder.

"Do you use Rolaids?" he asked.

"Yes," I replied. (It was true. I had stress that bothered my stomach from time to time.)

"Let me turn on the recorder and ask you a question," he said.

"Okay," I replied.

"How do you spell Rolaids®?" he asked.

I responded immediately, "R-O-L-A-I-D-S."

"All right. How would you like to try out for a Rolaids® commercial?" he asked.

"Sure, that sounds like fun," I said. I wondered what was up.

"Let's go across the street," he told me.

We walked over to the other side of Union Square. There on the corner was a setup with production staff and television cameras. Then I saw a familiar face: Roger Staubach, then the star quarterback for the Dallas Cowboys. He was standing on the sidewalk doing an on-the-street commercial with different people. I sat down and watched a couple of guys go through a very nervous, stumbling effort at trying to get the words out. I was sure I could do better. When my turn came, I went up and introduced myself to Roger. We chatted a little bit about the Raiders' move to Los Angeles and about football in general. I did a cut or two of the Rolaids® commercial. They seemed to like what I was doing. I ended up standing on the corner for about forty-five minutes while most of my predecessors had only been there for a very short time.

The commercial cut included me writing the word Rolaids out on some kind of a blackboard. Someone off camera asked the question "How do you spell relief?" and answered, "R-O-L-A-I-D-S" as I wrote the word Rolaids on the blackboard. We went through that several times. When we were finished, I walked back up to the fellow with the tape recorder and sat down.

"Well," he said, "We're going to take this back to the advertising agency and I'll let you know what happens. In the meantime, I need to give you something called consideration. Do you know what consideration is?"

"Well, I guess I do," I answered. "I've been a lawyer for almost twenty years."

"We need to have you fill out a little form and we'll give you $10 in consideration," he explained.

I jokingly responded that $10 didn't seem like much for my time since I usually charge $250 an hour. Then I asked him whether there was any chance that this commercial would really get on television. He said it was probably about a chance in a hundred, but they would let me know one way or another. I laughed off the experience, talked to my friends about it, and went home and told Liz. Then I forgot all about it.

About two months later, I received a large envelope in the mail from the Bates Advertising Agency. In it was a contract to join the Screen Actors Guild. I had to become a union member before they could use my face and words on the commercial. I was informed that I would be paid for the commercial based on how often it ran, although the formula for payment was so complicated, I never did figure it out. After I sent in the papers, we got a check shortly thereafter for several hundred dollars. The commercial didn't air much in California, but it wasn't long before my mother called me, squealing with delight, saying that she had seen me on television in a Rolaids® commercial. The same was true of some of my old fraternity friends and other people I knew around the country. I only saw the commercial a time or two, but it was pretty funny to see myself on television.

What wasn't funny was the money. It started to come in. The first check, as I said, was only for a few hundred dollars but within a week or so another check came in for about $400, then one for $800, and finally one for $1,000. This was money from heaven. At that time, the firm wasn't doing all that great and getting the money was terrific. My wife got so excited about the whole thing that she used to stand outside waiting for the postman every day to see if there was any mail from the Bates Advertising Agency with a check in it. When it was all said and done, I had earned about $15,000. Easy money. I should have been an actor. But then wasn't I already one in the courtroom? That was harder work and the money is not as easy. In any event, it was an interesting experience. I still have a videotape of one of the commercials. There I am with a full head of dark hair, standing with Roger Staubach, looking directly into the camera, and spelling R-O-L-A-I-D-S.

I loved my work and these were exciting times. Our new firm was making a name for itself and we were getting a good many cases. We weren't making a lot of money but we were having a lot of fun. My partners and I bonded and became like brothers. We worked and played together and had great times going to basketball games, football games, picnics, and playing dominos. Things were good at work. But on the home front, it was different.

# CHAPTER 19: BURNING OUT IN THE FAST LANE

From the mid-seventies to the mid-eighties, my life at home slowly became dark and difficult. There was the stress of trial after trial after trial. I loved the competition and enjoyed the work, but it was taking something out of me. I don't think people understand how stressful and difficult it is to be a trial lawyer. Every case was on a contingency basis. If I didn't win, I didn't get paid. And winning was oh-so-important. But I was also a guy who would try a tough case. I wasn't going to back down and I would take on any case at any time, as long as I felt that I had a reasonable chance of winning. So I was winning some cases and losing some. However, something continued to elude me: the magical million dollar verdict. Many of my peers were getting that great seven-figure verdict. It seemed that there were more and more of them in the seventies and early eighties. I tried several big cases that had a million dollar potential. I joked that I tried five-million-dollar cases but the juries disagreed with me on the value. These cases ended in defense verdicts. With each loss, I again vowed to try harder. But the stress was getting to me.

Of course, my toughest loss was Staples v. General Motors, the gas tank explosion case. Each subsequent loss haunted me and reminded me of the terrible pain I felt after that verdict.

The stress was mounting. I felt pressure from running my law firm and handling a heavy caseload. I was trying to balance being a family man and a good father with being an excellent trial lawyer and a fun party guy. The hard drinking and late nights were affecting me. Life was weighing me down.

In those days, I only knew two ways to handle stress. One was to work harder. The second was to drink harder. The latter was becoming a serious problem. I was convinced I would never become an alcoholic. I knew that my father was an alcoholic as were almost all the men in my family. But I wasn't going to become an alcoholic. Why? Because I was too smart. I not only had a college education, but I had a law degree! None of my ancestors were educated. I was smarter than them. Still, I definitely didn't want to quit drinking. I was arrogant in my thinking about alcohol. I have since learned that is denial. But I was very resistant to the idea that I might be an alcoholic. *Not me!*

During the week, my drinking pattern was confined almost entirely to the evening. By the time the workday was done, I not only wanted a drink, but I needed one. I had to have that drink by about 5:30 p.m. On the way home from work, I would hit the bar, have a couple of drinks, then go home and have another big drink or two before dinner. Liz was becoming increasingly concerned about my drinking. She tried to serve dinner as soon as I got home from work so that I wouldn't have time to have a second or even a third drink. It was an odd kind of race, but I found that if I just filled a bigger glass and drank faster, I'd get to the high I needed. So I would "win" the dinner race while losing my sobriety.

During dinner, I would have a glass or two of wine. If I had work to do, I would put on a pot of coffee and drink that after dinner to stay alert. Then, towards the end of the evening, I would have a couple of after-dinner drinks. I literally knocked myself out in order to sleep at night. I was numbing the pain of the stress and the struggles that I felt with my work. My marriage and being a father added to my stress. Forming a new law firm certainly hadn't helped. I was now on my own and had to make it myself without older, more experienced partners. I was now the senior partner. People relied on me to carry the load of the new firm. The load was getting heavy.

I didn't drink at lunch very often. When I did, it wasn't good. I simply ended up being more under the influence by the time I came home. But I never drank at lunch during trial and I never had a bottle in my desk. *I wasn't some drunk just staggering around! I wasn't an alcoholic, right?* In fact, I was a functioning alcoholic because I needed alcohol and used it every day. Liz and I were beginning to argue bitterly about my drinking. She was concerned about me. Of course, I was defensive and denied that my drinking was a serious problem.

Something else was also going on in my life. I must say I am not proud to talk about this part of my life, but I vowed honesty in this book and honesty it will be. My fast lane, after-work drinks evolved into evening drinking. Then to bars. And then to women.

I always loved women. I thought they loved me. I convinced myself that maybe I could just have my cake and eat it too with a little date here and there. As things deteriorated at home and my sex life with Liz fell apart, I felt somehow more justified in trying to find someone to satisfy me outside the home. This only added to my stress and increased my drinking. Much of my behavior was common among trial lawyers at that time. However, that didn't make it right. I felt guilty and this caused more stress, ergo more drinking.

My drinking at the bars went something like this: The bar was dark and inviting. The music was hot. The place was packed. One of the great spots in Oakland for party people was The Elegant Farmer, located in Jack London Square. I was supposed to be at the basketball game. By that time, the Golden State Warriors were really slipping and I wasn't interested anyway. I wanted to be where the action was. The juke box played some of my favorite music: "I Can't Help Myself (Sugar Pie Honey Bunch)" by The Four Tops. (I love to dance to that hard-pounding rhythm.) Then came "In The Midnight Hour" by Wilson Pickett. (I was ready to find somebody in the midnight hour.) Then finally, "Light My Fire" by The Doors. (I was ready to have my fire lit.) The music put me over the edge.

I did my typical routine. I would be in the bar for four hours and drink approximately sixteen bar scotches. That's only four an hour, or one every fifteen minutes. On a slow night, I might do three drinks in an hour. That meant I could spend five hours in the bar, have fifteen drinks, be ready to drive home with just enough alcohol to maintain a good solid buzz, yet still remain functional. So I thought!

The midnight hour approached and I went to the public telephone (nobody had cell phones in the seventies.) I dialed the number:

"Hi Fern, how are you doing?" I asked.

"Great," she responded, "It's good to hear from you."

"Do you mind if I stop by for a drink on my way home tonight?" I asked.

"I'd love it," she replied, her voice inviting.

"Thanks," I said, "I'll see you soon."

I parked around the corner from her building and walked to her door. I knocked softly. She opened the door and stood there in her robe and nightgown. I stepped inside. I saw the bottle of scotch with some soda and ice on the bar. It was the midnight hour. I was ready to light my fire. I was in trouble.

I woke up the next morning alone in my bed at home. That wasn't unusual after a long night out. I struggled mightily to remember what had happened at the end of the evening. I was having blackouts and I couldn't recall what, if any, conversation I'd had with Liz when I finally came home. I know it had been late and I'm sure it wasn't good. What the hell kind of excuse had I made up? Did we go back to the bar after the basketball game? I think so. Did my car break down again? Unsure. But something else was wrong. I felt it. Something had happened last night that had scared me. I couldn't remember the details. I knew Liz would be cold and wouldn't talk to me. Perhaps that was just as well. Anyway, something told me to go to my car. I walked down to the garage and checked on my little sports car. I drove a baby blue Mercedes 350SL and I loved it.

I opened the door to the garage and was stunned to see my beautiful blue car covered with green stuff. *What the hell had happened?* I looked more closely at my car. It was some sort of vegetation. Then it all came back to me. *Holy Crap!* I remember that I had fallen asleep while I was driving home, up on Joaquin Miller Road in Oakland. I had crossed over the center divider, mowing through the oleander bushes, and ending up clear across the road facing oncoming traffic. Fortunately it was after two in the morning and no one was coming at me. That scared the hell out of me, but not enough to make me quit drinking. Not yet.

I was lying to my wife. She knew it and I knew it. But she pretended I that I was telling the truth and I pretended that lying to Liz wasn't that important. However, it wasn't just about lying to Liz. That was wrong, and I did feel bad about it, although not enough to stop. There was something else that was more important. I was lying to myself. I wasn't living with integrity. I was losing touch with my values. I certainly was not in touch with my soul. I wasn't even sure I had one. How could I be, when I was living in the fast lane and pretending to myself that things were okay. There was no time for me to seriously reflect on who I was and why I was here. I was just putting one foot in front of the other every day. Work and drink. Drink and work and more of the same.

To make matters worse I began to drink alone. I also started sneaking drinks. When Liz left the kitchen after dinner, I would slip back and chug a swig of scotch straight out of the bottle. I needed to stay high and keep the alcohol in my system until I passed out or drifted off into a drunken slumber.

I was depressed. Depression had never been a part of my life and I hated it. But I couldn't see my way out. I tried therapy, but of course I lied to the therapist about my drinking and what was really going on in my life. Obviously, I didn't think I had a problem, so the therapy didn't work. Liz and I also went to counseling. But I lied my way through those meetings, too. As a result, counseling didn't work either. I was stuck in a rut and couldn't get out.

I don't want to imply that I did not have any happy times during those years. My two lovely daughters Lisa and Jenny were growing up and I enjoyed my time with them. I tried to spend as much time with them as I could. They were both good kids. I loved to laugh, play, and joke with them. I also loved my first daughter Catherine, although I didn't see her as often as I would have liked. Georgia had remarried and her husband was a teacher. He took a job teaching at an army base in Frankfurt, Germany. One day I got a postcard that said I should send my child support payments to a new address at the overseas army base. Just like that, Catherine was pulled out of my life for two years, making it difficult for us to remain close during that time.

I also had a wonderful dachshund dog named Sam. I enjoyed my times with him and he loved me unconditionally. I have always had a peculiar sense of humor. One of my most memorable pranks involved my dog Sam and my doctor Bruce Lawrence. Bruce was my family doctor that I regularly went to. I met him at the athletic club where I would go from time to time to get massages or to do a little exercise. He and I were friends as well as patient and physician. However, he was obsessed with tests. Blood tests, urine tests, and the worst of all: tests for colon cancer. That meant that you had to take a sample of your feces with a little wooden stick, put it an envelope, and mail it back to him. Not a pleasant task. No one likes that test. I sure didn't. So one day, when I was out on the patio cleaning up some of Sam's messes, a bright idea hit me. It would be simple to just take that little popsicle stick and take a few of Sam's samples and send them back. That was much easier and it would get that doctor off my back.

So off the sample went in the mail to my friend Bruce. A few days later, I called his office to get the test results. He cheerfully informed me that all of my tests were normal, including the stool sample. At this stage, I 'fessed up and told him that I was so glad that my dog Sam didn't have cancer. Well, I don't think Bruce has ever gotten over that prank. This took place some twenty-plus years ago, yet I still hear from Bruce about Sam's stool sample. A little humor goes a long way.

\* \* \*

However, I was still drinking heavily. I tried to deal with the problem on my own. First, I cut out all martinis then I cut back on scotch. Soon all I was drinking was wine, but I wasn't handling it well. My doctor told me my liver was irritated. I took vitamins and tried to stay healthy. I attempted to limit my drinking, but I wasn't successful. I was looking for any solution, except the most obvious.

By the early eighties, my drinking was even worse. Liz became more frustrated and concerned. We grew further apart. Frequently she would sleep in the guest bedroom.

Two instances in the early eighties clearly illustrated my increasingly severe alcoholism. The first was in May 1983, when my mother celebrated her seventieth birthday. Liz wasn't very interested in traveling back to Ogden, Utah, so my sister and I decided to throw a surprise birthday party for Mom. I didn't really care if Liz went. Frankly, I was happy to go by myself so I wouldn't be nagged about my drinking. I decided to drive my little sports car to Utah. My former law partner, Bill Gibbs, was in town, and I asked him if he would like to accompany me on at least part of the drive. He knew some people in Ventura, so we drove to Utah via Ventura, Los Angeles, and Las Vegas. Bill accompanied me. We put the top down on the car and drank beer as we cruised down Highway 1.

Drinking beer while driving is not a good idea. After I dropped Bill off, I drove on to Las Vegas where I partied and gambled. I got up the next morning at about 10:00 a.m. and headed out. Shortly after I started, I popped open a beer can. Right about then a red light came up behind me and I was stopped by a cop. I was speeding. Fortunately, I was able to slip the beer back in the cooler. Luckily for me, he didn't know that I had been drinking. He simply gave me a speeding ticket. This was another warning sign of my serious alcohol abuse that I ignored.

I cruised on to Utah where we had a nice surprise party for my mother. My sister Pat was also out of control, smoking marijuana and snorting cocaine. We partied together for a few days and then I drove back. Although the trip was fun in a way, it was certainly a serious indication of me ignoring my responsibility to my family and to myself. It was as much a chance simply to get away and drink without being nagged by my wife as it was to celebrate my dear mother's birthday.

A year later, in 1984, my Kappa Delta fraternity had a big twenty-fifth reunion at Pomona College. I drove down there alone and met with my old friend Turkey and my other fraternity brothers. By that time, my drinking was really out of hand. I was under the influence during the entire two days of the reunion. I started drinking in the morning and kept on drinking until I finally passed out at night. Turkey had always been ready and willing to drink with me, but now even he was concerned about how much alcohol I was consuming. We actually got into a big argument about it. I angrily denied that he had any right to talk to me about drinking, even though in my heart I knew that I was losing my battle with the bottle. Once again, I was looking for an excuse to drink with somebody and to find any reason to party hard.

I could still function at the office, but at this point, even my law partners were worried about the impact the alcohol was having on my life. Liz grew increasingly concerned. Looking back now, it seems so simple: I just had to quit drinking. But at the time, I didn't want to quit drinking. Everything in my entire life that I had ever enjoyed had involved drinking: my wild times in high school, my great days in my fraternity, and the good times with my hard-drinking trial lawyer friends. Every football game I had attended as an Oakland Raiders season ticket holder involved booze. Every card game, including bridge and dominoes, all centered on drinking. Everything about my life that was fun, especially anything involving women, had always involved drinking. I wasn't sure I could make love without being under the influence. If I didn't drink, I couldn't be happy. At least that was what I told myself.

I knew I was in trouble. But I wasn't about to pray to God. I wasn't sure that was the way to go and I didn't want to be a hypocrite. I had *never* quit drinking. Not even for one day. So going on the wagon was not an option. Maybe I just didn't want to quit. Maybe I was weak. But I was stubbornly holding on to my deteriorating lifestyle. My second marriage was failing. I was afraid of losing my daughters, whom I loved deeply, even though I wasn't sure I was being a good father to them.

I knew Liz was thinking about leaving me. I really didn't blame her. There were too many late nights with lipstick on my collar and too many of my phony, stupid lies that demeaned us both. There was too much irritability caused by too much alcohol. I was stuck. I needed help. I was literally drowning myself. I was concerned about my liver. If I didn't quit drinking, I could die. I am not sure I really cared at that point. I was depressed and afraid. Afraid to lose my lifestyle. Afraid to lose my family. Afraid to lose my life. *What could I do?*

## CHAPTER 20: INTERVENTION

The answer to my dilemma came with sudden swiftness. It is a day I will never forget: June 11, 1984. It was a Saturday night and Liz had set up a dinner with some of our friends, the Potters. I really liked them. John and I both loved drinking, and we often spent New Year's Eve together and had a lot of fun. I was looking forward to having dinner and drinks with them down at a hotel on Hegenberger Road in Oakland. It was an easy place for both of us to meet. Liz planned the dinner for 5:30 p.m. It was a bit early, but that was okay with me. That meant a little more time in the bar to drink before dinner. We walked into the hotel right on time and I turned to head into the bar.

"No, we are going this way," Liz said as she intercepted me. "They are meeting us in the coffee shop."

*Coffee shop?* It didn't compute for a minute. *Why are we meeting in the coffee shop?*

The coffee shop was deserted except for four men sitting at a table over in the corner. As I approached, I recognized some of them. One man was Bill Gibbs, my former law partner. He had returned from Texas and had remained a good friend. Another man was Edwin (Ed) Train Caldwell, a trial lawyer I knew from San Francisco. Burke M. Critchfield was also there. He was a lawyer in the Pleasanton-Livermore area whom I knew casually. There was a stranger with them. I approached the table with a sense of confusion and rising concern.

Liz turned to me. She looked serious as she said "Gary these men want to talk to you about drinking." I was puzzled.

"So do you want to have a drink?" I asked.

No. They didn't want to have a drink. That wasn't what this was about. It was something that I had never heard of: *an intervention*. This was a term that I have come to learn well since then.

With some reluctance, I sat down and heard them go around the table and tell me how serious my drinking problem was. They were honestly concerned for me. I was drinking too much and everyone knew it. I was even passing out at parties now and then and getting in trouble at work if I drank at lunch. Liz had asked them to meet with me and see if they could get me into a program to quit drinking. I sat quietly as I listened to them. I was becoming embarrassed as they berated me.

I blew up and looked at them.

"What right do you have to talk to me about drinking?" I demanded.

"Are any of you better lawyers than I am? Are you getting better verdicts than I am?"

No.

"Then what the hell right do you have to sit down and tell me that I should go into a program and quit drinking? Quite frankly, it is none of your business."

I stood up in anger and stomped out of the room. Liz followed quietly behind me. The Potters weren't coming. She had lied to me. She set me up. I was ashamed and full of self-righteous anger. We drove home in stony silence. When we got home, it was still early.

I distinctly remember turning to Liz and saying, "Well you don't expect me not to have a drink after a thing like that, do you?"

I went into the kitchen and fixed myself a stiff scotch and soda. I retreated to the front room and sat there alone, thinking and drinking. I nursed the drink and before long I started a second one.

But something had happened. They had hit me where it hurt—my pride. Their public humiliation of me pierced my self-inflated ego. It felt like I had been slapped across the face. Obviously I wasn't kidding anyone about how serious my drinking was. The only person I was kidding was me. I knew Liz was ready to leave me. She was sitting in the other room, crying softly. After an hour or so, I walked in and sat down next to her on the bed.

"Liz, I don't want you to leave me," I began. "I know that I am drinking too much and I am going to tell you something that I have never said before. I am going to quit. Starting tomorrow, I will quit drinking."

Although she was skeptical, she believed me and we made up. Within the next week or so, we had planned to go to Hawaii and we were able to take off and have an enjoyable vacation. This was the first vacation I had ever had without any alcohol. We had a wonderful time.

At the time, I was seeing a therapist about my drinking. I was concerned that tests showed that my liver was irritated so I had tried to cut back on my drinking. However, I hadn't really decided to quit so we weren't really getting anywhere in therapy. My therapist was also a physician and an expert in his field. He advised me that if I quit drinking cold turkey, he was worried that I would experience delirium tremors. My alcohol intake was that serious. Fortunately, that didn't happen. Immediately after I stopped drinking, I began to feel better. Within a week, I felt fabulous. My head cleared and as a result, my life changed forever.

I probably should have joined an A.A. program or gone to a rehab center. That was what the intervention was about. But I got turned off by Alcoholics Anonymous when I was a nineteen-year-old student at Citrus Junior College when my biological father, Jack, dragged me to a meeting. It was a total drag. Listening to all those old people sitting around and talking about having been drunks on the street didn't appeal to me. I wasn't that kind of a drinker. I was smarter than that. Or so I told myself. And I definitely didn't want to quit drinking. So, even years later, I was resistant to an A.A. program. But I knew that I had to quit and I knew that I had to make a dramatic change in my life. And so I did.

I began learning about drinking and alcoholism. I began reading a great book called the *Courage to Change: Personal Conversations About Alcoholism with Dennis Wholey*, a collection of stories by famous people who had overcome alcoholism was helpful. Other similar books inspired me. I decided I would be my independent self and maintain sobriety on my own. I vowed that I was never going to get in trouble with drinking again. I decided to live instead of die.

Fortunately, we had a place that we shared with another couple down at Pajaro Dunes, a lovely development of homes on a beach on Monterey Bay, just west of Watsonville, California. Going down there over weekends and spending time with the kids was healing. I began to read everything I could, not only about alcohol abuse, but other books that helped me find out who I was.

What made me drink the way I did? What made me get in trouble the way I did? Who was I? These were the fundamental questions that have been asked by philosophers and religious leaders throughout history. I wanted to find the answer on my own, so I began to read books. Over the next few years, I read between 250 and 300 books on religion, philosophy, self-help, and related matters. This led me to experience a true spiritual awakening.

During this process, I learned something very important. I didn't have to have a drink to have a good time. When I went to a party, nobody gave a damn about what I put in my glass. They didn't know whether it was soda, cola, or anything else. I dabbled with non-alcoholic beer for awhile, but for the most part I just avoided alcohol. Soon I found I could have a good time at the parties. I could even remember them too!

There was another wonderful benefit to quitting drinking. My mind cleared I found that I had a lot of extra time. I now had time in the evenings, when I could read and relax. I had time when I could be awake and alert. It was like I suddenly added three or four hours to every day of my life. I was living twenty-eight to thirty-hour days instead of the old twenty-four hour days. I could do so much more. I was also much more alert.

I had never really had a big problem with hangovers. I had found a simple solution some years before. I would always take an Alka-Seltzer® at night before I went to bed. Doing this helped clear my head and keep my stomach from getting too sour. Now I didn't need to do that. I slept better. I felt better.

I exercised. I had a physical, spiritual, and psychological awakening.

My productivity at work improved. I had kidded myself for years that my drinking didn't really affect my work. In one way it didn't. I didn't drink during the day or during trial and I could function as a lawyer. Although I didn't have hangovers, my energy was much better after I cleared the alcohol out of my system. My concentration was better. My judgment was better. Most of all, I had a tremendous amount of new energy. In fact, I was a better lawyer.

Since my terrible loss in the Staples v. General Motors exploding gas tank case, I had tried four other major cases. However, I still didn't have my million dollar verdict. I wanted it desperately. My ego had always wanted it. But now it was different. Now I was ready. Spiritually ready. I really believed that the Universe would give me what I wanted, as long as it was consistent with my client's interest. I had to have the right case for both me and my client—a case that would be right for us both to try. And the Universe responded. The right case was at hand.

## CHAPTER 21: THE ENVELOPE, PLEASE

The bailiff announced that he would be bringing the jury up shortly. I told him we were ready. I was sitting at counsel table on the right hand side of the courtroom next to the jury. That is where the plaintiff's lawyer always sits. My partner, Steve Cavalli, was seated next to me on my left. He was nervous. This was his first big trial. He had worked hard on the case and we had won important pre-trial motions due to his hard work. However, he never sat through a big jury trial like this, so his role was only to take notes. I was ready to start picking the jury and giving my opening statement.

It was March of 1985. I had been sober for nine months and I felt good. I had approached this case differently from any other. Not in terms of preparation. You always had to do the same hard work to get ready for a trial. It was my mental attitude that was different. I felt in touch with myself. I felt like I was so much in contact with the Universe. Spirituality and integrity were now a part of my trial preparation. I had to try to make sure that everything I did was for the greater good for all concerned and most importantly for my client.

I had a great client in Scott Morris. He had suffered a very severe injury in 1979 when he was only nineteen years old. He was working part-time for a subsidiary of the Weibel Winery Company called Finer Filter Products. This little company made its own filter pads. Wine could be filtered through these pads to remove impurities. The machines they used to compress the filter pads were pretty crude. They would take cardboard-like material and press down on it with a very strong platen.

This would compress the material to only a few centimeters of thickness. But the machines were old and they were dangerous. They looked a little bit like a dry-cleaning press. However, the machines required Scott to put both of his hands in there in order to place the filters before they were compressed. Then he would pull his hands out and press the starter button which would cause the top platten to drop quickly and compress the filter material.

Any machine that requires you to put both hands in is inherently dangerous, but the old one he was working on was like a huge animal trap waiting to clamp down on him. Unbeknownst to Scott, this old machine was manufactured in the thirties and had begun to cycle on its own, without anyone pushing the starter button. Once the machine started, it was difficult to hit the off button. Other workers had complained about this, but the supervisors ignored them. Unfortunately, Scott didn't know about these malfunctions.

In 1979, Scott was at work as usual. He was a good and prompt worker. One day he was working on the machine by himself. He put both of his hands in the machine and carefully began to put the filter in place, something he had done many times before. Suddenly, the huge platen dropped on his hands and began to compress them. His hands were trapped and his bones were breaking. Scott screamed for help. Some other workers came, but they didn't know how to turn off the machine. The only way they could do it was manually. They struggled mightily to lift the heavy platen. One of Scott's fellow workers estimated that Scott's hands remained crushed in the machine for ten minutes. Finally, Scott was able to pull his hands out. Another coworker described the scene with horror, saying that

Scott's hands looked like flattened pancakes. He couldn't even distinguish the fingers. Another coworker described Scott's hands as "two transparent dinner plates."

In excruciating pain, Scott was rushed to the hospital. There was serious question about whether he might lose one or both hands. Fortunately, a good hand surgeon helped Scott. Scott's hands were severely damaged, primarily his right hand. He ended up losing only one finger. Even so, for a very long time, Scott could do absolutely nothing with his hands other than to hold them up in the air. He had to be fed and was treated like a baby. It was particularly embarrassing for Scott to have his parents clean him after using the bathroom.

Scott's injury was one of the worst hand injuries that I had ever seen. We promptly filed a lawsuit. However, it was difficult to get cases to trial and this case was no different. Scott's case had a long and difficult history. At one point, it was actually thrown out by a judge who stayed the action, contending that Scott couldn't sue his employer because of the so-called "exclusive remedy rule." The judge ruled that Scott only had a workers' compensation case and could not bring a civil case for his injuries. Fortunately, because the company Scott worked for was different than his employer according to his pay stubs, we were able to prevail on the judge to change his mind on a motion for reconsideration. Once that very difficult legal hurdle was overcome, we were ready to proceed to trial. By the time Scott's case went to trial, it was six years since his injury. We'd had to actually extend the time that a case needs to go to trial, which is five years in California. Meanwhile, much to his credit, Scott had moved on in his life and enrolled at the University of California at Berkeley. He was receiving good grades and doing well.

The defense wanted to settle the case, contending that Scott was better off than he was before his injury. After all, they argued, without his injury, Scott would have never received such a good education. The defendant said Scott probably would have become a warehouseman like his father or would have done some type of manual labor. To the defense, the terrible injury to Scott's hands, which had caused him unending pain, emotional distress, and problems with all of his relationships, was not very important. In fact, they had done Scott a favor by injuring him. If you went with the defense view, Scott should pay the company a bonus for getting him a good education and elevating his stature in the world.

Needless to say, the defense's contention didn't set well with us. It certainly didn't set well with Scott. When settlement negotiations started shortly before the trial, Scott was determined to proceed. If he won the money, that was fine. But he wanted to prove that he was right and that workers shouldn't be submitted to these horribly dangerous working conditions. We made a final demand to settle the case for $2 million. The defense didn't think we were serious. They offered a few hundred thousand dollars. At one time, there was an indication that we might settle the case for $1 million, although that was never firmly put on the table since the defense wasn't interested in settling.

By the time we were ready for trial, Scott wasn't interested in that settlement. Neither was I. My partner, Steve Cavalli, had worked hard on the case from the beginning and he was serving as second chair. We were prepared and we didn't think the other side was. Although the lawyer trying the case was very experienced and had been practicing much longer than I had, we were ahead of the game.

As soon as the bailiff announced that he was going to call up the jury, the defense attorney turned to me.

"Let's talk for a minute," he whispered to me from the other end of the table.

"Okay," I replied.

"Well, we're ready to settle," he stated.

I looked at him.

"Oh? Yes?" I responded.

"Yes," the defense lawyer continued, "My client has finally agreed that they will pay you the million dollars."

"Well, that million-dollar offer was withdrawn," I retorted.

"I know," he countered. "But go ahead and tell your client. I know he'll take it."

I said that I would pass the offer on to Scott. We then started selecting the jury. That night, Steve Cavalli and I had a long heart-to-heart conversation with Scott. In those days, a million dollars was a huge amount of money to turn down. But Scott insisted—he wanted to try the case. Steve Cavalli was concerned. However, he was ready to follow my lead.

That night, I sat alone in my room and asked for guidance and help. My intuition told me that trying the case was the right thing to do. We had a fair judge and the jury was looking pretty good. More importantly, I was in sync with my client. I felt spiritually, mentally, and legally ready.

The next day we returned to court to finish jury selection.

I sat down and turned casually to the defense attorney sitting at the counsel table.

"No," I said, "We're not interested in the million dollars."

The color drained from his face.

"You're telling me you're turning down a million dollars on this case?" he stammered.

The answer was yes.

He couldn't believe it.

So, the case went to trial and the defense pushed their contention that their bad deed had actually caused Scott to become a better person and how happy Scott should be that the defendant injured him. Needless to say, the jury didn't like that contention. In closing argument, the defense suggested that an award of $375,000 total, including medical expenses, a lifetime loss of earnings, and all his pain and suffering, was fair.

The case had gone well. I had talked to lawyers all over the country about trying a hand injury case. I was concerned about how to argue the case, since I had never tried a case quite like this. My friend Browne Greene from Los Angeles had just won a excellent verdict on a hand injury case and he gave me some very good help. I found out something interesting things about hand injuries. I learned how important our hands are to us. We talk with our hands. Men are "handsome." Quality goods are handmade. But most importantly, we caress and love with our hands. We play with our children with our hands. A person with a serious hand injury is unable to adequately communicate affection to his or her loved ones. Someone with injured hands suffers one of the gravest injuries that a person can have. My argument went well, but you never know about those things. I asked the jury for $8 million. The defense attorney and a number of his friends snickered. They thought I had overtried the case by asking for so much money. After a few days of deliberation, the jury made its decision.

We sat quietly at the counsel table while the jury walked into the courtroom. Waiting for the jury is always the most agonizing part of a trial. The last few minutes, and even a few seconds before the verdict is read, my heart always beats with excitement, fear, and anxiety. I felt sure we were going win, but it's never a sure thing. The verdict was read: *"We the jury find in favor of the Plaintiff, Scott Morris, and award damages in the sum of $5,500,000."* I was ecstatic! The defense attorney was stunned. I had won what I still believe was the largest hand injury verdict in the country at that time. My bad stream of tough cases had come to an end. And it was due to the new me. The sober me. The spiritual me.

There was one interesting postscript to the trial. The defense made a motion to reduce the verdict on the basis that the damages were excessive. It was a serious motion and we were concerned. Our research showed very few cases with such high damages for a similar kind of injury. At the new trial motion, the judge did something quite unusual. After each of us completed our arguments, the judge said that he would take the motion under submission. He had already made his decision. He had a written ruling. However, his decision was sealed in an envelope. He held it up and said:

"I'm handing this envelope to the clerk. It will not be opened until I am ready to announce the decision on the new trial motion. Now boys, would you like to talk settlement?" (Of course, in those days, almost all the lawyers were men.)

So, off we went into chambers and started serious settlement discussions. The negotiations lasted for a couple of weeks. The defendant offered a lot of money, something like $4 million. But we were standing pretty firm on reducing the case by only about ten percent. Finally we reached an impasse. We were in the judge's chambers.

"That's it!" he exclaimed, "I can't get this case settled."

He looked at both of us for a moment.

"Let's go in the courtroom," he instructed. "I'll read my decision."

As I sat at the counsel table my heart was beating almost as hard as it was before the verdict came in.

"The envelope, please," the judge said as he looked at his clerk.

It was like something you'd hear at the Academy Awards. He picked up the envelope, tore it open, and began to read his decision. It was a well-reasoned long decision, but the last few words were what was most important:

***"The damages are not excessive and the motion for new trial is denied."***

*We had won again!*

Fortunately, within a few months we were able to settle the case for almost full value.

The Scott Morris case changed everything in my life. Until that time, our firm shared office space with my former partner Ed Digardi. It had been seven years and we were ready to move on. Now we had the money to do it. Most importantly, my client was very happy. We were able to create a long-term, structured settlement that would give him a certain amount of money for many years into the future. I think Scott perceived me not only as a friend, but almost as a second father. I feel the same way about him. I always will.

*   *   *

We had a victory party at the Claremont Hotel in Berkeley. My mother came out from Utah. Wayne didn't make it. There still wasn't a real father in my life. It was always about Mom, winning for her and getting her praise.

It has now been over twenty years since that verdict. Scott and I are still friends. His life has gone on and he has done well. He is a real estate agent, got married, and has two children. There is still a special bond between us.[6]

Over the years, I have tried many cases. I am proud to have won some and I have lost some tough ones, but Scott Morris's case will always remain as the one that forever changed both of our lives. I won this case with integrity, sobriety, and spirituality. From then on, that was the way I tried all my cases.

The one note of sadness about Scott's trial concerns my mentor as a plaintiff's lawyer, Jesse Nichols. He was the senior partner who started the old firm. Throughout his life, he was always friendly, kind, and generous to me. Although he retired in the 1960s, he remained a part of the firm and we always kept an office available for him, even when he was in his eighties. He tried a lot of cases in his career and he had compassion for me. He understood what it was like to lose a case and he was sympathetic to my losses, including the Staples v. General Motors case. He continually told me that the most important thing about the case was the client. He was right. I know he wanted me to succeed. Unfortunately, he died about two months before the Scott Morris verdict. I wish he had been there. He was as close to a father figure as I ever had.

# CHAPTER 22: CHANGES AND CHALLENGES

I'm sitting quietly in the back bedroom. It is seven o'clock in the evening and the house is quiet. It's a strange place for me to be. We don't use our guest bedroom very often, although Liz often sleeps here when my snoring bothers her. I snored a lot when I was drinking, so Liz spent a lot of time here before my sobriety. Now this bedroom a place for me to be alone, to relax, and to go deeper into myself.

I pick up my Sony Walkman® and put on the headphones, fitting the left and the right earpieces snugly into my ears. I slip in my cassette tape and push play. The soft music starts. There are interesting tinkling sounds, along with birds singing and the gentle beating of drums that float into a deep and spiritual rhythm. This is not the kind of music I am used to. This isn't R & B. This is a deep, quiet, spiritual music that fills my soul. It is Kitaro.

I hadn't heard of Kitaro until recently. I've learned that he is one of the most popular musicians in the world, frequently playing to audiences as large as 50,000 people.[7] His spiritual, new age music was born in the foothills of Mt. Fuji in Japan, where he composes and conducts it. His music takes me deeper into my soul than I have ever been. I begin to feel a light band around my head as though I had put on a cap or a hat. Some would say I am moving into my seventh Chakra. I'm not so sure about that, but I know it feels good. I'm totally relaxed. I try to let go of all of my thoughts. My cases, my work as a trial lawyer, my family, everything. I want to do nothing but listen to the music. In so doing, I'm learning to use my right brain. As with most lawyers, I am very left-brained and have had trouble opening to the intuitive, creative, and artistic right side of my brain.

The music's spell seems to be working. I'm spending almost an hour each evening in the back bedroom listening to this music, meditating, and feeling the power of silence. This is something unusual for me. I feel more creative. More energetic. More refreshed, alert, and awake. I'm changing. There is a new me emerging, just like the caterpillar that leaves its cocoon and becomes a butterfly. I'm searching for my soul and I think I'm finding it. It feels good.

* * *

Late in the evening on June 3, 1986, I watched television and became angry. The election results were in. The voters had overwhelmingly passed a bad initiative that would severely limit the rights of consumers and wrongfully injured people to sue the responsible defendants.

California is one of the few states in the country where voters can changes the law by putting an initiative on the ballot. Someone simply drafts the law and gets enough signatures to qualify the initiative for the election. At one time, it was thought that these initiatives would help to the common people. They were thought to be populist or grassroots protections for people to change laws if the legislature was not responsive. Unfortunately, the opposite happened. Initiatives are sponsored big companies and sometimes big government. They want to change the laws to their benefit. The big-money interests pay anywhere from $1 to $3 per signature to qualify the initiative for the ballots. People rarely understand the details since the wording is often quite complex. So laws are passed by using slick public relations firms and advertising campaigns that cost millions of dollars. It's not a good system.

The 1986 initiative was known as Proposition 51. It involved a complicated legal issue about the liability of multiple defendants in a lawsuit to pay judgments. It sounded fair but it let responsible defendants off the hook and substantially changed settled law. In fact, it was nothing but a veil to allow defendants who wrongfully cause injuries to avoid some of their responsibility. It was the start of an attack on the right people have to bring civil lawsuits against defendants who have done wrong. It was the beginning of a movement called "tort reform." This is a term that I had not heard of until this initiative surfaced in late 1985. Tort reform is an issue that consumer advocates would fight for many years to come. Debunking the myth of tort reform, as spun so successfully by the public media hired by the CEOs of big-business, insurance companies, tobacco interests, and many others, would be at the heart of my legal career for many years.

The results of that election on June 3, 1986 affected me deeply. When Proposition 51 was first proposed in 1985, it was well thought out, well funded, and well organized by a smart political consultants. They went to the media with their thirty-second ads accusing trial lawyers of taking advantage of public entities, big business interests and others by filing excessive lawsuits. However, tort reform is really a way to just to make it harder for people to get justice in the courts and reduce legitimate jury awards; all to the benefit of the proponents—insurance companies, big business interests and big government (the State of California, big counties, cities, etc.) The statistics showed that there was no "lawsuit crisis" and in fact, court filings in civil cases were actually decreasing rather than increasing. However, facts were not important. The public relations campaign by big corporate interests and their television ads ignored the truth. When they launched their blitzkrieg campaign, no one was prepared to rebut their false public advertising. The only people who could fight them were the lawyers who represented the public, consumers, and injured parties. So the California Trial Lawyers Association (CTLA,) now known as the Consumer Attorneys of California (CAOC,)[8] came forward to oppose the initiative. However, we did not have any experience with such a thing. We are unprepared and election results showed it.

I was personally affected by the outcome of the election because I of my leadership role in the trial lawyers association. Peter Hinton, a fine trial lawyer from Walnut Creek, was president in 1986. Browne Greene, one of the best lawyers in the state and probably the top trial lawyer in Los Angeles in 1986, was president elect. I was asked to be in charge of fundraising by serving as chair of the association's political action committee. We hired political consultants, but we were late to the game. They told us that if we raised $5 million, we could easily defeat the initiative. Although we raised the money, it was to no avail. We had lost anyway. The entire process was deeply frustrating to me and to my colleagues.

I knew losing this initiative would weigh heavily on us. We would look weak and our opponents would come after us again. We were wounded and they smelled blood. I feared that we would soon be in a fight for our very existence and there was no one else to defend the civil justice system.

Browne Greene was a great leader in 1987, but the next elections would come in 1988. It was likely that I would be the association's president at that time. I had a personal stake in the tort reform fight. The injustice and unfairness of the entire campaign rankled me deeply. The night after the election, I vowed revenge. If we were to have another initiative battle, we would have to win it. And I would be in charge.

I spent many months traveling around the state trying to raise money for the initiative battle. Unfortunately, I slipped back into drinking. My drinking wasn't nearly as bad as it had been in 1984, but even a little wine could lead to big trouble for me.

One day, I had a few glasses at wine at lunch, which then turned into an afternoon, evening, and early morning binge of heavy drinking. I woke up at 4:30 a.m. in a place where I shouldn't have been. I was deeply embarrassed, not only because I was drinking, but because doing so was inconsistent with the spiritual values that I had developed. So my vow on June 3, 1986, was to not only to avenge our defeat in opposition to Proposition 51, but to do so with complete and utter sobriety. I vowed I would never touch another drop of alcohol again for the rest of my life. And I haven't.

\* \* \*

On a personal level, I read many nonfiction books. The subjects of philosophy, religion—especially Eastern religion and

Buddhism—psychology and self-help books all appealed to me. I made big changes in my thinking. I now perceived myself as a spiritual being on a spiritual path. One of the first books that motivated me was called *Out on a Limb* by Shirley MacLaine. It challenged me to embark on the same search that she took herself: How to find an answer to life's fundamental questions without traditional religion. That was my path too.

MacLaine's book explores Eastern religious philosophies and metaphysics.[9] MacLaine explores questions about her connection to the Universe. What is her soul? Did she live before? What is the meaning of these past lives? Many of the world's religions believe in some form of past life and certainly life after death. This is particularly true of the Eastern religions such as Buddhism. I asked myself the same questions.

There was no particular order to the books I read. I would go into a bookstore and let my intuition decide what felt good, looked good, or simply struck me as something I ought to read. I was particularly impressed with the books by Deepak Chopra and have read almost all of his books. I also read Dr. Wayne Dyer's book *You'll See It When You Believe It: The Way To Your Personal Transformation*. I read about past lives and many books by psychics. I studied channeling and getting in touch with spiritual entities in the Universe.

The literature I read was all very new and interesting. However, I'm a trained lawyer. I approach books with a sense of rationality: Do they make sense? Are they scientifically valid? Are they logical? Some of the books made more sense than others. However, ultimately, their message is something I have to feel using my own intuition. As I read all this literature,

I began to find a common thread of principles that I wanted to live by and still live by.

The overriding principle in all these books is always **love.** It is such a simple statement, yet so hard to put into practice, especially for a trial lawyer in a conflict-ridden profession. Can you love your opponent? Can you love them and fight vigorously against them at the same time? Perhaps it is a matter of perception. At the soul level, I believe we are all made of love. At the personality level it is quite different. When I deal with personalities or corporations that mistreat my clients, then I must fight with them for justice. Love and justice are hard concepts to reconcile.

An interesting principle is **Karma,** the Eastern concept that we have life issues that we must deal with. Simply stated, Karma can be defined as **"What goes around comes around."** If our past lives raised certain issues that were not resolved in that life, we will have to deal with those issues in a later life.

Another principle I live by is **"Ask and you shall receive."** If you open your mind to God and the Universe, ultimately you will get what you need. It may not be in the form you expect or come at the time you hope, but it will come in its own way.

A helpful concept is **"Live in the present."** Everything that happened in the past, whether last year, yesterday, or just a few minutes ago, lives only in our memory. When I worry about the past, I don't accomplish anything. If my mind fills with worry about the future, I can't function in the present. Worry doesn't help. Planning is okay, but I have to take life as it comes. Once I pull myself into the present, I find happiness.

This concept may be easily stated yet it is difficult to live with on a day to day basis, especially for a trial lawyer engaged in strategy and taught to think ahead.

Perhaps the most important concept that permeated my search and has stayed with me is **"All things happen for a reason."** Every event, no matter how big or small, comes to us for a reason. **"There are no coincidences."** I need to learn why things happen to me and to not bemoan or become angry about them. I can't simply be happy because something good happened. I need to understand the reasons. Usually, there are multiple reasons. As I grow in wisdom, I gain a deeper meaning for life events. I am able to tie patterns together in our lives and pull together my psychological knowledge into a spiritual understanding of who I am. This is an evolving life journey.

I worked hard on how I could apply these concepts to my work as a trial lawyer. I was not into idealistic philosophy if it didn't make sense in my life. The books I read helped me begin to understand my life's purpose. If our purpose in life is to become the best human beings we can be, we must move as far as we can with our spiritual growth and have a complete understanding of who we are and why we are here. There is no such thing as getting it all right. It is not a test. Each of us lives and learns in our own way. We come back again and again in many lives until we have experienced every human experience.

Understanding these principles may be easy; living by them is not. I'm a pragmatist. Spiritual concepts and psychological insight do little good if you can't integrate them into your life. I struggled to apply these concepts on a daily basis, especially working in as difficult a profession as mine. There is constant conflict. I am always fighting with people. There is a lot of stress in my daily work. However, I work at living by these ideals. In doing so, I have come in closer contact with my soul.

I started to meditate. I learned the concepts about the right brain and the left brain. Lawyers are left-brained and I was certainly no exception. I balanced my thinking and used more of my right brain. I read books that assisted in that regard. Listening to Kitaro helped.

The work and training I did helped me in my profession and in my personal life. Now I had another challenge. How could it help me move beyond being a courtroom lawyer? Could it help me become a leader? Would my new philosophy and lifestyle help me lead a group of strong, independent trial lawyers? I would soon to find out.

# CHAPTER 23: FIRST, LET'S KILL
## ALL THE LAWYERS

Browne Greene and others asked me to run for president of CTLA. They felt we needed a strong leader in 1988. My opponent, Peter Mills, an attorney from Sacramento, had been elected as CTLA's vice president four times. He was an officer in the association much longer than me. Unfortunately, he was not a leader. He was a nice guy, but many perceived him as weak and lacking the strong personality necessary to lead a statewide group of independent trial lawyers.

I agreed to run. A contested election took place in the fall of 1987. Fortunately, with the help of many people from the southern part of the state, including my good friend Browne Greene, who was president-elect, I was able to prevail by about a sixty percent to forty percent margin. Now I was ready to become president of CTLA in 1988, a very important year as it turned out. We had lost our big Proposition 51 in 1986 and now some huge initiatives were looming on the horizon for 1988. The members, especially the board of governors, were concerned about the association's future. Because I was relatively new to the leadership of the association, I needed to demonstrate my leadership ability.

\* \* \*

I am sitting quietly in my hotel room preparing to give the biggest speech of my career. I am trying to meditate and get in touch with my higher self. There will be a large audience and they are special to me. I want to speak to them from my heart. I want to integrate the spiritual philosophy that I have studied for the last few years of my sobriety into my talk today. I feel that if I speak from deep within my soul I can reach out and touch them.

My speech needed to say something more than the same old stuff about the importance of our educational programs and our political commitment. I had read an interesting article in a national trial lawyer magazine about lawyers of conscience. I decided that would be the theme of my speech.

As I walked into the grand ballroom, I was greeted by many friends who congratulated me on my upcoming presidency. The room was packed with almost 1,500 lawyers, spouses, and others. Liz was at my side as I sat at the head table overlooking the large audience. I was nervous, but ready.

Our outgoing president Browne Greene introduced me with his typically warm and heartfelt remarks. I stepped forward to the lectern and received the ceremonial president's gavel.[10] I took a deep breath and asked for guidance from my higher self as I began my remarks:

> "I think our commitment and the philosophy of our membership can best be summed up by Chicago Judge Richard L. Curry of Cook County Circuit Court in an article he penned for the April 1987 of *Trial*, the national magazine for the Association of Trial Lawyers of America (ATLA): "We don't cheat. We do not suborn. We do not fabricate. We do not lie to clients or for clients. We do not file

frivolous suits, and we do not answer or defend against claims of merit with tricks or chicanery. We teach clients that beyond the statutes and the cases there is a law within each of us. That's the law of conscience. Lawyers of conscience should set no limits when it comes to personal achievement but the mark of that achievement should not be measured by how much money is earned, but rather by the standard of conduct set up in daily practice. Such is the commitment being displayed today, every time a trial lawyer takes a case—a case that may stretch out over years with no assurance that he or she will ever be successful and thus ever receive compensation. It is precisely because of this commitment, however, those plaintiffs' attorneys have always batted on behalf of the general public against the insensitive and uncaring, removing from the marketplace such life endangering products as the Ford Pinto, the Dalkon Shield, and asbestos containing products. As lawyers, we may never try a case as perfectly as the fictional Perry Mason. But, we can aspire nevertheless to his high professional standards. Current public perception to the contrary, I believe that most lawyers already do."

The audience was silent as I continued. I concluded as follows:

"That is certainly true of the members of this association. I know that your commitment to justice and your willingness to fight for what is right and fair will carry us forward through the challenges of 1988. Let us devote ourselves to that commitment and that fight as lawyers of conscience."

As I stepped away from the podium, the audience rose as one in a standing ovation. I'm not sure if it was the power of my remarks or the importance of the occasion that led to this spontaneous outburst. However, I did know that I was now president and ready to do my best to lead the association.

Or was I the president? We had our first board meeting and I was ready to launch into the work to be done in 1988. However, it wasn't going to be that easy. My opponent had decided not to give up the battle. He read the fine print of the association's bylaws that said a member had to be an elected officer for one year before that person could run for president. I had held the office of parliamentarian the year before. I was elected parliamentarian on December 6, 1986 and I was sworn in as president on December 3, 1987. My opponent contended that I was three days short of being an officer and therefore in violation of the bylaws. He argued that he should become the rightful president by default and even filed a lawsuit in the Sacramento County Superior Court. He asked the court for an injunction preventing me from taking office. Much to everyone's shock, the judge granted the injunction, ordered my presidency invalid, and ruled that my opponent was the association's president. Needless to say, this created a huge problem. A monstrous cloud hung over my presidency. This was terrible because we needed to focus our efforts on the imminent initiative battle ahead. Fortunately, the association had an excellent lawyer in Joe Remcho. Joe immediately filed a writ in the appellate court. Within a month, the judge's ruling was overturned and I was formally declared president. Joe was my lawyer and a good friend until he died in 2003 from a tragic helicopter accident. He was a remarkable man who is missed by everyone who knew him.

I was legally declared president in late January 1988 and I needed to get busy. Although I was president, I wasn't well known throughout the state. In 1987, under the leadership of our president, Browne Greene, we negotiated the infamous "napkin settlement"[11] with some of our opponents in the Proposition 51 fight. Unfortunately, the napkin deal did not include insurance companies or certain public interest groups. Not long after that, these groups wanted their own laws on the November ballot. Soon initiatives were being qualified right and left. Finally, there were five initiatives on the ballot. I had my opportunity to avenge our defeat in1986. It wasn't going to be easy.

Our biggest concern was Proposition 106. This would have limited all lawyers' contingency fees to ten percent. It was sponsored by insurance companies and other big business interests that wanted to prevent people from hiring lawyers to sue them. Lawyers taking cases on a contingency fee basis could stand up to the insurance companies and big corporate interests, but not if the money the recovered were so low as to make it financially impossible to represent deserving clients. Proposition 106 would have effectively eliminated the contingency fee arrangement, closed the courthouse door to the average citizen, and ruined our profession. Since lawyers are not popular with most people, the idea of limiting their fees seemed like a good one. The public was unaware that the fee limits did not apply to corporate or insurance company lawyers. Although it was one-sided and unfair, the initiative sounded great to the general public.

The insurance companies put the fee limit initiative on the ballot for several of reasons. First, they didn't want accountability. Second, they didn't want to be sued. Third, they didn't want to have to fairly pay out benefits. It wasn't as much about lawyers as about the insurance industry hindering people from making claims.

Another reason the insurance industry put this initiative on the ballot was to kill our association. We were too powerful and they wanted to put us out of business. It was just like the famous Shakespeare quote from *King Henry VI, Part II:* "The first thing we do, let's kill all the lawyers." This is spoken ironically indicating that without lawyers, there would be no due process or democracy. This was the insurance companies' real agenda.

Our very survival was at stake. When Proposition 106 was initially polled, the results were between eighty-eight and ninety-two percent positive. Rarely has any proposition or initiative polled anywhere near as high. This meant that nearly everyone was in favor of limiting lawyers' fees. Many in our organization were absolutely convinced we could never win. I wasn't. I felt we could win—with the right strategy. We had good political consultants and we found a way to link our message to the people's general dislike of the insurance industry. They had two unpopular no-fault initiatives on the ballot. These would have changed the way insurance companies paid out claims to people who were injured in car accidents. It was a brazen attempt to reduce insurance company payouts.

CTLA filed a counter-initiative involving good driver rates that would hold insurance companies liable for bad faith lawsuits. Although the initiative was well-written, it had trouble since the insurance industry attacked it as being sponsored only by trial lawyers. The fate of these initiatives boiled down to the public's perceptions of the insurance industry and of trial lawyers.

Perhaps the most interesting initiative on the ballot was Proposition 103 filed by Ralph Nader and Harvey J. Rosenfield, two outstanding consumer advocates. Proposition 103, known as the "good driver initiative," would have radically changed the way insurance companies were regulated and required that insurance companies charge their rates based on driving records rather than where people lived. Although Nader and Rosenfield didn't have much funding, they certainly had credibility.

The members of our association were frightened. Most doubted that we could win. This was especially true of the fee limitation initiative. Many association leaders and the board members shared their doubts. As we moved into 1988, my work was cut out for me.

During that year, the insurance industry spent more than $75 million trying to pass their initiatives. We were faced with trying to raise an impossible amount of money: the $15 million our political consultant said it would take to win. This was so much more money than we had ever raised in any year that it seemed like an impossible task. But we rolled up our sleeves and went to work. I was fortunate to have an excellent executive director of the organization, Leonard (Lenny) Esquina, Jr., a lawyer we had recruited from Michigan. His young wife Robin E. Brewer also joined the staff as a fundraiser. Lenny, Robin, and the entire staff were a terrific help to me throughout my year as president.

With the help of a committed board and a strong executive committee, we organized and began fundraising around the state. It wasn't easy. There was fear and anxiety among the members of the executive committee. The board meetings were contentious because the so-called "advertising lawyers" were not well-liked by the traditional trial lawyers who did not advertise on television. I had to try to pull them all together to fight the same battle. Tensions ran high. People became angry and accusatory. I worked closely with our political consultants.

The decisions I supported were frequently challenged. Everyone had a different idea as to how to best run the campaign. Trying to control this strong and independent group of trial lawyers was an almost impossible task. Some of my closest allies in the leadership worried that I wasn't doing the job and back-channeled their own ideas to fight the initiative. Some were less critical of me, including my good friends Laurence (Larry) E. Drivon, the 1990 president of CTLA, Rick Simons, the 1998 president, and David S. Casey, Jr., later a president of CTLA and of the Association of Trial Lawyers of America, now called the American Association for Justice.[12]

I needed to move the leadership learning curve in a hurry. I studied and read everything I could find about being an effective leader. My role as president did not give me any real authority. I couldn't hire or fire anyone. I was simply an elected official. How do you lead a nonprofit organization? The board is elected. What is your power? Not much. You run the meeting. You set the agenda. You communicate. You facilitate. And especially, you listen. I learned what I could about leadership and worked very hard to prepare for many contentious executive committee and board meetings.

Since many of the meetings were out of the area and held in hotels, I meditated in my room a half hour before each meeting started. I tried to stay centered for what I knew would be difficult meetings with independent trial lawyers all wanting to have their own say on how things should be run. I needed to stay steady. They could not see fear or equivocation by their president. The association stayed together as we frantically raised money to run ads and get our message out to the public. In 1988, I made twenty-five trips to Southern California for board meetings, executive meetings, and lots and lots of fundraising. It was chaotic.

We needed to go on the air but television advertising time was very expensive. We simply had to raise the money or we would fail. It was a long, slow, difficult struggle. Towards the end of the initiative, we were forced to try to raise almost $800,000 a week! This was more than we had ever raised in a whole year or two in the past. But we had to do it to survive. And slowly, by some miracle, we seemed to get it done. Each week, we'd barely make enough to purchase our air time. The television ads were the key. That is where the initiatives were going to be won or lost. We had to stay on the air.

As election day neared, things became even more frantic. By then, I wasn't practicing law at all. I spent every minute of the day trying to raise money, talking to people, communicating with the media, and keeping the ship afloat. There were hundreds of calls from anxious people who worried that we were going to lose the election. I talked to all of them. Had I still been drinking, I could have never held myself together or been a leader.

By election night on November 8, 1988, our organization was frazzled, fractured, and fearful. There were still many who felt we could never win the election, although the polls showed that we at least had a decent chance of winning Proposition 106. We gathered in one of the ballrooms at the Biltmore Hotel in Los Angeles for the election night party. Our political consultant, Dick Woodward, was there with us. I had spent many hours with Dick and he had spent countless hours trying to allay our tired and fearful troops. We were worn out but cautiously optimistic.

The election results began to come in. The initiative we sponsored was losing. The insurance initiatives were also losing big. But Proposition 106—the one that would put us all out of business—looked to be passing. Everyone watched it. I could see fear in the eyes of our members.

I pulled Dick aside so that I could speak with him privately.

"Are you sure about your poll numbers?" I questioned. "Do you think we're going to win this thing?"

"Wait until the results come in," he replied. "We don't even have the results from Los Angeles or some of the other counties that will put us over the edge."

He seemed optimistic, but there was concern in his voice. My stomach was churning with anxiety.

I felt isolated. I don't think people knew quite what to say to me. There were some pats on the back and comments like let's hope we win. My future with the organization was at stake. My presidency was on the line. I had told them that we could win the battle. I had done everything I could. All year long, I was an optimistic voice among a sea of pessimists. Lenny Esquina, our executive director, and Robin E. Brewer, our chief fundraiser, were the only people who had shared my optimism.

Would Proposition 106 pass or fail? Slowly, ever so slowly, the numbers began to change. From fifty-five percent yes to forty-five percent no, we were down to fifty-two percent yes and forty-eight percent no. Then the numbers were about even. Finally, at about 1:00 a.m., the votes swung to our side. There were more "no" votes than "yes" votes. Proposition 106 was finally going down in defeat!

We won by a margin of fifty-three percent to forty-seven percent, much better than anyone had predicted. I was tired and went to bed. I woke up a hero. It was not just me who was the hero, but everyone was—the entire leadership and everybody involved.

I definitely do not want to take credit for winning this election. I was just one person among many who worked incredibly hard and gave until it hurt. There are so many people in the association who worked hard that I am hesitant to mention names for fear of leaving someone out, but I do especially want to give credit to Rick Simons, Larry E. Drivon, Gary M. Paul, David S. Casey, Jr., Harvey R. Levine, and Ian (Buddy) Herzog. Browne Greene, Bruce A. Broillet, and everyone in their entire law firm were relentless and never stopped working. There are too many to mention by name.

Proposition 103 also passed, which was wonderful. Now the consumer advocates could fight with the insurance industry. We could get back to practicing law. The insurance industry would certainly think twice before taking us on again!

Just because someone is a good trial lawyer does not automatically make that person a good leader. The skills involved are quite different. I learned so much about leadership that year, what to do and what not to do. It was one of the most difficult and challenging years of my life, yet it was also one of the most satisfying. My sobriety, my psychological study, and my spiritual work had helped me become a leader.

1988 changed my life. I was now more than just another trial lawyer. I was considered a legitimate leader among my peers. I had avenged our 1986 loss of Proposition 51. People's attitudes about me changed. Many people considered me a hero and I certainly felt great about what I had done. However, not everything in 1988 was positive.

# CHAPTER 24: LESSONS FROM LOSING

There are a few moments in our lives that we never forget. One of those occurred for me on Saint Patrick's Day, 1988. I was in trial that day on a tough medical malpractice case that I was trying with my new partner, Steve Brewer. The litigation had been long and contentious. We had just begun the trial and were putting on our first witness. Because of the five-year statute of limitations in California, we had to start the trial within five years of the complaint being filed, or the court could dismiss the case. We had to get the case moving. The case involved a little girl who had received a brachial plexus injury, also called shoulder dystocia, during her birth. Her mother, Debbie Reibe, was my secretary. We sued Debbie's obstetrician alleging professional negligence during the birth. We said that the doctor had negligently pulled on the infant's arm to complete the birth. We argued that the doctor should have done a caesarian section instead. The obstetrician vigorously denied these charges.

The trial occurred at the beginning of my CTLA presidency. The initiative battles were getting into full swing and I was distracted by all of the activities I had to as president. This was also the first case Steve Brewer and I had tried together. We had worked hard to prepare the case.

About 10:30 a.m. on that first morning of trial, I had just called our first witness to the stand. Steve was sitting next to me, taking notes, and ready to help out. The bailiff walked to Steve and motioned for him to come over. Although this was unusual, I remained focused on my witness. The jury was listening intently to the testimony, as was the judge.

A few minutes later Steve returned, stepped into gallery, and approached me.

"Gary," he whispered in my ear, "We have to take a recess."

"Can't it wait until our eleven o'clock recess?" I replied curtly. "I'm right in the middle of this."

He looked at me intently. "No," he said.

His face was as white as a sheet.

"We have to take a break now," he insisted.

I requested leave of the court to take a short break and the judge invited us into chambers. Steve walked into the room holding one of those little pink phone message slips that everyone used in those days. When we sat down, he didn't say anything, he just handed me the message slip. The note read: **"Please tell Mr. Gwilliam that his mother died suddenly this morning. He should contact his stepfather, Wayne, as soon as possible."**

I was stunned. Mom and Wayne had been living in a trailer park in Scottsdale, Arizona where they spent their winters and in Ogden, Utah where they spent their summers. I knew Mom had problems with congestive heart failure and her health wasn't great, but she was only seventy-four years old. I thought she was doing well.

Needless to say, I was shocked. I didn't really know what to do or how to feel. I started to cry, but I felt embarrassed to be so emotional in front of the judge, the defense attorney, and Steve. Fortunately, the judge was very compassionate and indicated that he would immediately recess the jury and get back to them about what was to be done.

The recess lasted several days since I had to immediately pack up and go back to Utah for the funeral. Mom's body was shipped from Arizona to Utah and I was in charge of arranging the funeral and giving Mom's eulogy. All of my life my mother had been there for me. I realized that so much of my motivation throughout my entire life had been to please her. She had loved me unconditionally all her life. I'd loved her and done everything I could to be the good son even through my dark and difficult times. She really had never judged me and had always forgiven me for my faults. In her eyes, I was the perfect number one son.

\* \* \*

I stood up, took a deep breath, and walked slowly to the podium. I was getting ready to give the most important presentation and argument I had ever given. No doubt about it. Nothing compared to this. I wanted to speak with logic and clarity, but I knew I might succumb to the emotion of the moment.

I paused at the podium and looked out over the audience. I was usually quite comfortable in speaking. Not only had I spoken in courtrooms for years, but I had given numerous speeches to different audiences. This one was different. The subject of my talk—my client if you will—was behind me. Unfortunately, she couldn't see me nor could she hear me. She lay quietly in her coffin. She was my mother. I took a deep breath and began to speak. This was her eulogy:[13]

182

"I want to thank you all for being here and for the kind words that have been said about my mother. I want to talk about who my mother was and the success and difficulties she had in her life. I also want to talk about her family and speak directly to some of you. Lastly, I want to talk about what my mother meant to me.

Her first husband was an alcoholic and she had to leave him when her first and only son was two years old. Not too long after, she met Wayne and married him on December 15, 1940. Her life at first was that of a typical housewife. One day, all of that changed when she hosted what was known as a "Stanley Party." She was encouraged to begin putting on parties herself and before long became an extremely successful saleswoman. In the forties and early fifties, it was difficult for women to have careers, but she did so and eventually became the branch manager for the entire Northwest Region for Stanley Home Products.

After some years of success, she began to struggle with a series of illnesses. She had rheumatic fever as a child and developed congestive heart failure in her fifties. She was forced to retire early and had extremely serious heart surgery in 1968. The doctors placed a pig valve in her heart which they replaced fifteen years later. Unfortunately, she also suffered the most dreaded of all female diseases: breast cancer. She had a full mastectomy and fortunately recovered. A few years ago she had a brain aneurysm. When she was in her early seventies, she had brain surgery.

Mom knew that her health was not good. However, she never feared death. She and I discussed this on several occasions and she knew she would leave this earth when her time came. Fortunately, it came peacefully and easily. She was at the Laundromat in her trailer park in Scottsdale, Arizona. She was waiting for the dryer to finish its cycle and reading a book. This was typical of her. I can so clearly visualize her sitting there. The book dropped to the floor and she slumped forward. Her heart had given out on her. She died peacefully and without pain. This was exactly how she would like to go. She would never want to cause any trouble for her family because of illness.

I think the most important aspect of my mother's personality was her strong, positive attitude. She read Norman Vincent Peale's *The Power of Positive Thinking* when she was in her fifties. She lived by those principles. She tried to help me live the same way and encouraged me to have a positive attitude about life.

While she only had a high school diploma, I was very surprised that when she was age fifty-nine, she showed me an oil painting. She said she had painted it. I joked with her that it must have been a paint-by-numbers kit. Those were popular do-it-yourself paintings that gave you numbers for each different color. You simply filled in the blanks with the correct color. No, she said. She painted it herself. In fact, she had a great talent for painting. She continued painting for the next fifteen years until she died at the age of seventy-four. Two of her paintings still hang in my office and most of her family had been given her paintings of scenery and mountains. So she not only had sales talent, but artistic talent."

In my eulogy, I addressed each of the important members of her family. They were her siblings: my Aunt Rose and Aunt Betty, my Uncle Vincent, and also Wayne's sister Vivian, who was like another sister to Mom, even though Vivian was really her sister-in-law. Vivian also worked for Stanley Home Products and she and Mom were very close. I addressed my sister Pat and her only daughter, Fortune, who were grieving deeply. I asked them not to feel guilt, which I knew they did because of their own struggles with drug addiction.

Lastly, I spoke directly to my stepfather, Wayne, and told him what a good husband he had been to my mother for nearly forty-seven years. I read a card from my wife, Liz, and a beautiful statement from my fifteen-year-old daughter Lisa.

Then I turned to my own feelings about my mother. I felt her spirit. I knew she was in the afterlife and even as I spoke to the audience, I felt I was speaking her words. It was almost as though I were channeling her spirit to those whom she loved. It was a unique and unusual feeling. When all was said and done, the eulogy may have been the best "argument" I have ever given. It was certainly the hardest and the most emotional. I think my "client" would have been proud of me, even though she lay quietly in her coffin. I still needed her approval, even after her death.

Mom was loved by everyone. The funeral was huge and people from all over came to pay their respects. But, I was still a lawyer. I had an obligation to my client in court and I had to go back to work. After giving an emotional eulogy, I now headed back to California to complete the trial. I also needed to get back to my duties as CTLA president.

The trial would have been difficult under any circumstances. I probably wouldn't have won it anyway. It was a close and difficult case. I lost it. It was a tough loss because I was very close to the injured girl and her mother. Debbie was not only my secretary, but a friend. We remain friends to this day.

A strange, interesting, and unpredictable consequence came from this difficult loss. I had a string of victories before I lost that case. But this loss got me to thinking about how hard we attorneys take our losses. I felt terrible after losing this most recent verdict. I remembered how I felt when I lost that big case against General Motors some years before. This time, I had a lot of excuses: Mom died; I was president of CTLA; I was distracted; this was a tough malpractice case. But none of that seemed to make any difference. I blamed myself. That was always what I did when I lost. I think that is what everybody does when they lose.

I tried to get in touch with my feelings. Why did I feel a sense of shame and self-blame at losing this case? This time I would approach the loss differently than the Staples v. General Motors case of nearly ten years earlier.

I went into the office on the Saturday following the jury's verdict. I pulled out a yellow pad. I drew a line down the middle. On one side of the line I wrote down the things that were bad about the loss. On the other side, I wrote down anything that could be positive about the experience. I didn't expect much to be positive, but I was surprised. On the bad side I didn't get any money. On the good side my client really appreciated my efforts. I had made a friend for life. Furthermore, I had tried my first case with my new associate, Steve Brewer. Our work was solidified and he was to go on to become my partner and a great friend. Our work together was important. I learned a lot about this type of medical malpractice. I had also tried the case against a very fine defense lawyer. Even though this was a difficult loss, I learned a lot about how to try a case. The positive side of the ledger seemed to go on. Maybe I was learning about what losing really means.

As a result of this case, I decided to write an article about how lawyers deal with their losses. No one had ever written such an article. Lawyers don't like to talk about losing. Who does? Winning is everything, whether it is in trial, sports, or politics. Win, win, win. Nobody wants to talk about losing. A loser is a loser. Who wants to come in second in a lawsuit?

I researched what Vince Lombardi and Theodore Roosevelt had said about winning. There is much to be said about fighting the battle, having the courage to go on, having the compassion that comes from losing. I wrote an article called "The Art of Losing."[14] That article was published in national and state law journals and many people provided me with positive feedback. People appreciated that someone was willing to write about a very real subject: How we deal with the pain of our losing and why it is important to us[15]

So, in an odd kind of way, I had won for losing. And last, but not least, I had greatly reduced my own fear of losing. Losing my mother led to a great insight on my part. It would help me answer the critical questions that haunt so many of us. What is death? Can we be in contact with people's souls after they have died? My mother's death would help me find the answers to these questions.

I decided to try to get in touch with my mother's soul. I was more in touch with my soul than I had been for years. I had learned so much about my soul from all of the books I had read. In particular, *Anam Cara: A Book Of Celtic Wisdom* written by John O'Donohue was most relevant. The words Anam Cara mean soul friend. The idea that I found to be most profound was: "Your soul is not in your body; your body is in your soul." The soul is a larger entity that simply surrounds the body we inhabit during the short time we are on Earth. The soul is not limited. This concept comforts me. All of our souls are connected, particularly with persons who are close to us. So after my mother died, I decided to make a concentrated effort to see if I could really get in touch with her. If I got in touch with Mom, I would know it at a deep, intuitive level. My soul would know that I was in touch with her soul.

Around this time, I had joined a men's group led by a very fine therapist in Oakland, Mordechai Mitnick. I went to Mordechai one day and discussed the idea of contacting my mother's soul myself, not by using an alleged medium who would turn off the lights and move a table around. Mordechai told me to come to him next time with the best photograph I had of my mother. I did so. He indicated that we were going to do what he called "mat work." On the floor was a simple cotton mattress. He told me lay down on my back on top of the mattress. I put my mother's photograph next to me. Mordechai sat on the floor positioned behind my head where I couldn't see him. He put his hands on my chest. He instructed me do some very shallow breathing that would help put me into an altered state. He told me to visualize my mother. I wasn't quite sure where we were going with this. Meditation has never been easy for me. Yet, before long I found myself transformed into a state where I felt like I was outside my body, into an altered state of consciousness.

Soon I felt my mother's presence. Then I saw her. I didn't see her the way she had looked when she had been in her body. I saw her in a soul state. More importantly, I heard her. She talked to me. She said everything was all right. She wanted to know if I had any questions. I began to speak out loud and as I did, I could hear wise, simple answers given to the questions that I asked. Of course, she was there for me and had always loved me. We made a decision to come in this life together and to learn from each other. She was moving on to another dimension in her spiritual state but she would be with me until I died. Then our souls would reunite.

I don't know if my mother was really "there" in the room with me. However, I certainly felt her presence. That was all that really mattered to me. The session was very comforting and satisfying. It made good sense. It helped relieve the grief that I felt from her death. If we were truly in contact at the soul level—if I could contact her anytime—then the loss of her body and not being able to talk to her wasn't such a problem. I had known through my work that many people who have lost loved ones frequently feel in contact with them after their death.

Being in touch with Mom's soul was a profound experience. I went to Mordechai a few more times and did the mat work with him until I felt that I could contact my mother on my own. I felt that everything was good between us. I had a sense of understanding about why we had come together and what our lives were about. She had died at a particular time for a reason. My life was going on for a reason. I got a sense of knowing when I would die. I know exactly when it will be. It will be when I am ready. It will be when I have competed all of the work that I was meant to do in this life. This doesn't mean I can set a date or time for it. It simply means that it is part of my larger plan in the Universe, a plan my soul set in motion before I incarnated into my body. It is a plan that I cannot understand with my human mind.

My death will happen for a reason. Not just for me, but for everyone around me, whether they are my children, my grandchildren, my wife, my friends, my law partners, or anyone else.

My death will have a purpose, just as all deaths do. All events have a purpose. Everything happens for a reason. Figuring out the reason is the tough job.

My study of life and death is ongoing. I don't want to imply that the work I did was easy. I spend many long, hard hours reading, studying, and thinking seriously about these issues. I have read several hundred books on the subjects. I have spent many hours alone meditating. I have listened to subliminal tapes. I have talked to psychics, had past life readings, and worked with spiritual counselors. All of this has helped. It is an ongoing process. Life is a journey. Hopefully, it's a journey to self-understanding.

In some strange way the loss of my mother and the Reibe case are tied together. The loss of my mother helped me understand death. My analysis in "The Art of Losing" article following the Reibe case has helped me understand how lawyers can and should deal with losses. The positive feedback I have received from people all over the country is very satisfying. So, the confluence of these two losses has given me great insight for which I am most grateful.

1988 was a most interesting year, a year of leadership and professional growth, a year of winning and losing, and most of all, a year of enormous personal growth in my life journey.

# CHAPTER 25: LEAVING LIZ

1990 was a year of internal struggle, change, and transformation. I bought a handsome leather-bound journal and began to record entries about my life beginning on January 1, 1990. I'd been making entries in different booklets and smaller tablets since 1987, but in 1990, I decided to do some serious journaling. I'm so glad that I did. Reviewing my journal notes has brought back vivid memories of my life changes: how hard I worked at them, how hard they were, and how it all worked out.

Most of the entries deal with my relationship with Liz. We'd been together for twenty years, married for nineteen. We'd had such a wonderful relationship in our early years in the seventies but work stress, alcohol, and my infidelities had changed things.

It was now almost six years since I first quit drinking and four years since June of 1986 when I finally put alcohol behind me. I was working hard on my self-development. I was reading books about spiritual growth, metaphysics, and psychology. Metaphysics was especially interesting to me. Meta means beyond, so I use the term loosely to mean beyond the physical, those things we cannot see or hear. I was engaged in hypnosis therapy, working with psychics and past-life therapists. I was open to anything that would help answer questions about my life issues: Who am I? What is my life's purpose? How can I be happy?

By 1990 another issue was in the forefront. What was I to do about my relationship with Liz? It was not going well.

My January 1, 1990 diary entry set out where I was in my life. I was fifty-two years old. My life had changed dramatically in the last several years. I was working hard on exercising, trying to lose some weight, and staying mentally sharp. I was extremely active in our law firm and had a heavy caseload. But mostly, I was searching for answers.

I was working with Marilyn Gordon, a hypnotherapist. We had started working on weight loss. One day, something quite amazing happened. During the course of hypnosis, I stepped out of myself and began channeling an entity that seemed to come from Egypt. I know this seems strange. It was quite strange to me. I could hear my own voice but I wasn't processing the information through my left brain. It was just coming out of me. Whatever this was, it was wonderful. The experience answered the basic life questions. It came and was very powerful. I haven't talked much about this to other people. My life is strange enough as it is without complicating it with metaphysics, channeling, tarot cards, psychic readings, past life work, etc. But that is who I am. The channeling only lasted for a few years. I'm out of touch with it now, but at the time it helped me with my life's greatest crisis: What to do about my dear wife Liz and where was I to go in my life.

Liz and I bickered frequently. She was depressed. She didn't know it at first, but later through counseling she became aware of her depression. One of the primary symptoms of depression is irritability. Also, I certainly wasn't perfect. I was working hard and stressed out. Frequently small issues would blow up into big arguments. Liz was a bit obsessive-compulsive and I didn't tolerate that well. We would get along for a little while and then lose our tempers about the silliest things. But these fights were serious and our relationship deteriorated.

I was determined either to make a success of the relationship or leave it with integrity. Leaving Liz was very frightening. I had never been on my own. I had always been with women or around them, beginning with Mom and the matriarchy. Could I really leave my home? I had two wonderful kids who were fifteen and seventeen. I had a dachshund named Sam. I loved them with all my heart. I loved my house, a beautiful four-bedroom home up near Skyline High School in the Oakland hills. The whole idea of moving out was repugnant and frightening.

Time and time again Liz and I spoke about our relationship and how difficult it was. Fortunately, we had our house down at Pajaro Dunes. I was able go there alone from time to time, to write in my journal, and try to get my head straight. I read everything I could get my hands on that I thought might help. My work with Marilyn Gordon and my channeling was giving me advice, but the advice I was receiving was not specific. I had to follow my own feelings. I had to trust the Universe. Things would happen in their own due course. If I was filled with love—not only for Liz but for all those around me—everything would be fine. What wonderful platitudes. I believe them deeply. But what was I to do? It was hard to even think of another divorce. And I couldn't stand the idea of leaving my children.

On Valentine's Day 1990, I was alone at Pajaro Dunes. I wrote about a recent struggle I had settling a difficult case and reviewing some of my work issues. I reflected on my life and thought about my spiritual connection. I wrote:

> *"As I think about what are my dominant emotions—happy or sad—optimistic—angry, etc., I realize that most of my negative emotions come when I am in conflict with my wife. That is the area of most irritability. This is an important revelation and I must deal with it."*

Another example of my struggle was my entry on February 19, 1990:

> *"The question to ponder is what am I becoming? Where am I going? Where do I want to go? When I have some answers then I can visualize and manifest the result. The result is confusion, ambiguity, ambivalence, and uncertainty. These emotions do not often bother me but I have them now. I feel again at a crossroads with my career, family, and future. It's more important than ever that I receive good advice from my higher self, from my guides. I'll work on some meditation and keep seeing Marilyn Gordon. Don't rush it; go with the flow. Live in the present as you plan for the future—most important—unconditional love."*

I worked hard to stay in contact with whatever I could in the Universe. My mother's spirit was with me. I felt a connection with her and I also felt in contact with my higher self.

But all that didn't make it a lot easier. On March 13 I wrote:

*"Liz and I had a serious talk after our beach walk yesterday and I'm putting some of my goals and feelings on paper. Maybe we can have a rational discussion about where we're going and how to resolve our conflicts. I must admit that I'm ambivalent and in a dilemma—perhaps another sign of my 'midlife crisis' or being at the crossroads of my life. Liz is definitely at the same point."*

Liz and I continued to struggle along. However, it wasn't all bad. We took an interesting and wonderful trip to the Mayan area of the Yucatan Peninsula in Mexico. We went to a concert with my favorite new age artist, Kitaro. It was terrific.

I read an interesting book called *The Warrior Within: A Guide to Inner Power* by Shale Paul. In June 1990, I met Paul in Colorado and spent a few days with him. I continued to struggle with trying to find answers to my relationship questions. He suggested I write an autobiography of my entire life. I did that in an abbreviated form and it was helpful, but I still didn't know what to do about Liz and me.

At the same time, some strange things happened at the law firm. We had an unexplained theft of $7,500 that definitely looked as though someone inside the office had stolen it. It created a huge upset in our firm. We had never had a problem like that—I had prided myself on my good relationships with our staff and with my partners. We later learned that one of the construction workers employed by the building had opened our safe and taken the money. It was but another example of the difficulties of 1990 that seemed so prevalent.

\* \* \*

On April 29 I went to an exposition of new age and metaphysical matters in San Francisco. I noticed a woman who advertised that she would do an intuitive reading for $15. Something attracted me to her. She knew nothing about me. I was dressed casually in slacks and a sweater and there was nothing to indicate that was a lawyer or was married. The woman smiled and I sat down across from her.

"I would like to talk to you about something," I said.

"What about?" she asked.

"Relationships," I replied.

"Is there someone special you want to talk about?" she inquired.

"Yes."

"What is her name?"

"Liz."

At that point she sat back, closed her eyes, and went into a meditative state for a few minutes. Then she wrote Liz in cursive in the air with her finger. When she finished, she opened her eyes and looked at me and said something I will never forget:

"That relationship is over."

I was stunned. It was so direct and unequivocal. It was upsetting.

"Well, you don't know anything about her or me. How

could you say that?" I demanded.

"Well, that's what my guides tell me," she stated.

Intuitively, I knew that she was right, but I wasn't ready to accept it. I told her that I wanted to see her again, which I did in May and had a more detailed reading. She reiterated the same thing and said something even more important. She told me I was going to meet someone before the end of the year. I wasn't even ready to leave Liz. Her reading seemed so true and so honest. But I was still full of fear, anxiety, and ambivalence. *Could I trust this information?*

"When might I meet this other person?" I asked as my session ended.

"By the end of the year. Probably by October or November," she replied.

The woman, Dr. Susan Stuart, was a clairvoyant and I planned to meet with her again in June to discuss this further. *How weird.* I hadn't even made a decision to leave Liz. We were still trying to work out our relationship.

As a general rule, I do not accept "predictions" from psychics. If their information is valuable, intuitive, and makes sense, then I listen to it. If not, I reject it. I'm a lawyer. I think logically and rationally. I just don't accept stuff unless it seems rational. But something about Susan's comments seemed so profound. Something inside me told me she was right. Still, I had uncertainty.

Towards the end of May, Mike Hatchwell, a friend of mine, died. He had been on the CTLA board when I was president of the association. I was a friend of his widow, Renee, so Liz and I went to the funeral down to Southern California.

On the flight back, Liz and I were very emotional. There may have been something about the memorial service that opened us up. For the very first time, I seriously raised the question with Liz about whether we should separate. My journal entry of May 29, 1990 describes my feelings:

> *"Just got back from Mike Hatchwell's memorial service—Liz and I had a serious talk re: our future—it was open, honest, and upsetting—especially to her.*
>
> *I mentioned a book I was reading at the time, which, interestingly enough, discussed the fear of criticism and being afraid to leave an unhappy marriage.*
>
> *Is this another message to me? Am I imagining this? I must work out my thoughts here—Ambiguity again—It's hard!"*

My next entry on June 1, 1990 encapsulates the struggle that Liz and I were having:

> *"Liz and I have been having serious heart-to-heart talks all week. She badly wants to hold the marriage together—declares her love and all of her affection. She's going to see Barbara Lewis* [a therapist] *and we will try to go to Southern California to see Lee Coit* [a man who had written

a book about relationships.] *Maybe we will get to Pajaro Dunes in a couple of weeks. I love her and feel her pain — great fear of abandonment and living alone — 'like a hole in her stomach.' I am committed to try and work with her."*

We continued to have serious discussions about our relationship that summer. We would get along pretty well, and even have a satisfying sexual experience. Then we would withdraw and have a terrible argument. It was on again, off again. I was ambivalent about what to do.

At the end of June we decided to go to Spain. My daughter, Lisa, was going to spend some time over there with a student exchange program so the four of us went. After dropping off Lisa, Liz, Jenny, and I finished the trip. Liz and I really enjoyed ourselves, but when we returned home, the problems arose again. Liz and I would get along for a while and then something would happen that would make both of us realize that our relationship simply wasn't working. On August 26, 1990 I wrote:

*"I'm struggling again with Liz and my feelings. We did an exercise from the book, <u>Getting the Love You Want: A Guide For Couples,</u> and had a long discussion in which I was negative about our progress and the problems in our relationship. Liz is depressed again and I have ambivalent feelings. How can I be honest with these old barriers between us? Am I being a perfectionist? Do I truly*

*love Liz and want to be totally committed to her for the rest of my life? Do I want to be a bachelor? What the hell do I want?? I need some help."*

In the meantime, Liz was starting to see her therapist, Barbara Lewis. I went together with her once and then we decided not to do couples counseling since it was better for Liz to see the therapist on her own.

In September 1990, Liz and I did something that brought us to finality. We went to a weekend relationship seminar with a man named Lee Coit. It was a group session in which we had to deal very honestly with our feelings. I think by the end of the session we both knew the answer. There was no hate between us. We knew we really loved each other. But the passion was gone. We couldn't be intimate any longer. The marriage was over. It was time for us to move on. It was finally clear to me. My September 23, 1990 entry tells the story of the end of my second marriage:

*"This last week has been the most significant in many years for me—perhaps in my lifetime.*

*I told Liz of my decision to move out on Wednesday evening. I phrased it in the most spiritual of ways. I had indeed reached this decision after consulting my inner self and I knew it to be right. I referred to her statement at the end of the Lee Coit seminar: 'I know what I have to do' i.e., let me go. She was very upset that night and into the next day.*

*However, when I came home from work the next
day something dramatic had happened. She had
changed. She said she had accepted the decision
and knew it was right for both of us. I felt like I
was listening to a new woman. She then told me
that after our conversation she had sat quietly in
the bedroom that morning in tears and frustration
and had the most amazing spiritual experience of
her life. She was in tears and asked God for help.
Then a light came over her and she felt at peace for
almost the first time in her life. She knew herself
that it was time for us to leave, that our separation
was the right thing. It was the best conversation
we had had in over fifteen years. For my part, I
felt a huge load lifted from me and I am now ready
for some freedom."*

This profound spiritual experience transformed Liz. She
accepted our separation and was ready to move forward with it,
even though we both knew it would be painful. For my part,
I also felt that her spiritual experience gave me the answer I
had been looking for. I wanted to leave Liz with integrity. We
both had to be right with it, for ourselves, and especially for our
children. I was determined that our separation would be done
with mutual love, integrity, and compassion.

Shortly thereafter, we had one final counseling session
with a psychiatrist whose sole area of specialty was how to tell
children about a coming divorce. This was a huge issue for us.
We had not spoken to the kids about what was going on, although

I'm certain they were aware of our difficulties. His advice was good:

"You should make a decision as to when to tell the kids and as soon as that happens, you [Gary] must immediately move out. Do not stay in the house for even one night because the kids will think that they can help put the relationship back together."

We decided on a move-out date that would be after Jenny's birthday on October 21, 1990. Liz was also going back to the east coast with Lisa, who was preparing to enter college. I found a nice apartment on Lake Merritt near my office. On the last Thursday in October we told the kids. It was very difficult. They both cried and were upset.

However, I followed Dr. Nestor's advice. I picked up what clothes I had in the house, threw them into my little sports car, and drove off to my new apartment on the lake. That afternoon, I had been to a memorial service for Rick Rankin, a well-known defense attorney who had practiced law in Oakland. This experience seemed to add to my feelings of nostalgia and sadness. I felt his family's grief. I was also grieving. I was grieving for the loss of a relationship. Divorce is like death. There are similar feelings of grief, pain, and sadness.

My apartment was lonely. Yet, I knew that I needed to be alone. I'd noted this in my journal. For the first time in my life I was truly on my own. I wasn't living with a woman at my side. I needed to make sure that I could do this. In a strange way, it greatly strengthened me. I proved to myself that I could live without Mom. I could live without a wife or a woman. I had to sleep in a bed alone. Of course, I would have preferred to have a woman with me, but not just any woman. I left my wife Liz with integrity. I loved my kids. I loved my dog. I loved my house and I missed them all—most of all, of course, my children. But I had to make it on my own. I would accept whatever happened. I felt that all my hard work over the many years since I had quit drinking was coming to fruition. I felt the Universe was going to bring me what I needed. What I had asked for. A truly spiritual relationship. A soul mate. But there was no predicting when or if it would come.

# CHAPTER 26: A PREDICTION COMES TRUE

On Friday November 9, 1990 I was in La Jolla, California for the annual CTLA convention. Two years before I had been president. Now I was there alone for the first time. My friends and colleagues knew Liz, so I had to explain that we had separated. People were understanding and compassionate, but I felt strange and alone, somehow distant from the couples and friends I had known for so many years. The first night there, I had an in-room massage by a very strong, heavyset woman. Massages are a meditative experience for me. I've had many of them over the years. This one was particularly powerful. Maybe it was because I was alone and my feelings were so raw and open. I felt in touch with my soul, my guides, and my higher self. Somehow or another, I knew everything was going to be all right. But I was still in pain. I was still grieving the loss of my marriage.

The next day, I attended the usual educational sessions. I looked forward to the luncheon. Each year the association gives out different awards and this year I was the chair of the awards committee. I had worked with staff and the lawyers to decide who would get the awards for trial lawyer of the year, trial judge of the year, appellate judge of the year, etc. I presented an award to a wonderful judge from Alameda County named Jacqueline Taber. She was one of the pioneering women of the law in our community. The awards ceremony went well.

We were outdoors in a big tent and the weather was perfect. Then the program came to a close, at least according to my agenda. But our president, Buddy Herzog, rose to present another award. Buddy and I had our problems when I was president of the association. He was a strong-willed guy and we had occasional differences. The same was true of a good number of my board members at the time. We had since put all of that behind us and we were now good friends.

I looked over at our executive director, Bobbie Frayne.

"Hey, what's going on?" I exclaimed. "The awards are supposed to be over!"

"Just be quiet for a minute Gary," she replied.

Buddy Herzog started to talk about somebody. Then it hit me. *It was me!* I'll never forget his words. He was talking about a man who had literally saved the association by stepping forward in our time of need. He used a John Wayne analogy: a man who wasn't afraid and was ready to lead the organization when others were fearful. I was stunned. I was not ready for this. I was already tired, raw, and strung out. Usually, you have a little time to think about how to respond to an award. But this was a shock. I literally had no more than a minute to prepare a response.

I slowly walked to the stage. I felt a tremendous amount of emotion. I hadn't been sure how much the association really appreciated me until that moment. I looked out over the sea of faces and all the friends around me, all smiling and appreciative. I don't know that I have ever felt more loved by an audience in my life. I could only find a few words to express my emotions. So I said:

"I have been in this organization for a long time. Being president was hard. You know that it was a

206

sacrifice for me. Would I do it again? The answer is yes. I'd sacrifice anything for the causes we fight for. This is the greatest group I have ever known and I love you all."

As soon as I said that, the audience stood up in unison and cheered. I could actually feel a tremendous wave of emotion coming towards me. I could feel their love for me. It was overwhelming. I broke into tears. It was one of the most memorable experiences of my life.

That evening, I was with my friend, Ed Caldwell, who helped me quit drinking at my intervention. I didn't usually attend A.A. meetings, but the trial lawyers were having a special late-night, candlelight ceremony for those in recovery. There was a candle in the center of the room and no other light. I had never attended such a ceremony but I went at Ed's urging. I wasn't ready to return to my room. It was about 11:00 p.m. when I entered the room. There were five of us who knew each other well. Steve Pingel, a good lawyer and a friend, was there with a woman. She sat quietly through the ceremony which lasted almost an hour.

During that time, each of us talked at some length about our drinking experiences and where we were now. I spoke last. I talked not only about how much better off I was after quitting drinking, but about everything good that had happened to me since that time, including my verdicts, and most importantly, my work with the trial lawyers. On the professional front my life was great. On the personal front it was a struggle. I talked about the reason I left Liz. I needed to be on my own. I talked about leaving her with integrity and how I felt the Universe would take care of me. When I was finished, the mysterious woman with Steve spoke up.

"Can I say something?" she asked.

"Of course," I responded.

"Gary," she said to me intently, "I just want to tell you that I really appreciate your integrity. So many men leave their marriages for another woman. You left because you knew it was the right thing. I left my own marriage the same way a number of years ago. I really wish you the best and simply wanted to say that."

I appreciated her comments but assumed she was dating Steve, so I didn't really think much more about it. I returned to my room alone.

Lilly told me later what happened to her. She needed to drive back to Los Angeles early the next morning. She had been separated for sixteen years and had dated a lot of men, but never had a serious relationship. As she began the drive back, she had a strong, nagging thought running through her mind: **You should call him**. *Why should I call him? He's an alcoholic. He's coming off his second marriage. He's a two-time loser and an alcoholic. This is not exactly what one thinks about for good relationship.* But the thought persisted: **Call him.** It stayed with her.

The next day, she went to the hypnotherapist she was seeing for anxiety about taking the California Bar Exam. She told him about me and then asked him a question:

"Michael, I met a man this weekend. He has been married twice and has just separated from his wife. He's had alcohol problems. But I have this sense that I should call him. It seems weird, don't you think?"

Michael looked directly into her eyes.

"You should call him," he answered firmly, "Do it."

Lilly had never called a man in her life. But she took his advice and called.

On Wednesday after the conference, I was still buzzed about receiving the award, but was back to the hectic life of my law practice. When I came into the office, the receptionist handed me a phone message slip. It was from a Lilly Phalen (her name was incorrectly spelled—it should have been Phelan) with a telephone number.[16] The message said something about meeting me last Saturday at the convention. I returned the call but she wasn't there so I left a message. We played phone tag for a while, but were finally able to speak to each other one evening a couple of days later. She was nervous as she started the conversation:

"Well, Gary, I just wanted to call you and tell you again how much I appreciate the integrity you have shown in leaving your marriage. . ." She was struggling.

"Oh yes," I offered, "I remember, you're Steve Pingel's girlfriend."

"No," she stammered, "I'm not his girlfriend. We are just friends."

"Oh, I see," I said. There was an awkward pause.

"So, did you call to say that maybe you'd like to get to know me better?" I asked.

"That would be all right," she answered.

"Well, I'd love to meet you and get together some time,"

I offered.

"I've got a daughter up in Pleasanton" she replied, "And I do get up your way now and then."

"Well, that's great," I said. "Maybe we can get together over the holiday." I was thinking of Thanksgiving, only a couple of weeks off.

"That would be a good idea," Lilly responded. "Maybe I could get up there for New Year's."

"New Year's?" That seems like a long way off. How about Thanksgiving?" I suggested.

Lilly said she would check whether she could get time off work. She later called and said that she would come up over the Thanksgiving weekend. She said she could see her daughter at the same time and we could go out to dinner on Saturday night. I suggested that she fly out from the Burbank airport near where she lived and I could meet her at the Oakland airport. I was surprised when she said that she would rather drive.

"You're going to drive all the way up here on Saturday and drive all the way back on Sunday?" I asked.

"Yes," she said. She explained that she had to go to work the next week.

"That seems like a lot of driving," I commented.

"Well, I just like to drive," she said.

"Okay." I thought to myself, this woman must really love to drive."

* * *

On November 16, 1990, I noted in my journal that I met "my mysterious Lilly" and that she was coming up to meet me on the Saturday after Thanksgiving.

Then on November 24, 1990 I wrote in my journal:

> *"High anticipation. I am waiting for Lilly Phelan who has driven up from LA to meet me and have dinner tonight. What an enigmatic and mysterious woman she is. It's like waiting for a blind date."*

That Saturday afternoon I sat quietly alone in my apartment. I thought to myself:

> *"Here I am, fifty-three years old. Married twice and going through a divorce. An alcoholic who has struggled with his relationships and is now trying to get it right. A woman is driving five-hundred miles to have a date with me. I hardly know how to go about dating after being married for so long. At least not this kind of date. What does it all mean?"*

Lilly arrived a little late, shortly after five o'clock. I had asked her what kind of wine she liked to drink and she indicated white. So I had a bottle of Chardonnay for her and a bottle of non-alcoholic wine for me. Lilly was a little flustered when she came into the apartment. Actually, I had a very nice place. It was on the eighteenth floor, overlooking Lake Merritt. It is particularly pretty at night because of the "necklace of lights," small lights stringing all the way around the lake, making the view quite beautiful after dark.

Lilly had a couple of glasses of wine and I had my glass of non-alcoholic wine. We began to talk. It was the most amazing, open discussion that I had ever had. I decided that everything I told Lilly was going to be the truth. I was going to be completely honest. This was the new me: total honesty. So I talked about my life and she talked about hers.

We were getting to know each other. After she had her third glass of wine we went to a nice dinner in Berkeley. She was still a little nervous and ordered another glass of wine with dinner. That was fine with me, but as a former drinker I was now a drink counter. After she had her fifth glass of wine, I began to wonder. A strange thought began to creep up in the back of my mind. *What an interesting woman, am I running into someone with an alcohol problem? How Karmic would that be?* The thought soon passed. Lilly was charming and I took pleasure in her company.

We returned to the apartment. I put on a little slow music and we danced. I enjoyed our conversation and was attracted to Lilly. However, it wasn't about sex. It was just about feeling comfortable with somebody I had just met. Then, after dancing for a few minutes I heard a voice. It was a voice I will never forget. It was in my head and said very simply: **"This is her."** *What was that?* I couldn't believe it. Then the voice again said, **"This is her."** Immediately, I had an incredible vision of Lilly and me living a life together where we traveled all over the world and we had the most wonderful relationship I could ever imagine. The vision lasted only a matter of seconds; it was like a flash. I didn't know what to think. *Was it my imagination? Was it my guides? My higher source? Was it God? Was Susan Stuart's prediction coming true?* Whatever it was, it was powerful.

Lilly and I had only known each other for about three hours so I guess the next thing I said to her sounded pretty strange:

"You know Lilly," I said, "I want to tell you something that's really going to sound weird."

"What's that?" she asked.

"Well," I said, "I'm in love with you and we're going to spend the rest of our lives together." I said this not as a question, but simply as a fact. She looked at me but didn't respond. I wondered if she felt the same way, but maybe she thought I was crazy. Somehow or other, I think she knew the same thing.

"Who knows?" she replied with a smile.

It was getting late. Lilly had said she might spend the night with her daughter but it was obvious that she shouldn't drive. Not after six glasses of wine. She didn't seem drunk, just very relaxed.

Not too long before, I had bought a book called *Journey of The Heart: The Path of Conscious Love* by John Welwood. It was on my coffee table. I hadn't started to read it but something made me think that I should read it to her. I don't know why I felt like reading a book, but I did. Maybe I was rusty or uneasy about how to get into the physical stuff. It didn't seem the time for that. So I began to read the book. The writing was beautiful and poetic, however, before long, Lilly started to nod off. It was time to go to bed. *Now what?*

I had a two-bedroom apartment. There was a nice big

water bed in my master bedroom and a small pullout bed in the second bedroom. I gave Lilly a choice saying, "You can sleep in the small pullout bed in this little dinky bedroom or you can share this big beautiful water bed with me in this nice, bigger bedroom."

I guess the choice was easy. Strangely, the evening wasn't about sex. Although we were holding and kissing some, that wasn't the point. It was as if we had known each other for years. I felt totally comfortable with her. She felt totally comfortable with me. As we got in bed, I read some more and soon we both drifted off to sleep.

Lilly later told me that she had never had slept overnight with any man she had dated. When she was with another man, she always got up and drove home. But she said that she had a better night's sleep with me than she'd had in years. I felt the same way.

The next morning, we were still talking about why we had this incredible sense of companionship, of already knowing each other, and of being so connected. I had talked to her a bit about past lives the night before so I asked Lilly if she would like to get a past-life reading.

I'm not sure what brought that into my head but it just seemed natural. She was ready for it. I called a hypnotherapist named Kay Heatherly who had given me a couple of past life readings. She said that if we came over right away she could see us. We walked into her living room hand in hand and sat down quietly. Lilly and I were acting like we had known each other for years, yet we hadn't even been together for twenty-four hours.

Kay said she would give us three readings. She quietly

channeled in her own guides then gave us our first reading.

It was very interesting. We had lived as brother and sister in Europe in the seventeenth or eighteenth century. We lived on our parents' large estate. When they died, we stayed on and managed the estate together. We each married and had our own families. We had a long and loving life, totally platonic. We had lived together from the time we were born until the time we died. We were always very close. This seemed to explain why Lilly and I felt we had always known each other and why we were immediately so comfortable together.

In the second reading, Lilly was a little girl about eight years old and I was her father. We had a loving relationship. I have three daughters, so that appealed to me. This was another reason why we might feel so close, especially around the Thanksgiving holiday.

"Well, these are nice readings," I said to Kay. "I guess we've had these wonderful, platonic lives together. Do you think you can find anything more passionate there for another life?" Of course I was just kidding. But the next life was something else.

In our third reading, our genders were reversed. I was the woman and Lilly was the man. She was a temple high priest in Egypt. I was married and a worshipper in the temple. But the priest, Lilly, seduced me and we began a wild and passionate affair. Very forbidden. Very sexy. Very exciting.

After the readings we walked out in a bit of a daze. It seemed like we'd always known each other and yet we hadn't even had a full day together. We went to the Good Earth Restaurant to get a bite to eat. I was trying to process all of this information. I think Lilly was doing the same. While Lilly went to the restroom, I waited to order. Suddenly I broke into laughter. It all seemed so funny and I just couldn't stop laughing.

"What's wrong?" she asked when she returned to the table.

"I don't know, Lilly." I answered. "This is the funniest damn thing. I don't know whether I'm your brother or your father. I don't know whether you're a man or a woman. I don't know what the hell is going on but you look great to me. Let's go back to the apartment and make love."

And we did. She stayed another night which was absolutely wonderful. We were in love. It seemed like we had always been in love. We felt so connected. It wasn't like anything I've ever felt before or since, at least not in this life.

*  *  *

I distinctly remember walking in the office on Monday morning after Lilly had gone home. My law partner and longtime friend, Eric Ivary, was there. He had been supportive throughout my divorce and knew of my struggles. I went into his office and shut the door.

"I want to tell you something amazing, Eric" I said.

"What's that?" he asked.

"This weekend an angel from heaven dropped into my life," I answered.

It's a quote he will always remember. And it was true. I had trusted in the Universe and the Universe had given me what I wanted. The next entry in my journal is descriptive of my feelings.

*"Tuesday December 4, 1990: Wow these last days are hard to describe. I guess quite simply I've fallen madly in love with my Lilly. What a time we have had* . . . [I described at some length our evening and our past life readings] . . . *before she left, she left a beautiful note on my bed that Monday and said how much she cared for me and how much she wanted to get together again."*

My long entry in my journal continued:

*"I only know this I love this woman and I know she loves me. She told me after the first two nights that it was the best weekend of her life and she loved me like no other before. I believed her and feel the same. It's like being a kid yet this is a deep and mature connection it's not just physical. I opened up as wide as I could and bared my feelings about other women. Indeed last weekend some of them actually called. But that didn't affect Lilly. No judgments, just unconditional love. She confided her deepest concerns about her career to me, her struggles with the bar exam, and her past relationships. But mostly it was <u>new</u>. A transformation for both of us."*

The next weekend we got together again and went to see Susan Stuart in Marin. We had a wonderful reading with her and it was quite amazing. Susan didn't remember the details of the reading she had given me where she told me that I was going to meet this beautiful woman before the year's end. However, our readings with Susan confirmed that Lilly and I were truly soul mates. In one reading we weren't really in a human state. We were like twin towers of light in a spiritual dimension, working together in a metaphysical way. It is hard to describe, but it seemed like we were truly spiritual beings and earth mates. To me, that is what the word soul mate means. We are souls together. We are also mates in this life. We have to work together both spiritually and psychologically and that's what we decided to do.

In a strange way, I feel that Lilly is almost an incarnation of my mother. Lilly also looks similar to the way Mom looked when she was young. Oddly enough, I also resemble Lilly's father, who died in 1982. Although our parents are dead, we are strangely in touch with them through our relationship. We have worked on understanding what this means. It is this connection that helps us understand at a very deep level how our relationship works.

We did inner child work, getting in touch with our lives as young children. Little Lilly and little Gary, kids who were just three and four years old. We dug up old pictures of ourselves, which we still keep in our bedroom. They remind us of what our lives were like as children and how that affects us today.

Over the next few years, I learned more about my relationship with my mother and what had formed me as a man than I had in my thirty years of two previous marriages. I finally understood my need to be wanted by women. But I didn't need that anymore. Lilly is all I ever needed, all I ever wanted, and all I care about. I found monogamy with Lilly ten times more exciting and interesting than all of my past relationships put together.

We did the hard work that needs to be done in a relationship: psychological analysis, metaphysical study, inner child work, past life work. There were many honest discussions about who we were and how we came together. We put it into practice.

Here's an interesting analogy that I think crystallizes who we are: Think of two candles burning brightly next to each other, one in each hand. Take the candles and slowly bring them together at the tip and watch the two flames join each other. They become one larger, brighter flame. That describes Lilly and me. We are joined together, two parts of one person. It is amazing how much you can really learn from another human being if you work at being in an open, beautiful, spiritual relationship.

Of course there is more to it than that. We had our differences that we had to deal with. Lilly had her fears and I had my self-righteous issues. She would think that I was interested in another woman. I wasn't and I would angrily deny it. This would lead to an argument. But after each argument, we came back together and learned from it. Slowly, over the years, these arguments have diminished as we have learned to really understand each other emotionally, psychologically, and spiritually. We have a couple of principles that we live by: We are always honest with each other and perhaps more importantly, we always insist that we physically come together in a loving way after any disagreement.

Underlying each argument is the fear that we might not be loved by the other. This is so true of many relationships. That's what ends up causing anger and separation. Each party thinks the other doesn't love them. But Lilly and I know we are connected, not only psychologically, but spiritually. The spiritual connection helps us heal the psychological issues that are a part of our life. When Liz and I had arguments, we would usually sleep separately and go for days without speaking. This led to resentments and hurt feelings that were oftentimes never resolved. Lilly and I never do that. We always bring our disagreements to closure with love and understanding. Although the issues may remain in our lives we try to learn and grow from any disagreement.

We have something else important to a good relationship: a lot in common. Lilly is a psychiatric nurse and holds a master's degree. She has not only taught nursing but had also served as the dean of a nursing program. She worked with mentally ill people and people who were dying. She has many experiences with disabled, injured, and grieving patients. I have had similar experiences with my clients. Lilly is also interested in law and has her law degree. Obviously, the law is my life. So our interests in psychology and law keep us interested in each other's work. Therefore our relationship continues to grow and flourish.

# CHAPTER 27: A COMMITMENT CEREMONY
## AND A BIRTHDAY WEDDING

I think the term "soul mate" is way overused. It has become a cliché. But Lilly and I are true soul mates. We made a decision to come into this life and go our own ways until November 24, 1990. Then like two railroad tracks joining together, we merged. It was meant to be at that point in time. Not a minute before and not a minute later. It was our Karma. We were each ready for a serious, spiritual, deep relationship. It was as if we had planned this all of our lives and were now ready to live it out, and quite frankly, that's what happened. Lilly and I began a relationship filled with fun, love, excitement, and interpersonal work. We traveled to Hawaii in January 1991 and had an incredible experience. It was Lilly's first trip there and both of us will never forget it.

We are serious about understanding who we are, psychologically and spiritually. We began a process of deep psycho-spiritual analysis. It was hard work, but good work, and quite rewarding.

Lilly and I had an issue in our relationship which was quite common in second and third marriages—our children. Although we knew we had a lifelong bond, but we were not ready to get married in the early years of our relationship. Still, we wanted our children to know that this wasn't just an affair or some boyfriend/girlfriend relationship. We wanted them to know we were in a long-term, serious, and loving relationship. We wanted them to accept us. We wanted them to get to know and accept each other. We wanted an extended family.

Lilly and I have seen many couples in new relationships that have a great deal of difficulty with their stepchildren. Frequently, the children don't accept the new relationship. Sometimes there are custody battles. The former spouse can resent the new relationship. We wanted to work hard to find a way to avoid these problems.

Our divorce experiences were quite different. When Lilly and I met, she and her former husband Ed were separated for sixteen years. She had left Ed because they had grown apart. She wanted a career and he wanted her to be a stay-at-home mom. There wasn't any drinking involved nor were there any affairs. Lilly needed her independence. After Lilly ended her marriage in Chicago, she moved to Southern California and continued to further her career. She obtained a master's degree in psychiatric nursing and got a law degree.

Ed had primary custody of the kids in Chicago, but eventually he remarried and moved the kids to Northern California. Lilly always maintained a close and loving relationship with her children but their separation had been difficult. She was anxious to have a closer relationship with them now that they were young adults. Her daughter, Liz, was single and working in Pleasanton. Her son Pat attended graduate school in New York.

My situation was quite different. I had left my first wife, Georgia, when my oldest daughter, Catherine, was only a year old. Georgia had full custody of Catherine and visitation was difficult. At one point, Georgia moved to Europe and took Catherine along without my consent. As a result, I lost contact with Catherine for several years when she was in her early teens. I had never been as close to her as I would have liked. Furthermore, Georgia still resented my relationship with Liz. This also made visitation difficult. Liz had loved Catherine, but had been uneasy with visitation because it always involved a difficult, if not nasty, confrontation with Georgia.

Soon after Lilly and I met, Lilly wanted to meet Catherine. I hoped my new relationship with Lilly would help bring me and Catherine closer together. Lilly and I began to visit Catherine in Seattle on a regular basis, and as a result, we became closer.

My daughters Lisa and Jenny were seventeen and fifteen when I separated from Liz in 1990. Liz and I tried not to be critical of each other, especially around the kids. Although divorce always causes some trauma to the children, I wanted my kids to meet and get to know Lilly and to accept her. Lilly was not "the other woman" in the separation. Liz understood that and encouraged the girls to spend as much time with me as possible. Still, my relationship with Lilly happened so soon after my separation from Liz that it was bound to cause some problems.

Lilly and I began the long, steady, process of integrating these five very different, young people into an extended family. Gradually, we introduced all of the children to each other at family events, such as graduations and holiday celebrations.

Lisa graduated from high school shortly after Lilly and I began our relationship. Lisa then moved to New York to attend Sarah Lawrence College. Two years later, Jenny graduated from high school and moved to San Luis Obispo to attend college. She later moved to San Diego to attend community college.

My former wife Liz's only brother, Roger, lived in southern California at the time. He was quite close to Lisa and Jenny and was a source of emotional support for Jenny. In the meantime, Lilly's daughter, Liz Phelan, went back to school and moved to New York to get a degree in social work.

A couple of things happened to bring all of us closer together and eventually satisfy our desire to have a loving extended family. First, Lilly and I decided to hold a "commitment ceremony." We weren't ready to get married, but we wanted to have our family and children, as well as our friends, know that we were in a serious, long-term relationship. How could we accomplish this without having a marriage ceremony?

I came up with the idea that we should have everyone gather together in a beautiful place to have a celebration of our relationship. We arranged this in Hawaii at the chapel on the grounds of the Grand Wailea Hotel in the Wailea area of Maui. We held our ceremony on November 25, 1995 at 5:00 p.m. This was the Saturday after Thanksgiving, exactly five years after the time of our first meeting at my apartment on Lake Merritt. We invited all of the kids, as well as my law partners, their wives, and a few close friends. The commitment ceremony also coincided with the trial lawyers' seminar being held at a nearby hotel.

We sent out invitations that said that there should be no gifts. The invitation read "Your presence is our gift." We still have the invitation on a plaque on our kitchen wall. It was a great success. During the ceremony, Lilly and I read poetry to each other and stood in front of a group of about thirty people and publicly proclaimed our love and lifelong commitment to each other. No one presided over the ceremony, although we did have some musical accompaniment. We had accomplished our purpose. Our close relationship was clear to everyone.

The second thing that cemented our extended family relationship was our travels together. Lilly and I took all of our children (except for Lisa, who was in school) on a trip to Europe in 1994. The kids all met each other in Rome. They each flew in from different parts of the country and spent a week traveling together through Italy. My daughter Catherine, who was engaged at the time (although that later fell through) also brought her then-fiancée and my daughter Jenny brought along Tom, who is now her husband. The trip was very meaningful. By the time it was all over, the kids had formed wonderful, permanent friendships with each other.

So Lilly and I were in good shape with our families, but what about marriage? Lilly and I had been together for six and a half years but I wasn't ready for another marriage and neither was she. Instead, we began to travel extensively. The vision that I'd had on that first night of November 24, 1990 had came true. Lilly and I have traveled all over the world together, including Europe, two trips to Africa, Fiji, Australia, New Zealand, South America, and many cruises. We traveled a lot, had a great deal of fun, and were enjoying our wonderful, loving relationship.

In 1994, we bought a house together in Alamo. I shared all of my finances with Lilly and she was as well off financially as though we were married. We would frequently ask ourselves "Why should we get married? How will it help us?" However, when we traveled abroad, we often found out that people had difficultly with the term "significant other" and didn't quite understand our relationship.

In 1996 we asked ourselves a different question: "Why not get married?" We had been together for over six years. What was the problem? By then we were both ready. So we decided to get married on my sixtieth birthday. I told Lilly that if we got married on my birthday, I would never forget our anniversary. She agreed. My sixtieth birthday was the best birthday of my life!

By then we had many friends throughout the trial lawyer community. We had integrated Lilly's friends and mine into our life. Our five kids got along well. They were happy to see us get hitched. So we did it.

We wrote our own vows. We don't go to church regularly, but we found a nice little Methodist church nearby, the oldest church in Lafayette, California. We had a wonderful ceremony on May 18, 1997, my sixtieth birthday. The weather was quite warm and now my law partners, who were all in my wedding, continually remind me of this. It was great day. Everyone there knew us well and loved us, just as we loved them.

Our reception at the Round Hill Country Club near our home was quite a party! When you throw the party and pay for it, you get to call all the shots. So I did something I'd always wanted to do. I stood on stage and sang to Lilly. I guess it's my Welsh background. Welsh guys love to sing. I can't say I sang well, but I sang for fun. Two songs: "Oh, Pretty Woman" by Roy Orbison (one of my great heroes) and "Unchained Melody" by The Righteous Brothers. Fortunately, I had a big band to back me up. Lilly danced as I sang and everyone joined in. It was the most fantastic day of my life.

For our honeymoon, Lilly and I did something unusual. We rented an RV and drove 4,500 miles up the California, Oregon, and Washington coasts, and on into British Columbia. We went to Jasper, British Columbia and returned through the Canadian Rockies. We drove through Glacier National Park, Yellowstone, down through Utah, and then on to Lake Tahoe. We were gone seven weeks and I uncharacteristically grew a beard. It was a magnificent time, although sleeping in the RV was a little difficult since Lilly and I prefer hotels. That RV trip is probably our once in a lifetime experience. We did it once, and that was enough. Our wedding and honeymoon were fabulous, as is our life. The vision I had that first night we met has come true.

* * *

During the 1990s, I continued to try a lot of cases, as I had done throughout my career. However, it was different. Now I had my own personal jury consultant, a shadow juror, and a companion. I could confide in someone about case strategy, my anxiety and standard fears lawyers have during the trial. There was someone there to help me relieve the stress and who understood exactly what I was going through every day of the trial. Of course, that someone was Lilly.

Lilly helped me both objectively and subjectively. She was more conservative and cautious about cases than I was. She had medical training and was able to more quickly see problems with a case. As an advocate, it is easy for me to completely believe in my client and be ready to charge forward. Lilly could see the "warts" of the case and was quick to warn me about them. I respected her opinions because they helped me remain objective.

On the subjective level, it was great to have someone who understood exactly what the stress of the trial was. Lilly was there from the early morning until late at night when we went to bed together. She understood how hard I worked and the difficulties and intricacies of the trial. As a trial lawyer, it is hard to explain to a spouse or significant other exactly what takes place in a trial, especially if that person is not in court. Describing everything taking place during trial each day is tiresome and drains my energy. I didn't need to do that with Lilly. She was there with me and understood it all. Our work together was important. Lilly not only attended trials with me but also encouraged me to speak to various trial lawyer groups. As our relationship developed, I began talking with other lawyers about their personal problems. I began to speak with them about things Lilly said were "real."

# PART THREE

# CHAPTER 28: SPEAKING ABOUT WHAT'S REAL

My God, what a beautiful day. From our window on the tenth floor I could see a good part of the lake and the snow-covered mountains around it. It was spring in Lake Tahoe. There is hardly a more beautiful place in the world.

Lilly and I had a nice room at Harvey's, where we liked to stay for the CTLA convention held every year in Lake Tahoe. I have attended and spoken at the convention for many years, talking on many subject concerning trial practice: winning arguments, best opening statements, effective cross-examination, getting the most out of a trial practice, how to pick the best jury, etc. I was ready to speak again, but this time it was to be different. It was 1992 and the subject wasn't trials, trial lawyers or trial practice. It was going to be personal, very personal.

About thirty minutes before my speech, I sat quietly in our room and looked out at the beautiful view while trying to get myself in the right place. I needed to be ready to open myself up, completely and honestly. I would bare my soul. I would talk about issues that are real to trial lawyers: drinking too much, damaging relationships, and being workaholics. These issues are important and rarely spoken about at trial lawyer conventions.

I had a new title for my talk: "How To Get a Winning Verdict In Your Personal Life." I had given a similar talk to a few smaller groups and got a good response. However, this was going to be a large audience. I was going to talk to friends, colleagues, and complete strangers about my life. I wasn't going to talk about cases I had won or my work as president of the association a couple of years ago. This talk was about my losses, my drinking, my failed marriages, and working too hard. I was going to lay bare my struggle to try to keep balance in my life as a trial lawyer. I hoped my story would help others become more aware of these real issues. If they did, I knew they would be come better lawyers.

I was nervous as I walked into the room. It was a typical hotel conference room set up with long tables facing front and running parallel to each other. There was an aisle down the center. Lilly took a seat at one of the tables where the audience sits. I spoke with a few lawyers I knew and others soon filled the room.

In a way, I had a captive audience. My lecture qualified for continuing legal education credits in the field of ethics. In California, ethics is a required subject and lawyers must get their credits every three years. However, this wasn't your typical ethics class. I wouldn't talk about conflicts of interest, rules of professional conduct, or disciplinary procedures. I was going to talk about preventive ethics. The talk would focus on how we can become better lawyers by being in balance with ourselves and in touch with our values. If we do that, we will always be ethical lawyers.

Usually when there are speakers, there is a lectern or podium on a stage, with an adjacent long table where three or four speakers wait before giving their thirty-minute talk. I did not want to sit on stage at a table, or speak from a lectern. I wanted to be with the audience so I could connect with them, just like I would with a jury. For my program, there were only two chairs at the front of the room facing the rows of tables.

One of the chairs was occupied by a man who would

also speak to the group. A technician was fitting him with microphones so that we could walk around as we spoke. The man was the person who saved my career. He was the man who saved my life. He was the one who had been involved in my difficult, confrontational intervention several years before. His name was Ed Caldwell and he has become one of my closest friends. He was qualified to speak on the subject of alcohol since he helped found The Other Bar, a confidential counseling and referral resource for California lawyers, judges, law students, and their families for help with alcoholism, drug abuse, and related personal problems. The organization was founded on the principle of anonymity and provides services in strict confidentiality. Ed had worked with hundreds of us and saved many careers and lives. I was pleased that he was speaking with me. I sat next to him as the technician attached my microphone. I touched Ed's arm and thanked him for being there.

Ed and I wanted to develop an audience connection and, ultimately, audience participation in our unusual program. At 9:00 a.m. the room was almost full. People seemed curious about the presentation. The convention brochure included only a brief description of our talk. I took a deep breath, stood up, and looked around the room. I immediately began speaking:

> "When I was president of this association a couple
> of years ago, I saw a tremendous amount of stress,
> anxiety, and real fear on the part of my fellow trial
> lawyers. Our very existence was threatened by
> the initiatives on the ballot. We were fighting for
> survival that year. It wasn't about winning cases,

making money, or getting business. It was about staying alive for our clients and staying alive to battle powerful corporations that no one else in this country could do.

When my year was over, I decided it was time to start talking about something different: the real problems we face as trial lawyers: stress, overwork, and difficulties with our relationships. Lawyers in general and trial lawyers especially, have one of the highest divorce rates in the country. When I started law school, the chances of a first marriage surviving were less than one in ten. That means a ninety-plus percent divorce rate. Lawyers suffer from alcohol and substance abuse problems at a rate much higher than the general population. Depression and suicide rates are also much higher. A recent State Bar study indicated that as high as seventy percent of the lawyers were not happy in their profession. Over fifty percent said they wouldn't become a lawyer again if they were to start over. Perhaps we trial lawyers do a little better in this regard, since we believe so strongly in our clients' causes and have a choice in the cases we take. Still, I've seen all of these issues arise with my fellow trial lawyers. Many of my former partners, friends, and colleagues have died from heart attacks and other stress-related issues.

We ought to address these subjects. In order to do so, I need to make it personal. I want to tell you personally the story of my twenty-five years as a trial lawyer and how I have responded to these challenges. I've had two failed marriages and twenty-plus years of alcohol abuse. Then, thanks to the help of my good friend Ed Caldwell, I recovered and I was clean and sober when I led your organization in 1988."

I held up a book. It was called *The Soul of the Law* by Benjamin Sells. I told the audience that Sells was a trial lawyer for ten years, then he became a therapist. He treats only trial lawyers, certainly an unusual route for a therapist. However, his work gave him a special understanding about what causes much of our stress, depression, and relationship problems. I quoted a portion of his book where he eloquently described how lawyers become objectified. I summarized his thesis as follows:

"How Lawyers Objectify Themselves and Others: We are trained to solve problems in a detached and objective manner. We see and handle others' problems without becoming emotionally involved. In law school we are taught the 'reasonable person' standard and we begin to take on the persona of the reasonable person. Left-brained. Analytical. Logical. This is the way we solve our problems at work. Unfortunately, we take these same solution skills home. They don't work there."

I spoke about how I learned the skills of argument, how I put together facts to advocate my client's position, and how I quickly and effectively counter the other side's position. So, I explained, when an argument came up with my wife, I was ready. I was skilled at argument. I thrust, then counterthrusted. I tore her position to pieces. I advocated effectively. I could easily win any argument with my wife. She wasn't trained as I was. Then there were the kids. They didn't even have a chance. Before they could get their views out of their mouths, I was ready to counter every potential argument they might have. The were not going to out-argue a trial lawyer! I did all of this without emotion. I was detached as I articulated my point reasonably and logically. So I "won" those arguments.

However, by doing that, I lost touch with my family and even myself. By being so detached and reasonable, I was not in touch with my own feelings. I couldn't see or understand my family's emotions. I put on a suit of armor to fight my battles at work and I couldn't take it off when I got home. I told the audience that this is a common problem with lawyers, often leading to family stress. It plays a part in our high divorce rate.

Next, I talked about how to balance our work lives with our family lives. The more successful we are professionally, the less time we have for family. This is an issue virtually every trial lawyer can relate to.

At this point, I asked for participation from the audience. I urged lawyers to give me examples of how they found balance in their work. One lawyer said that he dealt with the problem by blocking out every Wednesday afternoon for the "Jeremy case." He instructed his secretary to never to allow anything to get in the way of that special appointment. So every Wednesday, the lawyer left the office to see his son Jeremy play baseball or just spent time with him. A great idea! Soon the audience was abuzz with hands up and people getting involved in an honest and open discussion about how to deal with these issues.

Next, Ed Caldwell stood up and began talking about his experiences with alcohol. He was very frank and honest about his difficult struggle. It was as though he were sharing at an A.A. meeting. It was touching and meaningful because it was his story. Soon, another person spoke frankly about his own substance abuse problems. Lawyers shared in an open and honest way, something that I had never seen at any legal conference. Time flew. The meeting was a success. It was the start of what would be many similar programs offered in the future.

\* \* \*

In the seventies, I had heard of attorney Gene Bambic, a powerful lawyer who had a great record of success. He served as vice president of CTLA and spoke frequently at our conventions and seminars. I had met him casually, but didn't know him very well.

He had problems with alcohol and then started using

237

cocaine. His life spun out of control, and before long, many of his clients filed State Bar complaints against him. Stories about his conduct filled the local newspapers. The federal government investigated him for stealing client funds and charged him with a serious felony. Gene thought that he could fight the government's charges. He thought he could win in court, just as he had done for his clients so many times before. However, his arrogance got the best of him and a state prosecutor went after him big time.

Gene pled guilty to two serious felonies and various federal charges. The newspaper headlines screamed his name. He was vilified. People who didn't like trial lawyers to begin with used Gene's conviction to smear the reputations of all of us. Even in his own profession, Gene became hated and reviled. Gene lost everything: money, friends, and, ultimately, his liberty. In 1983 Gene was sentenced to serve four years in state prison.

The trial lawyer community forgot about him. Nobody wanted to talk about his case. No one mentioned his name. As far as they were concerned, Gene got what he deserved and "a pox on his house."

I had almost forgotten about Gene Bambic until I ran into him at the CTLA convention that was being held at the Sheraton Palace Hotel in San Francisco. It had been over ten years since his conviction. I recognized Gene and said hello. Gene was not part of the convention but was visiting a friend who was attending. He and I talked for a bit and then decided to have lunch together.

He was a changed man. There was none of the old arrogance about him. He served more than two years in prison and was still on parole. He was disbarred and not allowed to practice law. He had quit drinking and that change enabled him to begin a new life. He was honest and sincere about his recovery and he really wanted to make amends for the embarrassment he caused his colleagues. I sensed Gene wanted to tell his story, yet there was no one who would listen. Moreover, I suspected many lawyers wouldn't even go within twenty feet of him. I could sense his humiliation. He was also totally broke and with his background, it was nearly impossible for him to earn a living.

I wondered if Gene would speak at one of my lectures and be "Exhibit A" for what happens to trial lawyers who abuse substances, lose their values, and ultimately lose touch with their souls. It is one thing for me to step in front of a group of lawyers as a successful leader of the organization. It is quite different for Gene. I strongly encouraged him to come to my upcoming seminar in Lake Tahoe. I offered to help him out financially so that he could make the trip. After a lot of thought and trepidation, Gene took me up on my offer. This led to one of the most dramatic confrontations I had ever seen.

The seminar started as usual. Ed Caldwell and I talked about our personal backgrounds. Then I introduced Gene Bambic. Gene was visibly nervous. Hardly anyone recognized him. It had been many years since he had been to any trial lawyers' meetings. I gave a little background about what had happened to Gene and then asked him to step forward. He walked uncertainly to the front of the room and faced the audience. He was palpably nervous. At first, he spoke slowly and hesitatingly about his difficult experience. This wasn't the Gene Bambic we used to know. This was a different man. This man was humbled and changed by his prison experience. But

Gene spoke honestly and courageously. Everyone in the room understood that Gene was giving them a message: Don't do what I did, learn from my mistakes. Gene was emotional to the point of tears.

Then the unthinkable happened. Larry Drivon stood up. I had known Larry for years. He had been on my board and had served as CTLA's president in 1990. He is a beloved leader and a powerful figure in our association. I did not expect him to speak. He turned and looked directly at Gene Bambic. Larry's words were strong and powerful:

> "I used to know Gene Bambic. We worked on cases together. I respected him. He was a great lawyer. I wanted to follow in his footsteps. Then he betrayed my clients and he betrayed me. I was angry with him, not only for what he did to me and my clients, but for what he did to his profession. I wasn't sure I ever wanted to see him again. Yet now I can see that he has paid dearly for these transgressions."

At that point, Larry got up from his seat and began walking to the front of the room. He approached Gene with open arms.

"I forgive you," Larry said. "I'm so sorry for all the hell you've been through."

The two men hugged each other.

There it was: Two trial lawyers, tears streaming down their faces, in an unrehearsed and dramatic moment of honesty, humility, and forgiveness. I could barely keep it together. I never expected or planned such a thing to happen. The moment was unforgettable. They walked off together, arm-in-arm, to reminisce about old times while I completed the program. It was a smashing success.

Each speech I give is different. Although I may cover the same basic material, I don't do it with notes. There is no firm outline about what I am going to say or when. I speak from the heart. It is not always easy and some sessions are more successful than others.

Most of my talks are to fellow trial lawyers who know me. I am comfortable with them. I am one of them and feel at home. Occasionally, I give lectures to larger groups whose members do not know me. I was invited to speak at the University of the Pacific McGeorge School of Law in Sacramento. My talk was part of a legal conference that was not sponsored by trial lawyers. This wasn't a trial lawyers' convention. This was a different audience altogether.

When I walked into the lecture hall at McGeorge, I was surprised. It was a Saturday morning and the place was full, with over six hundred people in the auditorium. I did not expect a crowd that big. I had never spoken to a crowd that large.

I sat alone at the table next to the lectern. I looked out at the sea of faces and hardly recognized anyone. However, there in the very front row was a malpractice defense attorney from the Bay Area. He smiled and nodded at me, and I did the same. *My God, I am going to speak to a bunch of strangers and now to a defense attorney!* I was not ready to talk to my adversaries about these personal issues. When facing an opponent, we are supposed to be confident, self-assured, and strong at all times. Here I was, ready to bare my soul and talk about my losses, my drinking, and my marital failures. But there was something about this strange place that put me at ease.

After being introduced by a stranger, I started my talk by admitting how nervous I was. I told them how difficult it was to stand in front of strangers and tell my story with total honesty. I told them that I was not there to be a guru—definitely not. I said that I would tell them a story of a trial lawyer and urge them to learn from my mistakes, and not my successes. Then I opened up. I spoke about my life, my drinking, my infidelities, my divorces, my struggles, and my losses. I assumed they knew about my successes. Before long, the words just flowed out of me without forethought. I spoke for nearly an hour without using notes. The audience remained silent. When I finished and thanked them, there was a moment or two of silence. Lawyers are not used to talks like this—especially not at educational conventions. Then, almost as one, the audience rose and gave me a standing ovation.

\* \* \*

Sometimes I wonder why I continue to open up and bare my soul during these lectures. I am never paid for speaking. Occasionally, I accept small expense reimbursements, but only if I travel to other parts of the country. Of course it is nice to have some recognition, but it would be a lot easier to talk about my successes. So why do I do it?

In 1959, when my fraternity advisor, Fred Sontag, said to me, "Have you ever thought of being a lawyer?" it struck a chord. Later I realized that I was always meant to be a lawyer. Not just to try cases and help clients, but to do more: to help my fellow trial lawyers deal with their personal issues so that they can become better lawyers. Intuitively, for some years I have realized that this is important, yet it only came into clearer focus after I had a past life reading.

In this past life I had been a lawyer in Rome. I had been a corrupt lawyer. During my career, I did nothing but act in my own self-interest. I had been dishonest, unethical, and completely self-centered. My life as a Roman lawyer was an utter failure. The past life therapist suggested that perhaps my life as a lawyer this time around was to atone for my earlier one. That made sense to me. I don't always automatically accept past life readings. Some have more meaning than others. This one seemed real to me. It felt right that one of the purposes of my present life is to atone for my past sins. In part, this idea has prompted me to write this book and remains one of the reasons why I continue to work in the legal profession to help my fellow trial lawyers.

# CHAPTER 29: A MEN'S GROUP AND
# WOMEN'S ISSUES

My lectures to trial lawyers led me to give serious thought to the nature and make up of trial lawyers. I am particularly interested in how gender roles affect our work. When I went to law school, there were only a couple of women in our class. Law, and especially trial work, had been considered "men's work." It is a tough profession, similar to the military, police work, construction work, and many other traditional "male vocations." However, women have increasingly entered the legal profession, and by the mid-1990s, almost a third of all law school graduates were women.[17] What did this mean for our traditionally male profession?

My wife, Lilly, is a strong feminist. I consider myself an advocate for women's causes and have represented many women with gender discrimination and harassment issues. So I am quite aware of the emerging feminist movement. Unfortunately, there was no corresponding movement for men. I felt it was time for us men to start dealing with our issues as women had done with theirs.

When I returned from my honeymoon with Lilly at the end of summer in 1997, I formed a men's group. In the group were trial lawyers who would openly and honestly discuss our personal and professional problems. Discussions would include how to deal with women coming into the profession. We would also talk about personal issues.

I had read some interesting books on the emerging "men's movement." One book suggested that men only had three roles in society: providers, protectors, and procreators. That is all that men were good for. We were there to provide for our family, to protect them, and to inseminate women so they could procreate. That definition of men seems far too limited to me. I wanted to get some experienced male trial lawyers to discuss gender issues in these changing times.

\* \* \*

It was October 8, 1997. I sat alone in the front room of my house a little before seven o'clock waiting for my friends to arrive. Lilly was upstairs where she wouldn't hear us. This was a men's-only night. It was a time for a group of experienced trial lawyers, acquainted to one degree or another, to meet, open up, and talk about personal issues. This was new! Traditional, tough trial lawyers don't do that kind of thing. We shunned "group therapy." That was for wimps. But times were changing. Maybe it was a time for us to learn from the other sex about open communications and the importance of honestly expressing our feelings. It had been working for me for a number of years. Would it work for my friends?

There were eight of us in this group. First was my partner, Eric Ivary. I had known Eric for a long time before we become law partners and I knew that his life was bringing him to a point where he needed to talk about these issues. Because I wasn't so sure about my other law partners, I didn't invite them, not that they really wanted to come. Then there was Mike Brown, my former partner from the old Nichols firm back in the seventies. He and I were good friends and he was enthusiastic about joining the group. In addition, there was Lee Sanders, a highly intelligent and intellectual trial lawyer.[18] He also had interests in such things as Greek history and the esotericism of the origins of democracy. He was also going through some life changes and he was ready to talk among friends. Next, there was Michael (Mike) P. McCabe who had been a trial lawyer for many years then became a mediator. I didn't know Mike well, but thought he would fit in, and he agreed to join us.

The fifth member of the group was Michael (Mike) P. Semansky. He had attended a number of my lectures and frequently joined in, helping create an honest and open discussion of his problems with substance abuse. He was just right for the group. I also invited Stephen (Steve) L.R. McNichols, Jr. We had another interesting connection since he was a member of my old Kappa Delta fraternity from Pomona College, although he graduated a few years after me. Last, there was William (Bill) B. Smith, one of the top trial lawyers in San Francisco. Over the years, Bill and I became friends and I felt there were issues he might want to discuss with us.

I also asked a few other people to join our group, but they were not able to make it. One was David (Dave) S. Hobler, who had become a great friend and who also attended some of my lectures. He also did some of his own lectures and discussed very openly the terrible tragedy that took place in his own life when his son's spinal cord was damaged in a horrible accident. Unfortunately, Dave was not able to come because the distance from his home in Marin County was too great. The same was true of my old friend Ed Caldwell, who would have been a natural in the group, but he was tied up with his Other Bar meetings and the commute was too long for him. So there were just the eight of us.

Before they arrived, I thought back on my experience with a men's group a number of years earlier. I was working with Mordechai Mitnick who helped me bring to fruition the idea of forming my own men's group. I had also read about men's groups and was ready to do the best I could to lead one.

The doorbell rang. The first person of the group arrived. Before long, the eight of us were seated in a circle around the L-shaped couch in my front room. A fire was burning in the fireplace and I offered tea, water, or coffee to the group. There was no alcohol. When everyone settled in, I started. I was holding in my hand an interesting little artifact. It looked like a mini totem pole decorated with brightly colored images, similar to those that are on the totems of the Native Americans from the great northwest. It is called a talking stick. I spoke first:

> "Thanks for coming tonight. I know all of you, and I know some of you know each other and some are not so well acquainted. We will soon get to know each other well. There are a few rules of our men's group that need to be honored by all of us. The first is total and complete confidentiality. Everything said within the group stays within the group. We need to feel free to speak with complete honesty, knowing that nothing said here will leave this room. We also need to be committed to speak honestly and openly about issues that are important

to us. We are not here to talk about law, our law practices, or legal cases. We are here to talk about personal issues, whether they be relationships, health, finances, or any other personal issues. Lastly, I also need you to make a commitment to the group to stay with the group for as long as we agree to continue our meetings.

In order to allow each of us to speak our own piece and talk about what is going on in our lives I will be using this talking stick. Anyone who wants to speak should take the talking stick and talk about their issues. We will discuss them with you openly and honestly. Then when you are done, you should pass it onto the next member who can then talk about what is going on in his life and any express any concerns he wants to share."

With that, I passed the talking stick to Eric. So began an interesting and unusual process for us all. We met for two hours and agreed to try to get together every two weeks or so. Unfortunately, the group lasted for only a little over a year because of consistent difficulties in working with our schedules.

When we disband in early 1999, I think we all felt a bit of nostalgia. I am still in close contact with all of these people and I hope that one of these days we may get together for dinner and reminisce about old times. The whole process was most satisfying. We were able to share intimate feelings and experiences that we couldn't talk about in any other setting.

* * *

What is the significance of so many women in the legal profession? I have given a lot of thought to this subject. Women are making some profound, if subtle, changes in the way that lawyers deal with conflict resolution. In the civil field, our work is about resolving conflicts between parties over civil wrongs (torts) and related issues. The traditional male way of dealing with these conflicts was to resolve them in something called a trial. Battle is the way men have traditionally resolved conflicts whether in a courtroom or a battlefield When nations resolve conflicts in this manner, they call it war. It has been an unfortunate and unhealthy method of conflict resolution for thousands of years. Wars and warriors. Men fighting to the death on the battle ground. Who will win? Who will lose? And, do the winners really win or do they ultimately succumb in later battles or wars? Are trials the best way to resolve conflicts? I believe they are a necessary and important part of conflict resolution, but only a part.

How about women? How are they different? War isn't their thing. That is not the way they resolve conflicts. They prefer to negotiate and talk. In law this new way of resolving conflict is called mediation. Interestingly enough, it is a fundamental outgrowth of who we are as men and women. As little boys and little girls, we grow up with different ways of resolving our conflicts. If the boys get into it with each other they either get into a fight or almost a fight. Somebody wins or loses. But the matter is resolved and we move on. Usually, it is a pretty quick process. Not so with little girls. They don't fight (or rarely do.) No, they just talk. They talk and talk and talk and talk. They drive us boys absolutely nuts. Sometimes, they spend days and nights talking, but eventually they resolve their conflict without bloody noses or pain. They seem to have a win-win way of doing so. For the most part, they end up as friends and not as combatants.

I think women coming into the law are fundamentally changing the way lawyers resolve conflicts. We are trying to find a better, win-win way of resolving matters through mediation. Trials are important, but only as a last resort. Trials should be avoided at all costs and this is exactly what is happening. There are far fewer trials today than there used to be. Lawyers coming into the practice during the last twenty-five years or so, since about 1980, will never try a fraction of the cases that lawyers of my generation did. And lawyers of the generation before me tried even more cases than we did. Maybe the law is better off for the women coming into it. We can take pride in ourselves as we enter a new era of conflict resolution in the twenty-first century.

A good example of the new woman trial lawyer is Mary E. Alexander. Mary started her practice with Robert (Bob) E. Cartwright, Sr. in San Francisco during the mid-eighties. She rose through the ranks of CTLA and became president in 1996. She helped lead an initiative battle of her own and did an amazing job. She is active nationally and became president of the Association of Trial Lawyers of America in 2003. She is one of the most widely respected trial lawyers in the country and I consider her to be one of my good friends. She is the quintessential blend of femininity and assertive strength. She is blazing the way for all of us to accept women trial lawyers.

Maybe male trial lawyers can learn something else from the women trial lawyers: It is okay to talk. It is okay to open up about who we are. It doesn't indicate weakness. I do not consider myself weak, nor do I consider those trial lawyers who honestly and openly express themselves to be weak. Weakness comes from fear and fear often leads to fighting because you are trying to protect something that you are afraid will be taken from you. Strength and power come from letting go of fear. Good trial lawyers know this. We have been through the battles. Peace is the better way.

There have been women's groups for many years. Now it is time for more men's groups. It is time for men and women to join together and discuss these issues openly and honestly. I am trying to do my small part to help us trial lawyers learn these fundamentals. We need to change with the times.

# CHAPTER 30: TRIAL: ART OR SPORT?

Civil trial lawyers who began practicing law after 1980 will not try many cases. It's just a fact. Of course, trying cases isn't the only way to become a successful lawyer. Many lawyers are now developing new skills in the area of negotiation and mediation. However, I am an old-school trial lawyer that often thinks trial first and settlement second.

As I look back over my long career, it is becoming increasingly clear to me how difficult it is to be a trial lawyer. It is a life full of conflict where I never win anything that I don't take from the other side. My clients want their money and the defendants don't want to part with it. I try cases against big and more powerful interests, such as large corporations, insurance companies, and public entities including the State of California and the United States government. These defendants do not like to be sued. They don't like me and they don't like my clients. I have to fight for everything that I get. But fighting, trials, and being in conflict for many years takes its toll, especially when you handle that conflict by working harder and drinking more. But over the past twenty years, all of this has changed for me. I now try cases differently and see my career through different eyes.

As I tried case after case during the sixties, seventies, and eighties, the stress became immense. On the mornings of trial, I frequently had a nervous coughing episode, usually in the shower. I had dry heaves and almost retched. It was a way of releasing stress. I have heard that athletes experience the same kind thing. However, once I got into trial and "struck the first blow," I felt better.

During those years, I frequently drew analogies between my work and that of a boxer. It was a fight. One on one. Head to head. Mano a mano. I could score a knockout or get a decision. Or I could go down for the count. Somebody was going to win and somebody was going to lose. Trials were for tough guys. (There were few female attorneys in those days.) To me, being a trial lawyer was similar to being the tough guy in my high school gang or being the macho kid in my college fraternity.

However, when I quit drinking and began the journey down my spiritual path, something happened. I started to see trials in a different way. As I explores my spirituality, I put myself in a place of love and forgiveness, rather than being swept up in anger and resentment. Thus, I learned that I needed to approach my trials in a different way. I now think of the trial as my art. It is my creative expression: less conflict and more communication.

A trial is really perhaps best envisioned as a stage play. The trial lawyers is the producer who puts up the money (case costs) and decides which cases will go on stage (on trial.) He is also the director who decides how the play is to be presented. While the director's cast of characters consists of actors, the lawyer's case of characters consists of parties and witnesses. Instead of actors speaking their lines from a script, the witnesses give their testimony based on the truth. The way actors speak their lines is an important part of the production, just as the manner in which the witnesses testify is an important part of the trial. By speaking their lines, the actors tell a story, just like the witnesses tell a story through their testimony. The director (the lawyer) decides which themes to emphasize and which actors (witnesses) will be on the stage (the stand) first. During trial, the lawyer also plays the role of the actor and is on stage at all times.

The lawyer's goal is to present the client's case as a cohesive story that will grip the audience's attention. The "audience" is small, consisting of only twelve people: the members of the jury. However, there is a difference. Unlike the theater, where only one play is on stage at a time, the lawyer's "play" competes with another play taking place at the same time and on the same stage. The other play is being staged by another director (the defense attorney) who has a different theme and another set of actors (witnesses.) The audience (the members of the jury) must decide which play they like the best. The "reviews" of the lawyers' "plays" are in the form of a jury verdict that tells them who won and who lost. The trial is really a combination of a stage play and a debate, presided over by a person in a black robe who makes sure that the rules are followed and makes important decisions that can affect how the play (the trial) is presented.

With this in mind, I try to visualize my trials as artistic endeavors rather than as knock-down, drag-out sporting events. This proves more satisfying to me and less stressful. I also feel I am doing something creatively important rather than just beating up on somebody—or getting beat up. In this way, I am more relaxed during trial. I now see my career in a more satisfying way. Instead of looking back on my trial record as a boxer would with 145 wins and 30 losses, I look back on my career as having produced a great number of plays, some more successful than others. Some of these creative endeavors were very good, even though I may have had a prejudiced audience (jury) who didn't appreciate my work or like my client.

Most people never think of a lawyer as an artist. Not hardly! They still see us as fighters, sometimes even sharks. But I know lawyers. I know many fabulous trial lawyers who are talented artists. Many put on creative plays in the courtroom but are never rewarded. A lot of them do better work than me. Most are my friends and I care deeply for them.

A person's work is important to him or her. Work is certainly important to me. However, my life has to be something more than just winning money verdicts. I believe that I am doing something important. Something creative. Even more importantly, something helpful to my client. Something altruistic. It has taken a long time for me to get to this place in my career, but it feels good.

\* \* \*

Trials are public events. There is great glory in winning and great shame in losing. It is the fear of losing that primarily motivates most of us. I have seen great trial lawyers whose entire motivation in trying cases is simply never to lose. They have almost life-threatening fear of losing. Any loss is extremely painful. They are similar to many athletes. The high of a win isn't nearly as motivating as the terrible fear of a loss. I know. I've been there. Yet, if you try many cases you will lose some.

So how do we deal with the fear of losing? Or, why should we? First, if we are less motivated by fear we will do a better job. We will go into a trial more relaxed and ready. Think of the great athlete Michael Jordan getting ready to go into the seventh game of the championship basketball series. This isn't a man pacing up and down the sidelines, all fired up and trying to pump himself up even more. No, quite the contrary. He is relaxing quietly. He is getting into his zone. Being in a state of relaxation makes him a much better athlete.

The same is true for a trial lawyer. If we are all pumped up with caffeine, sugar, and a whole bunch of adrenaline, we are not going to perform as well. Having a high degree of fear leads to a surge of adrenaline. So what can we do to reduce our racing heart and get into that relaxed zone? How can we be relaxed and still be competitive?

Here is how I approach it: I do not just want to win the case. First, I have to know that I am right. I do not try a case unless I believe in my client's cause. So I work hard to prepare the case. I do all I ethically can to win, but I have to be prepared to accept a loss.

The client and I have to do this together. We must face the possibility of losing. We talk about it and visualize it. Then we do the harder thing—turn the trial over to a higher source or a higher power. We must trust in the Universe, our guides, our higher selves, God, or whatever you want to call it. We have to trust that the outcome will be the right one. We have to believe that all things happen for a reason. This is the fundamental principle that must guide us in trial. If it is our destiny to win, so be it. If it is our destiny to lose, we must be ready to accept it. Of course, we must do our best to win but only with integrity and honesty. We have to fight hard to win, yet accept that we might lose. We have to try to understand that we cannot completely control the outcome.

Trial lawyers are by nature egotists. I am no exception. In talking about trials, lawyers always talk about "I won it" or "I lost it." I, I, I. It's all about me. It's all about the trial lawyer. But that really isn't true. A jury trial is far beyond our control. Rarely do trial lawyers fully comprehend that obvious fact. We only see it from our own perspective. But let's think about it for a minute:

A trial always involves twelve independent jurors, each with his or her deep-seated beliefs and prejudices. Even though we question them during the jury selection process, we really don't know them. We do know, however, that more and more jurors are full of preconceptions and have strong prejudices about the civil justice system. Many jurors feel that lawsuits are frivolous, that jury awards are out of control, and that trials cost us too much money (i.e., tort reform jurors.) As trial lawyers, we do the best we can with limited challenges to get a fair jury. However, that jury still had a mind of its own—actually, twelve of them.

We certainly cannot control our judge. We rarely know the inherent prejudices or biases of any judge and they are notoriously unpredictable. They make rulings that can suddenly change everything in the trial. Clearly, we can't control that. We trial lawyers must do our best to argue our case but a judge will always have a mind of his or her own. We have to accept that hard fact.

Then there are the witnesses. How often do witnesses surprise us on the witness stand? Any lawyer who has tried more than a few cases knows what that experience is like. We do our best to prepare a witness trial, but we never know what will happen. This is especially true when a witness's simple slip of the tongue causes the case to be lost instantly.

Another important factor beyond our control is the defense lawyer. That lawyer wants to win the case as badly as we do. He or she may be very capable and probably has his or her own surprises for us in trial. We can't control that. Frequently, we don't give the other side credit for a win—we just think of it as our loss.

Last but not least, there is our client. No matter how well we think he or she may perform, we are never sure. Good clients make good results. Bad clients make bad results. It's axiomatic.

So, obviously, we are not in control of everything that happens in the courtroom. There are so many dynamics that we can't begin to control them. Outside influences in the news may affect the jurors or something may happen to any juror personally. Often we never know about these intangible factors and we can do nothing about them.

Over time, I begin to realize that control is the problem. The absolute need to try to control everything is what leads to the fear of losing. Many lawyers fear losing control over their case. Their egos are at stake. This is the essence of the fear of losing. Lawyers become control addicts motivated primarily by fear. They will do anything to win. As a result, those lawyers all too often lose their values. How often do we see this in sports? Or in business? It is human nature. The need to win or, more importantly, the fear of losing may cause us to do things that normally we would never do, such as tell a lie, hide evidence, or misrepresent things to the judge and to the jury. If we do that, we lose our values. We lose our integrity. We lose touch with our soul. Even if we win, we are still losers.

Thus, we must try our cases with integrity. We have to try and stay in touch with our client's needs and be ready to accept the trial's outcome. We need to let go of the control and just do the best we can. If we approach cases this way, we are much better off. Even in the unhappy event of a loss, we will be able to move beyond it and learn from the experience. We must not let the feelings from the loss fester and turn into anger and bitterness. In doing so, we become better human beings as well as better lawyers.

## CHAPTER 31: BECOMING A HOLISTIC LAWYER

My spiritual journey over many years taught me to see my relationship with my clients quite differently. Most lawyers in my field are consumer advocates. It is their job to take an injured client's case and get the best result they can for the client. The "best result" is almost always money. How much money can we get for them? We take our cases on a contingency basis. The more the client gets, the more we get. It becomes easy to define ourselves as successes when we get our clients a lot of money. But it is not that simple.

Any lawyer who has been in this field for long realizes that giving clients money does not necessarily make them happy. Quite the contrary: Getting money can cause great problems in the client's life. Therefore, I decided some years ago to take a different approach in my practice.

For a long time, I had criticized the medical profession for being overspecialized. Doctors simply take one part of the body and treat it, whether it is a broken bone, delivering a baby, performing an operation, or treating a disease. The days of the old-time family medical practitioner are mostly gone. Nowadays, there are few kindly doctors who make house calls and understand their patient's needs. Few doctors see patients as whole people—the holistic doctor—are fast disappearing, if you can find them at all. Almost everyone in the medical field is a specialist of one kind or another. There are few holistic doctors.

We lawyers, I realized, are falling into the same trap. We are becoming more and more specialized. The day of the family lawyer who knew his client well is fading. So I decided to try to become a holistic lawyer.

A number of years ago I joined a boutique organization called the International Alliance of Holistic Lawyers, in which I maintain a membership. I love their premise that our job as lawyers is to work with the whole person, to help them deal with any legal problem within the context of their other life issues. Thus, we try to help the client in ways beyond simply solving their immediate legal problems. This is especially true of clients who suffer serious injuries, disabilities, as grieving the death of a loved one, or who have been wrongfully terminated from their jobs. Their lives are turned upside down. They struggle, often times not only with injuries, but with serious psychological problems. They experience pain and suffering, as well as emotional distress, loss of self-esteem, anger, or frustration. I almost always ensure that my clients receive good counseling. In general, it is helpful for them to get help from a psychologist or trained therapist.

Moreover, it is rare that a person's injury affects only them. Those around the injured person are also deeply affected. An injury to the plaintiff is also an injury to his or her entire family. Lawyers need to recognize this. Our job is to help our clients deal with their injury or tragedy. Sometimes we have to answer questions or deal with other matters that don't seem directly related to the legal job at hand (getting them money.) We need to get to know the client to deal with their whole persona. We have to understand who the client is and learn about their family background. It is important to have a deep understanding of all of the ramifications of the injury or insult to the person, and those close to him or her. Being a holistic lawyer helps us to be better trial lawyers. Once we know our clients inside and out, we can do a much better job of representing them. Far too many lawyers do not take the time, energy, or interest to delve into who their clients really are. These lawyers are happy to just take the superficial route. In my opinion, that is not sufficient. You are not doing your client justice if you only get them money. We need to help our clients as fellow human beings.

When all is said and done and our client's case is over, we usually do get them some money. But how do the clients feel about that? Do they feel like the lawyer twisted their arm to get a settlement they did not like? Were they "sold down the river?" Have you made a friend or are you going to never see that client again? Most good lawyers pride themselves on having long-term relationships with clients. It is not about how much money the lawyer gets them, it is about how the lawyer helped them.

Browne Greene, a good friend of mine and an excellent trial lawyer from Los Angeles, recently received a prestigious award from a consumer organization. Browne has won innumerable multi-million-dollar verdicts and is considered one of the best lawyers in the country. However, when he received his award, he didn't talk about his many verdicts. He didn't talk about his wins. He read a letter from his client thanking him so much for helping her family through a difficult time. The letter is actually from two young girls who had lost both of their parents in a terrible automobile accident. Browne helped them through the long litigation process and they appreciated his caring, help, and compassion. Browne brought these two little girls with him to the ceremony and they appeared visibly grateful for his help. For Browne Greene, it isn't merely about the money. For the really good lawyers, it never is. These trial lawyers take the attorney-client relationship to a deeper level. They become holistic lawyers.

## CHAPTER 32: GOING IN A NEW DIRECTION

My trial work up into the early nineties had been almost exclusively injury related. However, in 1992 I had the opportunity to try a different kind of case. This led me to change the direction of my career.

Lana Ambruster was a young insurance adjuster working for California Casualty Insurance Company. She had a little experience before California Casualty hired her as a new bodily injury insurance adjuster in June 1990. Lana was single but engaged and ready to get married. When Lana asked for a week off for her honeymoon, her office manager startled her by commenting, "That's fine, but I just hope you don't come back pregnant. I don't want any more pregnant women around this office."

Lana wasn't sure whether or not he was kidding. He seemed serious. He had made similar comments to other women in the office.

Not too long after her honeymoon, she learned she was pregnant. She didn't say anything around the office, since she was still concerned about her manager's comment. He had made even more comments that now made her think he was serious about not wanting pregnant women working for him. Eventually she had to tell him. She went into his office and nervously explained to him that she was pregnant. His face darkened and she knew he was unhappy. He said nothing and she left the room. Almost immediately thereafter, Lana's work performance in the office was challenged. She had always done good job, but now her cases were being audited and within a month she received a negative performance review. Thirty days later, she was terminated for "poor performance." But she knew the real reason.

She came to our office and we considered a wrongful termination case based on pregnancy discrimination. At the time, few such cases had been tried since California law had only recently changed to protect the rights of pregnant workers. A lawsuit was filed and before long, we were ready for trial in the Santa Clara County Superior Court in San Jose. In the meantime, Lana had her baby but life had become very difficult. She spent a year living with her in-laws while off work. Lana was able to find another job so her lost wages totaled only $30,000 but her emotional distress claim was quite severe. I thought the case had some real potential and finally, after protracted negotiations, I agreed to settle it for $150,000. The defense insisted that they would never pay more than $100,000, so the case went to trial.

The trial went well, with one exception. During Lana's testimony, she began to hesitate and get nervous on the stand. She started giving I-don't-remember answers. Fortunately, during a recess Lilly came to the rescue and my jury consultant immediately saw the problem. Lana had to be firm about her testimony and not equivocate. During the break, Lilly and I had a serious talk with her and when Lana returned to the stand she straightened up and things went well.

The jury became increasingly angry at the denials and lies of the manager and other insurance company employees. My argument went well and the jury awarded $1 million in emotional distress damages. Then we went to trial on the second phase of the case for punitive damages. That award was $1.7

265

million. The total verdict of $2.7 million dollars was the largest pregnancy discrimination verdict in the country. I was on my way to becoming an employment lawyer!

As the years went on, I continued to specialize in more employment law work, culminating in one of the most interesting cases I ever tried—not once, but twice.

Dee Kotla worked at the Lawrence Livermore Lab as a computer technologist in 1996. She had been there for more than twelve years and had a perfect record. She loved her job and it sustained her.

Dee had a very difficult background. She was in foster homes as an infant and struggled with being moved from place to place and never really having a stable family. She had been abused and gang-raped. When she was sixteen, she watched a young man shoot himself to death. She had been through abusive marriages. Yet somehow, Dee's job at the Livermore Lab saved her sanity. It enabled her to be successful and gave her self-esteem. The psychologist who later treated Dee indicated that her job was the one area of complete stability in her life. He opined that other than her children, her job was perhaps the most important thing in her life.

Dee has a strong sense of right and wrong. So when a manager on the job began harassing Kim Norman, one of Dee's coworkers, Dee spoke up. Kim complained about the manager's behavior and Dee said that she would testify for her. This wasn't the way it was done out there at the Lab. Although the organization gives lip service to people speaking up about these things, there is a well known culture of retaliation at the

Lawrence Livermore Laboratory. If you testify against the Lab, there will be ramifications. However, when Dee's deposition was taken in Kim's case, Dee testified honestly about incidents in Kim's sexual harassment case. The Lab lawyers were hostile to her during the deposition. As soon as it was finished the Lab and its lawyers retaliated against Dee. Within two months, the Lab investigated her for allegedly misusing her computer. Dee knew it was a pretext. They were retaliating against her because she testified as a witness in a sexual harassment case.

When the department head called Dee into his office on February 17, 1997, he abruptly fired her. Dee was devastated. She went home and brooded for a few hours then began to drink. She was ready to give up on life. Later that night, Dee overdosed on pills and attempted suicide. Fortunately, she was saved although she had to be hospitalized for several days. The Lab had achieved its goal and ruined Dee as a witness.[19] She was determined to fight the Lab. Dee tried to get reinstated. When that failed, she took a job paying substantially less than what she had been earning during her years at the Lab. To her credit, Dee performed well at her new job.

Many lawyers are afraid to take on the Lawrence Livermore Lab. It is funded by the Department of Energy and is part of the University of California, a notoriously difficult defendant against which to litigate. After three years of working with lawyers who did not want to fight the Lab, Dee came to our office in 2000. She was a pleasant client and had a good case. We went to trial during the spring of 2002. We received a $1 million verdict plus a significant award of attorney's fees.

The Lab appealed, and the case was reversed because the appellate court thought our expert witness's testimony was inappropriate. Dee was not ready to give up. She was ready to try the case again. When the Lab didn't offer her what she felt was fair, we went to trial for a second time. We had another long, four-week trial early in 2005. This time around, we had a better jury. They awarded Dee over $2 million. It was twice as much as her original verdict! In late 2005, Dee was finally paid.

Today, Dee Kotla is still working. She litigated her case against the Lab for eight years. It was not easy for her but she definitely became a better person and a stronger woman because of it. Dee became a union steward at her new job and is an outspoken advocate for others still working at the Lab. Her life gained new meaning. As a result of her difficult experience, Dee is more self-confident. She has grown and learned from this tragedy. If this had never happened to Dee, I wonder where she would be. I am sure that she would not have the strength and values that now define her. Dee turned a tragedy into a success. A bad thing happened to a good woman, but then her life got better.

I had always considered myself a specialist in personal injury law. I had handled every type of case including medical malpractice, products liability, government entity liability, premises liability (I tried nine slip and fall cases,) auto and truck injury cases, etc. With the Ambruster and Kotla cases my interests were going in a new direction towards representing workers who were harassed and discriminated on the job, whistleblowers and workers who were wrongfully terminated. My work in employment law coincided with my interest in a new and slightly different area of law: public interest law.

\* \* \*

During the mid-nineties, I became involved with an organization called Trial Lawyers for Public Justice (TLPJ,)[20] a unique public-interest law firm supported by a foundation consisting of 3,000 of the best lawyers in the country. The firm takes on issues that other lawyers won't, such as important environmental battles, consumer law matters, civil rights cases, and issues relating to court access.

For example, the organization has an active project fighting mandatory arbitration, something all of the big companies try to force on consumers so that they will waive their right to go into court and have a jury trial. Most mandatory arbitrations are totally slanted in favor of the companies. The companies put these arbitration clauses into their written agreements with clients, customers, and employees. This insidious invasion of the rights of the average person to pursue justice against the biggest and most powerful companies in the world is gaining momentum. Few are able to fight back. TLPJ is one of the few willing to fight. The work they have done in that regard is remarkable.

TLPJ also takes on Title IX cases involving women's rights to equal athletic programs in colleges. The Brown University case litigated by TLPJ was a landmark decision giving women's sports programs in college the right to equal treatment, enabling the women's programs to be competitive with the men's programs.[21] TLPJ also acts as the conscience of the community and has a project dedicated to making sure class action cases are litigated fairly and adequately on behalf of the class. On occasion, TLPJ's lawyers will intervene in class action settlements if the attorneys' fees outweigh the benefits to the class. TLPJ also strongly supports class actions in many different arenas. It is an unusual organization that vitally enhances the entire civil justice system.

Each summer, TLPJ holds an annual meeting and presents and award of "Trial Lawyer of the Year" to the year's most significant public interest. Nominations are usually announced in June and much of the legal community looks forward to what is the legal equivalent of the Academy Awards for the most outstanding public interest case of the year. These cases were recently gathered in a wonderful book written by Wesley J. Smith, *Fighting For Public Justice: Cases and Trial Lawyers That Made a Difference*, published in 2001. The book sets forth all of the cases nominated from 1983 through 2000 along with the winners for each year.

In 1995, I was honored to be nominated as Trial Lawyer of the Year for the work that our firm did on an important insurance bad-faith case. The case against the California State Automobile Association (CSAA,) Adams v. CSAA, et al., was filed in Alameda County Superior Court. We represented a large number of accident victims who were insured by CSAA, which was one of the major automobile insurance carriers in Northern California. It was a consolidated case with eighty individual plaintiffs. It was not a class action. The company had decided to cut back on benefits under the automobile medical payments coverage, which automatically pays a certain amount, usually about $5,000, for all medical expenses involved in an automobile accident case. It is coverage paid without regard to fault and had rarely been controversial.

However, in the early nineties, CSAA decided to reduce these payments by cutting off the insured's medical benefits if CSAA decided that the insured's medical expenses were not "reasonable and necessary." CSAA sent its insureds to CSAA's own doctors who would then determine whether the medical bills were necessary and reasonable. These so-called independent medical exams (IMEs) were biased. The doctors CSAA chose were from their "litigation stable" and almost uniformly backed up CSAA in saying that the medical bills were either not necessary or were unreasonable. CSAA aggressively refused to pay the medical expenses of any insureds who had soft tissue neck and back injuries or who were treated by chiropractors.

Our firm represented eighty of CSAA's insureds and took on major litigation that lasted for several years. We took 350 depositions before settling the case for a significant amount of money in a confidential settlement. Plaintiffs' trial lawyers in Northern California followed the case closely, as did many other lawyers throughout the country. Other big insurance carriers also watched the case. At that time few other insurance companies had so aggressively declined to pay first-party medical coverage. Our settlement forced CSAA to change its procedures entirely. After being defeated in court, CSAA stopped using these IMEs to reduce the amount of medical benefits paid to its insureds. This was a very high-risk case for our small firm because it involved numerous depositions and required our firm to advance several hundred thousand dollars in costs and expenses. However, the work we did was widely publicized and well received. Our result is one of the most important victories against abuse by insurance companies in the state. Because of our successful result in this case, TLPJ nominated me for Trial Lawyer of the Year in 1995. This was my first serious exposure to the organization.

In 1996 I was again nominated for my work in a different case. The 1996 case was Jeanette Adams v. City of Fremont. Although both cases shared the surname Adams, they were unrelated.

Adams v. the City of Fremont involved claims of serious police misconduct. In this case, the Fremont Police Department went into the backyard of Patrick Adams and fired thirty-five rounds of ammunition at him, killing him while he sat under a tree in his own yard. According to the trial testimony, an officer heard a gunshot so officers began pouring bullets into Patrick. From the evidence, it was clear that Patrick never pointed a gun at anyone other than himself and the only place he discharged his own gun was into his heart. It was never clear whether the police fired first and before Patrick shot himself. Although Patrick was threatening to commit suicide, he never confronted the police. He was clearly depressed and suicidal, but he was not a danger to anyone, other than to himself. My law partner Jim Chiosso and I litigated the case for several years and took many depositions to prove that the police procedures were entirely inappropriate and that the police could have easily resolved the situation with Mr. Adams without confronting him with guns and a police dog. The case resulted in a verdict of about $5 million, which at the time was one of the largest verdicts in the state for police misconduct. As a result, in 1996, TLPJ nominated Jim and me for the Trial Lawyer of the Year award.

Patrick Adams's case came to a very unfortunate ending. An appellate court reversed the entire decision and threw the case out on the basis that Patrick was trying to commit suicide. In my judgment, the long, rambling opinion was one of the worst ever written by a California appellate court. It was a classic example of two conservative justices trying to reach a particular result (throw the case out) without following the law. Although Justice J. Anthony Kline had prepared a well-written dissent, the California Supreme Court chose not to review the case, so it was dismissed. Neither our firm nor the Adams family ever collected a dime from the City of Fremont. It was a painful and expensive loss after experiencing a great win in the trial court, but that is one of the risks plaintiffs' lawyers take when we try tough cases on a contingency fee basis.

It was a great honor to be nominated for Trial Lawyer of the Year and this led to my increased interest in TLPJ. I told the TLPJ leadership that I would like to work with the organization and soon afterward was invited to become a member of their board. This, too, was quite an honor and I remained on the board for a couple of years. I was then asked to join the executive committee and eventually worked my way up through the officer position and become president of the organization from 2003 through 2004.

My leadership work with TLPJ has led to many new friends and acquaintances. The list of past presidents and members of the board is a who's who of the finest and most dedicated trial lawyers in the country. All of us serve without payment. Among the many friends I have through TLPJ include Mike Withey from Seattle, Washington. Mike graduated from Pomona College a few years after I did and he also turned out to be another reformed wild member of the KD fraternity. I also got to know Bill Snead from Albuquerque, New Mexico, Fred Baron and his wife Lisa Blue from Dallas, Texas, Peter Perlman from Lexington, Kentucky (a past president of ATLA,) Susan Saladoff from Ashland, Oregon, and Paul L. Stritmatter from Seattle, Washington. Paul is a past president of the Washington State Trial Lawyers Association and also a past president of the Washington State Bar Association. These people are some of the best trial lawyers in their states and in the country.

Another great friend of mine is Jeff Goldberg, a top medical malpractice attorney practicing in Chicago, Illinois. My executive committee was very supportive during my presidency and included Jeff Goldberg; Thomas M. Dempsey, a former TLPJ president and a former president of the Consumer Attorneys Association of Los Angeles; Al Brayton, a great asbestos lawyer and one of our most generous supporters (as is Jeff Goldberg;) Sandra Robinson, who will be TLPJ's first African-American president and who is a fine medical malpractice lawyer; Harry Deitzler, one of the best lawyers in West Virginia; Mona Lisa Wallace from North Carolina who is also one of the top trial lawyers in the country; and Gerson Smoger, an outstanding toxic tort lawyer who practices in Oakland, California and Dallas, Texas.

Being involved with TLPJ is very rewarding. I am learning a great deal about true public interest law, which is new to me. Some of TLPJ's areas of interest include environmental law, mandatory arbitration cases, and important issues of federal preemption as well as many other related consumer and civil rights issues. The TLPJ Foundation oversees the TLPJ law firm and helps law firms fund cases so that the TLPJ lawyers can take on public interest matters without regard to fee generation. Thus they can take on important cases that many law firms that have to maintain a profit couldn't or wouldn't be involved in. I remain on the board as a past president. The experience has been very rewarding and broadened my legal perspective.

My work with TLPJ led me once again into a challenging leadership situation. In 2002, the organization celebrated its twentieth anniversary and I became president-elect of the organization. The president that year was Paul Stritmatter from Washington state. The organization benefited greatly from Arthur Bryant, a very strong, respected, capable executive director. Arthur was the managing director of the law firm, the liaison to the TLPJ Foundation and one of the top public interest lawyers in the nation. He was recently named one of the top 100 lawyers in the country[22] a great honor. Arthur was more than the glue that held the organization together. He was its driving force and dominant personality. The president, the executive committee, and the board typically relied on him to help us deal with financial issues as well as managing a caseload of some of the most important public interest cases in the country. After TLPJ celebrated their twentieth anniversary at the annual ATLA convention in Atlanta, Georgia that summer, Paul was ready to roll as president and I was eager to follow as president elect. Then tragedy struck.

On August 27, 2002, Arthur, his wife and young son were returning from a convention of the Oregon Trial Lawyers Association in southern Oregon where he had been a speaker and participant. They started south to drive to their home in Oakland, California on a typical summer day. Then, out of nowhere, a pickup truck—driven by a negligent, uninsured and irresponsible driver— suddenly turned left in front of them on the two lane highway and tore open the entire left side of Arthur's small vehicle. He was crushed under the steering wheel and both of his legs were terribly fractured. He suffered a serious head injury and was in a coma.

His wife and child were less seriously injured. They took his unconscious, battered body to a local hospital where fortunately he received good care and survived. However, the injuries to his legs, arms and, particularly, to his head were quite severe. All of us at TLPJ were immediately notified of his terrible accident and did everything we could to help. Fortunately, two past presidents of the organization were in Oregon and able to liaise with the rest of the leadership. Susan Saladoff, the president in 2001, was in Ashland, Oregon and Jeff Foote, a president from ten years earlier and a talented lawyer from Portland, Oregon helped. We received regular reports on the status of Arthur's injuries. He was in a coma. We were concerned about whether he would have a brain injury and whether he would ever be able to return to his position guiding TLPJ.

Fortunately, Arthur made a slow but steady recovery. His mental faculties returned and he had numerous orthopedic surgeries, particularly on his legs. Unfortunately, he was out of commission for an entire year and was operating at less than full capacity during the following year when I became president. Paul L. Stritmatter and I, along with the entire executive committee had a huge void to fill. We had to take over running the organization and do everything we could to keep it afloat. Although we did a reasonably good job, the organization did suffer financially.

In the summer of 2003 at our convention in San Francisco, I stepped in as president and immediately was faced with a leadership crisis in two respects. Arthur was just coming back, but still wasn't one hundred percent. We had suffered by not having him present at our fundraisers and helping to run our meetings. We were falling deeply in debt and I needed to do everything I could to pull the organization together and pick up the slack. I began having monthly meetings with the executive committee which, fortunately, involved some highly capable people, especially Jeff Goldberg, my president-elect. We were all volunteers and busy attorneys with full schedules. In any event, we all worked hard to keep the organization going. Over a difficult but eventful year we pulled the organization out of its financial spiral. Our hard work had paid off and I was pleased to once again play an important leadership role in an organization near and dear to my heart.

By the end of my year in 2004, Arthur was back and was able to get the organization on its feet and once again, we were going to be in pretty good shape.

My work with TLPJ over the years has broadened and deepened my understanding of the civil justice system. During my entire career, I always cared deeply about civil justice, civil rights, and access to justice, and my commitment to fight for these issues grew stronger during my years with TLPJ.

Our entire civil justice is under attack under the guise of so-called "tort reform." This is nothing more than an attempt by the largest and most powerful companies in the world, including insurance companies, tobacco companies, oil companies, and many others to have their own way in the courts. Very few people can stand in their way. Trial lawyers, especially those hardworking, courageous lawyers at TLPJ, are among the forefront in fighting this difficult war every single day. I have been a part of that commitment and have fought these battles for many years. I intend to continue to do so.

# CHAPTER 33: GRIEF, GRIEF, AND MORE GRIEF

I have learned a great deal from my clients as their lawyer. However, I have only felt their tragedies vicariously. But there comes a time when we are personally tested. That time came for me in 2001.

By then my life was good. I had long been off alcohol and was a successful trial lawyer. I am a leader and active in trial lawyer organizations. I have a wonderful relationship with my wife Lilly. I have a good law firm partnership and work hard to form a close, almost family-like relationship with my four partners: Eric Ivary, Jim Chiosso, Steve Cavalli, and Steve Brewer.

Our firm: Gwilliam, Ivary, Chiosso, Cavalli & Brewer. The five of us had been together for many years. The youngest of us, Steve Brewer, came in 1986. He had been with the firm a mere fifteen years whereas Eric Ivary, Jim Chiosso, and Steve Cavalli had joined the firm between 1978 and 1981. We are like brothers. We are a family.

We had a good, successful firm, but like all firms we had our difficulties. We were never afraid to take on tough cases and sometimes that hurt the bottom line. We were generous in giving to causes in which we believed. Our goal was not simply to make money. First and foremost, we were in practice to do the right thing for our clients. But near the end of 2000, things began to change. Storm clouds were brewing on the horizon. I couldn't see them coming. One rarely can.

Near the end of 2000, my partner Eric Ivary tried a very difficult case. It took a lot out of him. He struggled with the stress of the trial, a divorce, and a subsequent remarriage. For a number of reasons, Eric decided that it was time to take an early retirement. He wanted to be a mediator. He had done a little of that work and he liked it. A number of other trial lawyers were going that route. It was sad to see him leave, but we made adjustments.

Then in May of 2001, the firm suffered its worst tragedy. Jim Chiosso had been a friend of mine for thirty years. I had practiced law with him for twenty-two years and we had tried many cases together. He was like a brother to me. He was a round, cheerful, Italian whom everyone loved. His demeanor brought ease and humor to our firm. I never met anyone who did not like Jim Chiosso. He was obsessed with food, restaurant menus, and was an amazing cook. Unfortunately, that led him to weigh 270 pounds on a 5'8" frame.

He was only fifty-eight years old when he had a heart attack. At first, it looked like things would be alright. He had bypass surgery and appeared to be doing well. My birthday is May 18 and I called Jim at home that night. He had just gotten out of the hospital. I told him that I would visit him the next day.

On Saturday May 19, at about 8:30 a.m. my phone rang. It was Steve Cavalli. Steve and Jim were very close. They were both Italian and they treated each other like family. Steve's voice was breaking up. Jim had collapsed at home and it didn't look good. He was being rushed to the hospital. However, within a few minutes of his arrival, Jim died. He had a knee replacement surgery the previous year making him prone to the massive blood clot that blocked the blood to his heart. It was just like a bullet had hit him. He didn't have a chance. He was gone, just like that. It was one of the biggest shocks of my life. He was too young to die. Sure, he was a little overweight and stressed out, but he was certainly not ready for death.

Jim is survived by his wife Judy and their two children. They were a wonderful couple and made a striking and unforgettable pair. Jim was round and overweight at 5'8" and Judy was tall and graceful at 6'2" in her stocking feet. They loved to joke about it and people loved them. They had two children that they adored. Their son Tony had just become a lawyer and their daughter Jaime was in high school. Jim never got a chance to see her graduate or to appreciate his son as a lawyer. Jim's death was huge blow to all of us.

Jim's death was compounded by another serious problem in my life. My former wife Liz had been diagnosed with a cancerous brain tumor in March. The prognosis was bad. Liz's condition worsened. She went through chemotherapy and lost her hair. She, Jim, and his wife Judy remained close even after Liz and I divorced, so Jim's death was a blow to Liz. The last public appearance Liz ever made was at Jim's memorial service.

Liz's condition worsened over the next month or so. Eventually, in early July, it was decided that she should be taken off life support. This was her choice. My daughters Lisa and Jenny were with her. They joined in her decision along with Liz's significant other. It was a tough choice, but the right one.

Everyone expected Liz to be gone within a day or so, but she held on. Finally, Liz died on July 13, 2001. It was Jim's birthday. Jim would have been fifty-nine—the same age as Liz.

That day Jim's wife Judy, who was very close to Liz, received a call on her cell phone while she was holding a memorial service for Jim in a Northern California grove of redwoods. Judy was informed of Liz's death. Later, Judy would tell an interesting story: As soon as she got the news that Liz had died, she looked up into the sky. There was a hawk lazily circling up above them. Perhaps it was a symbol of Liz's spirit, there with her and Jim. Judy felt that connection. I did too.

Liz's memorial service was held a few days after she died. She had one brother, Roger Cornell, who is a very fine dermatologist at The Scripps Research Institute. We always got along very well and still do. My daughters are close to him. He was in charge of Liz's memorial service. Although there were not going to be very many people speaking, I asked Roger if it would be all right if I said a couple of words. An ex-husband speaking at a funeral is perhaps a bit unusual. But there was something I wanted to say. Roger agreed.

The service was held at a lovely church in Walnut Creek. My kids were there, as was Lilly, my law partners, and their wives. All of them knew and loved Liz. There were also number of friends Liz had made in the years following our separation. I didn't know many of them. I was nervous, but I needed to say something. I needed to speak publicly about how I felt about Liz. I went to the podium and hesitated for a minute. Then I spoke:

> "As you all know, Liz was my former wife. We were together for twenty years and had two wonderful children. Although we divorced, I never quit caring for her and tried to be good to her. But

there's something else I want to tell you. If it wasn't for Liz, I wouldn't be here. She saved my life. She had the courage to do an intervention in 1984 that led to my quitting drinking. If that hadn't happened, I probably would have died and certainly would not have been here with my children and my wife and all the people I care about so much. So, Liz, I wanted to stand up here and thank you and let you know that I always cared for you and that our souls will always remain together."

I was in tears as I returned to my seat. However, it felt good. Even though it wasn't easy, it needed to be said. Leaving a marriage with integrity, honesty, and love is not easy. It certainly did not happen in my first marriage, but it did happen with Liz. I am very proud of that. I am now both a mother and father to my children, something I often tell them. But I always remind them of their mother's spirit. It is there when they need her, just like my mother's spirit is there for me. They understand. We are all souls inhabiting these human bodies until they wear out. But the souls remain in touch with us after death, if we are open to them.

\* \* \*

Jim's and Liz's deaths were a hard time for my family and for my firm. But 2001 wasn't done with me yet. There was of course September 11, 2001. Although I wasn't directly affected in the sense of knowing very many people at the Twin Towers, I did have the same pain, frustration, and empathy that everyone had over this tragic and senseless event. I felt the national grief and mourning as we all did.

September 11 had a terrible impact on lawyers, especially those practicing in the New York area. However, I'm especially proud of the trial lawyers' response to this tragedy. Leo Boyle was the president of ATLA in 2001. Leo is a great lawyer from Boston and he and I had become fast friends. He had heard me talk about my hand injury case for Scott Morris. He said he was impressed by my speech. He tried a lot of similar cases and we struck up and acquaintanceship that grew into a deep friendship. I had been there when he was sworn in as ATLA president and I knew that he would make an excellent leader. However, no one could have anticipated the events that took place on September 11, 2001. What he and the leaders of trial lawyer community did was truly remarkable. It was one of the greatest acts of generosity in the history of the law.

Not long after September 11, the government declared that there would be a fund set up to pay all of the victims of that terrible tragedy. The victims would therefore be saved the expense and emotional drain of litigation against the airline companies, the building owners, the government, and anyone else whose negligence might have partially contributed to the injuries and deaths. The fund was to be administered by a special master appointed by the government and the claims were to be paid off without fault. The intent was to get full compensation to the heirs of those who died and who had wrongful death claims and personal injury claims. It was a concept fully embraced by Leo and the ATLA leaders.

Lawyers handling cases like this would typically do so on a contingency basis, often taking a third of the compensation. These were big cases and there was a lot of money involved. However, Leo Boyle and the trial lawyers associations stepped up and said "No way. There will be no fees taken on this money." An organization called Trial Lawyers That Care was formed with Leo at the helm. It consisted of lawyers recruited from all over the country who gave their time free of charge to represent the victims and get them compensation. Not one dime of attorneys' fees was paid. The response was overwhelming. It is not well known to the public but, thanks to Leo Boyle and the leadership of the trial lawyers' bar, there were thousands of claims processed. The attorneys' fees that could have been charged would have been in the hundreds of millions, if not billions of dollars. This act showed the true generosity and caring of so many trial lawyers that is to this day unappreciated by many members of the public.

I had a chance to talk with Leo about his work when he came to San Francisco to speak to the Consumer Attorneys of California conference in the spring of 2002, several months into his presidency. Lilly and I met with him at the Fairmont Hotel in San Francisco. He was extremely busy and he looked tired. Being president of ATLA is a huge job that requires virtually twenty-four hours a day, seven days a week. He was working day and night and constantly traveling. There had been some controversy about Trial Lawyers That Care. Although the vast majority of lawyers had embraced it, there were a few dissenters. Leo had many issues on his plate and he was in a self-reflective mood. September 11 had affected him personally and he was still struggling with some of that grief. Lilly and I talked with him for a time about his presidency and what it meant. He questioned whether he was being a good leader and what he was accomplishing in the midst of his chaotic schedule. I listened to him. Then I felt compelled to share my thoughts with him.

"Leo," I said, "You know, September 11 is your legacy. You were chosen to be president during this most difficult time. Great leaders arise in times of tragedy, difficulty and loss. You accomplished something with the Trial Lawyers That Care organization and the tremendous generosity given to the September 11 victims that no other president of ATLA can ever match. You are a hero and a great leader for the work you've done and I just don't think you realize it."

I think Leo needed to hear that. He needed the encouragement. He needed to be able to see the forest for the trees. He greatly appreciated my perspective. I think what I said helped him and I felt good about it. Leo and I have a special relationship. It is easy to describe. We are the best of best friends and always will be. We are brothers in arms.

\* \* \*

Unfortunately, September 11 wasn't the end of my experiences with death in 2001. My sister, Pat, six years younger than me, turned fifty-eight in April of 2001. She was overweight and had health problems. She had finally kicked a very difficult drug addiction. She had suffered a terrible tragedy in 1994 when her daughter Fortune died of an overdose. Fortune was barely thirty years old at the time and was survived by her two young boys whom Pat loved dearly as her only grandchildren. Pat never got over the death of her daughter. I think Pat suffered from depression, as well as brain impairment from her long-term use of marijuana. However, she moved in with Wayne and to my great pleasure they got along well. He was ninety years old and she was there to take care of him.

On Halloween 2001, Wayne called. Pat had died in her sleep the night before, apparently of a heart attack. Soon I was on my way to another memorial service in Utah. Another death in that strange, weird year. After the service was completed I thought, "Well, I'll be glad when this damn year is over." But it wasn't over yet.

In 2001, I was an officer in the TLPJ Foundation. I was moving up the ranks and would become the president of the organization in a couple of years. The man I was following through the organization's leadership path was a friend named Larry Trattler, an excellent trial lawyer from Colorado. He and I had become quite close and talked about our personal lives over the years. He had gone through some difficult times, including a tough divorce. He had two sons, age twelve and seven, over whom he had custody.

In 2001, things were going well for Larry. He had met and married an amazing woman. She had a daughter about the same age as his sons. Their families were integrating well. Before long, Larry's new wife was pregnant. He was preparing for

Christmas with his new family and expectant wife. He seemed to be in good physical shape. He wasn't overweight and took good care of himself. However, on December 22, 2001, Larry suffered a sudden, massive heart attack. He slipped into a coma and never regained consciousness.

Larry hung on for a few days, but on December 28, 2001, his family made the difficult decision to take him off life support. Larry was only fifty-four. I never really got to know his widow Barbara or his children, but I knew Larry and I could feel their grief. The tragedy of the whole thing seemed pretty senseless. It was the end of 2001, and I had been forced to deal with death in a very personal way, several times over.

* * *

For some years before 2001, I thought I'd come to terms with death. I had seen so much of it vicariously and worked through it with my mother's death. I knew we are spiritual beings and our spirits don't die. I had read Dr. Elisabeth Kübler-Ross's book, *On Death and Dying*, and an especially helpful book by Stephen Levine called, *Who Dies? An Investigation of Conscious Living and Conscious Dying*. People who study death from a spiritual standpoint understand that life doesn't end when the body gives out. We are not our bodies. We are spiritual beings inhabiting those bodies. The body is in the soul, not the other way around. So we live on. But that doesn't lessen our grief when life ends.

We can't be with or talk to our loved ones after they die.

Yet I know Judy Chiosso still talked to Jim after he died. I know my daughters could feel their mother's spirit. I could be in touch with Liz, as well as Jim, Mom, Pat, and others. So why did all these deaths occur? All things happen for a reason. It was time to apply that principle to myself. Lilly and I talked about the terrible events of 2001 and tried to keep them in spiritual context. I grieved these losses. I ached for the loved ones who had been left behind. Now I was one of them. Yet I knew they were still with me if I needed them. I knew they were with their loved ones, their children, their spouses, and anyone who reached out to them. This is real to me. These are not just words. They are here when I need them and it gives me solace to know that. We are not our bodies. Our souls live on.

Every so often, when I am driving to court and I get worried or anxious, I sense that Jim is sitting right next to me, just like old times. I have a conversation with him just like I did in the years that we were together. He always makes me laugh and then I calm down. His spirit helps me. My sister Pat loved me with all her heart. When I feel a lack of love, I just need to think of her and it is there. And dear Liz, whom I loved yet didn't always treat as well as I should have. I know her soul is with me. It gives me comfort. I know she is with our daughters. I frequently remind them of her presence. I think they know it's really true.

Since 2001, I am in closer touch with my guides and the souls of my departed loved ones than I have ever been. I understand even better the pain of my clients who have suffered a loss by death. Death has touched me deeply, as eventually it will for all of us, whether it is our parents, siblings, friends, or even, God forbid, our children. I must accept these tragedies and learn from them. All things happen for a reason. The events of 2001 happened for a reason. Understanding the reasons is not always easy, but I need to continue to work at it. I'm doing the best I can.

# CHAPTER 34: FINDING MY TWO DADS

As Lilly and I continued our psycho-spiritual work, it became clear that I had another issue to deal with: my father issues. It was easy for me to deal with my mother issues since I always got along well with her. I had also been in touch with my mother's soul after she died and had come to terms with our relationship at the spiritual level. But how about the men in my life?

I had few strong male role models in my life. My mother had a brother, Vincent Anderson, who I always called Uncle Vince. He was a tough, athletic guy who had been in the service but also was a hard drinker and later a serious alcoholic. He was present early in my life, but not as I grew older. He certainly wasn't a very good role model in any event.

So as part of my ongoing psycho-spiritual analysis, I realized that I needed to come to terms with my father, or more accurately, with both of my fathers. I needed to understand my relationship with them at a deeper level. When Lilly came into my life, I began to work on that difficult problem. Both my stepfather, Wayne, and my biological father, Jack, were alive. I needed to understand them and come to more spiritual, honest, and better relationships with them if possible.

\* \* \*

Jack was out of the picture from the time I was two years old. I really didn't realize he existed until I was eight years old. After seeing him on only three short occasions, I moved in with him and his new family when I was eighteen years old. He always lectured me. I hated that. He spent more money than he earned and I didn't like his lifestyle. To make matters worse, after I lived in Glendora with him and his family, while I went to Citrus Junior College, he found another woman and left my lovely stepmother, Helen, and his three daughters. He never supported them properly. I found it necessary to start paying room and board. Suddenly I was supporting his family and he wasn't supporting me. *What was that all about?* This made me angry.

About that time, I needed some money from him for a very personal matter. It was an embarrassing situation but I felt that it was extremely necessary. I didn't know who to turn to, so I turned to him. I went to his house and told him my problem. Instead of helping me, he lectured me about my morals. I blew up and stormed off. We didn't talk again for almost twenty-five years.

Before I quit drinking and changed my life, I didn't want to have anything to do with him. After I changed, I decided to reach out to him. I reestablished contact in 1987 and had a short meeting with him near the end of that year. Although we opened up and had some communication, I didn't feel comfortable with Jack and I really hadn't made a serious effort to get to know him. Liz hadn't like him and hadn't been in favor of me seeing him. On the other hand, Lilly was interested in meeting him. She didn't carry any emotional baggage and felt strongly that I should try to forgive Jack.

So, in the summer of 1991, Lilly and I visited Jack. He lived in a small cracker box house in the little town of Fort Jones in Northern California. He was totally broke and his ego was deflated. Because he had never saved any money, at age seventy he had to work on a ranch shoveling horse manure just to survive. He had learned humility the hard way. When Lilly and I visited Jack, he was in his late seventies and had serious emphysema. He had smoked for sixty-three years — from the age of fifteen until he was seventy-eight.

For my part, I was ready to forgive him. I felt it was important since forgiveness has become a part of my life. Even so, I approached a meeting with some trepidation. So Lilly and I got in my little Mercedes sports car and drove up to see him. I was nervous. I knew I was going to try my best to see him as a fellow spiritual being that had made a decision to bring me into this life. I was also curious about his life and wanted to understand him better psychologically. That might help me better understand myself. However, forgiveness is hard.

Jack never supported me as a child. When I lived with him in college, he abandoned me and I had to help support his family. I couldn't help feeling that he didn't deserve any help from me.

We met in front of his little house and shook hands awkwardly. Lilly was able to observe the scene more objectively. She knew Jack loved me but had never been able to express it. He had been shut out of the family. She knew that I had never had much of a father and that I needed one.

Tears welled up in Lilly's eyes. We both looked at her.

"Please, you two," she begged, "Would you just hug each other?"

And we did. The ice was broken and we were finally able

to have the beginning of a father-son relationship. Afterwards, we started to communicate more directly.

It soon became obvious that Jack was desperately in need of money. I told him that I would not loan him money. I knew that Jack tended to try to borrow money from his other kids, but I wasn't going to be a part of that. I don't believe in loaning money to family. It only leads to trouble. But, I did tell him that if he needed some help, I would talk to him about it. He did need it.

I gave Jack $500 so that a ramp to the entrance of his house could be built, since he was now relegated to a wheelchair. Jack didn't ask for it. I just gave it to him. I told him it was a gift, not a loan. I had a lot of good reasons to justify why I would never give him anything. Jack never supported me, so why should I help him? But that line of thinking didn't help my spiritual growth. I decided to make amends with him before it was too late. This gesture really helped us bond. In addition, I gave Jack another $500 for a wheelchair that would lift up, making it easy for him to get out of the chair and less of a struggle when he went to bed.

One day, I quit calling him Jack. I called him Dad. I was fifty-five years old and he was eighty. I had never called anybody Dad. I had never said that to Wayne. So I had at least one Dad. It felt good.

Unfortunately, it lasted only three years. I distinctly remember when he died. Lilly and I had a long-planned trip to Europe. Shortly before we left, Dad had a severe stroke. It was not unexpected, given his advanced emphysema and his poor health in general. It was pretty clear that he probably wouldn't come out of it. I knew he wouldn't recognize me if I went to see him. Reluctantly, Lilly and I went on our trip. We were in a nice hotel in London when I got the call from his oldest daughter, my half-sister Shana. Dad had passed away. It didn't come as a surprise. Initially I didn't feel overwhelmed with grief. I knew it was coming. It was his time. I had made amends. However, something happened in that hotel room in London that I didn't expect.

I had always been told that Mom left Jack when I was a year old, so I wouldn't expect to have any memory of him. It turns out that was not quite the case. He told me that they separated when I was two years old. He and I were in close contact during those early years. He remembered that I used to knock on the bathroom door in the morning while he was spending his usual long time with his morning constitutional. I would rap on the door and say to him, with my childish pronunciation: "What cha' doin' Dad? Shabing?"

I got up at three o'clock in the morning on the night he died and sat quietly on a chair in a hotel room. I suddenly remembered Dad saying those words. It is amazing to remember something that happened when you are two years old. I remembered my father. But more importantly, I knew something else. I remembered that he disappeared from my life. As a child, I was too young to understand what was going on, but I knew he was gone. Nobody talked about him. I was told to forget about him, and I did. The matriarchy wanted him out of my life. But I grieved. Little kids can grieve in their infant way. I knew something was wrong. Something was missing. All my life I had missed my father. Unfortunately, I never really fully realized this until he died. All my life I had grieved for my forgotten father. As I sat in my darkened hotel room in London, I began to cry uncontrollably. I was finally able to feel my grief and let it out.

I feel good about finding him and being with him, even for those few, short years. His spirit is with me now. I have forgiven him and he has forgiven himself. His soul and mine are at peace. It feels good.

* * *

Then there is my second father Wayne. He is the man who came into my life when I was three years old and stole my mother from me. I felt I wasn't number one anymore and I didn't like it. He kept taking her into that bedroom. But what did I know about that when I was three years old? All I knew was that they would disappear into the other room and leave me sitting there. I was always a good boy and didn't complain. But I developed a sense of jealousy, frustration, and anger towards him.

Furthermore, Wayne never spent time or played with me. We never threw a ball back and forth. He took me to one movie when I was about six years old. It was a movie about mummies. He thought it was funny to scare me. It worked. It also increased my frustration and anger towards him.

Wayne didn't raise me. That was Mom's job. He couldn't discipline me. He and I had an uneasy, competitive relationship for the affections of my mother for all the years she was alive. All significant communication between Wayne and me came through my mother. She was the conduit between us. He and I never really sat down and had any serious conversation until the time she died.

I can't say that I hated him. I just didn't care for him. I didn't respect him. I certainly didn't think of him as my father. I never called him Dad. More importantly, I attributed every good part of my life, my personality, and my success to my mother. She was the one that made it for me and not him. All of my bad habits must have come from Wayne (or Jack.)

When Mom died on March 17, 1988, I was fifty years old. Following that, my relationship with Wayne began to change. I was especially pleased that he helped my poor sister Pat. She struggled through her addiction problems and eventually went to jail over some cocaine possession. He had never been close to her. He had been a judgmental guy who put her down. But to his credit, he began to take care of Pat after Mom died. He brought her back into his house and in time, they developed their own good relationship.

After Pat died in 2001, I began to visit Wayne on a regular basis in Utah. There was no one left in our immediate family, except him and me. By then, he was in his late eighties and still independent. He got out of the house every day and did his yard work. He was always very active. He cooked for himself and drove a car. I had to give him credit; he was very self-sufficient.

Gradually, I began to appreciate him. There were things about him that were not so bad. His health was terrific. His positive attitude about his health helped, and he passed this attitude on to me. My health is exceptionally good, partly due to my attitude. Maybe he helped me in that regard.

Through everything, Wayne always had a good sense of humor. However, he was a narrow-minded man. He didn't care much about reading, politics, or anything else. Life revolved around him and his little world. He never fully understood what I did as a lawyer, nor did he seem to really care. Maybe he was unable to comprehend it. But, I think, he always liked me. He probably loved me in his own way. I know he was proud of me and I began to feel a stronger sense of warmth and caring for him in those last few years. This man was always a hard worker who had supported and cared for me. My judgment of him had been too harsh based upon my juvenile attitudes, not the spiritual attitude I was now developing. So, as I had done with Jack, I began to call Wayne "Dad."

In 2004, Wayne was ninety-two years old and still living alone. I thought that I would probably have to help Wayne out financially and put him into a home. However, he lived so frugally that he managed so survive on about $900 a month in social security payments and some small dividends he received from a few shares of stock that he and Mom owned. He paid off his house and had very few needs.

But Wayne's health took a turn for the worse. He developed cancer in his bladder which progressed into his lungs. Then he had a fall and was hospitalized. Within a relatively short time, he became very thin and emaciated. He was never a very big man and was always kinds of skinny. But now he was really in bad shape. I worked very closely with Wayne's doctors and saw him frequently. I was now caring for him as if he were a child, giving him the kind of care that I had always hoped he would have given me. Somehow it felt good. I was doing something for him that I didn't have to do. It wasn't about whether he deserved it. It was the right thing to do.

I had always competed with Wayne for Mom's affection. My Oedipus complex had started when I was three years old. It had been there all of my life. Now Mom had been dead for sixteen years. I still resented and was angry with him on a subconscious level, but it was leaving me. Now things had changed. Now Wayne was the child and I was the parent. I was bigger and stronger than him. And finally, I had control over his life. Literally.

Wayne was in a coma and the decision had to be made to take him off of life support. I was the only one left in our family and I had the power of attorney to do it. He had been very firm in his opinion that he did not want to be kept alive on life support.

So I traveled to Ogden to see him. I walked into his room. His deteriorating medical condition was obvious. He looked like a skeleton with a little bit of wrinkled skin covering it. He was in a deep coma. I talked to him and he responded slightly. I told him I knew what had to be done and spoke to his doctor. I made the choice to take him off life support.

I stayed with Wayne and talked to him as he haltingly wheezed his last breaths. It is called a death rattle. If you ever hear it, you will never forget it. He seemed like a helpless infant and I felt like the parent. A parent who had to let him die. He had always said that he didn't want to stay around if it was his time to go. I began talking to him. I think he could hear me talking to him even though he couldn't respond. Then I did something that seemed so strange. I touched him. I put my hands on his chest and on his head. I had hardly ever touched him before, except to shake hands. Now I was caressing him like he was a baby. I told him that it was alright. I told him that he was going back to see Mom. I told him that he wouldn't really die, that we are all just spirits inhabiting these bodies. I spoke of things that I know to be true, things I could never talk to him about when he was well. I needed to say these things. I found myself crying. He was also my Dad. He had done the best he could. There was no need to judge him any more. I told him it was okay to die.

I looked down at Wayne for the last time. I had always been critical of him. I didn't think he was a good father. He wasn't much of a role model and hadn't been there emotionally for me.

But now I saw our relationship from a different perspective. A new question occurred to me, one that I had never asked myself before: *Had I been a good son to him?* I pondered that question as Wayne's life was slowly ebbing away. *Had I been there for him? Had I judged him too harshly? Had I not appreciated him?* I did spend more time with him after Mom and Pat died, but I hadn't gone to see him as often as he wanted. He was lonely and I was all he had left. Yes I tried, but maybe not hard enough. Maybe it wasn't all about me forgiving him, but about him forgiving me. We were two men born in different generations. Two souls whose paths were meant to travel together for awhile. I guess we had done the best we could.

I took a deep breath, kissed him on his forehead, and walked out of his room. Tears streamed down my face. I flew home and he died the next day.

After Wayne's funeral, I began to close out his small estate. Much to my surprise, Wayne left me a small inheritance. I had always assumed that I would have to support him when he got older, but Wayne had lived so frugally and was so healthy that he never used up all of his money. He owned his house free and clear, and even had some money in stocks and bonds. The money came from Mom as well as his contribution. It was a good legacy from my parents. I put the money to good use by funding a wonderful family vacation in Hawaii on Thanksgiving in 2005. All of our kids and grandkids came and we toasted Mom and Wayne, the people who had helped us make that fun family reunion possible.

Wayne was a better dad than I gave him credit for. Perhaps Jack was too. I had always felt that I didn't have a father. Now I realize that I had two fathers. But they were both gone. Now again, I had none.

## CHAPTER 35: WHY ME?

I recently celebrated being a trial lawyer in Oakland for forty years. During that time, I've sat across my desk from people who have had every kind of terrible thing you can imagine happen to them. People in wheelchairs. Scarred people. People who lost limbs. Brain injuries. Back injuries. Hand injuries. Leg injuries. You name it, I've seen it. Also people with diseases, including a number of cancer cases where their doctors didn't diagnose the disease in time. And parents with babies seriously disabled because their doctors didn't do a timely cesarean section. Among my cases, there were many deaths. Deaths of spouses. Deaths of parents and siblings. However, the worst thing that can happen to a person is to lose a child. I've never seen more gut-wrenching pain than that of parents who have had a child die. This was true whether the child was an infant or an adult. There's something about losing our children that is the very worst thing that can happen to us.

My clients are invariably good people. I took their cases because they had been wronged by someone. It could be as simple as an automobile accident or as complex as a product failure or medical negligence. In recent years I've seen people suffer from employment discrimination or being wrongfully terminated. I understand how important our jobs are to us and how deeply affected our self-esteem can become when we are treated wrongfully on the job after years of good service. Day after day, month after month, year after year, the same thing. Why did these terrible things happen to these good people?

It was the question I asked again and again. It was

a question my clients asked me. But I couldn't answer it. I didn't know. Maybe life was just unfair. Maybe there wasn't a God. Maybe there was no answer. But slowly, after years of observation and personal experience with life's tragedies I began to find the answer. At least for me.

I couldn't find the answer to this question until I found the answer to my own life's tragedies and losses. Twenty-five years of alcohol abuse. Two divorces. A loss of four premature infants. The deaths of my family and friends.

When I quit drinking in 1984 and began my soul journey, the answers began to appear. As I found my own soul, I began to get in touch with the souls of my clients. The answer lay therein. I had to answer life's basic questions. Why are we here? What is the purpose of our lives? I don't pretend to have all the answers but I've come to some of my own that give me satisfaction and they work for me.

I would frequently be involved with clients in their cases for many years. I would see how many of them changed and evolved from the time of the immediate tragedy until their legal issues were resolved. Invariably, they grew. It was painful, but they grew and changed. They became wiser, more compassionate, and tolerant. They began to understand the nature of pain. They began to empathize with people who had the same pain, suffering and loss. They were forced to deal with their own infirmities and deal with their own emotional issues. Frequently, counseling helped. So when their cases resolved many years later, they were oftentimes more in touch with life and themselves. They were wiser and stronger. This was not true of all of my clients. Some seemed to learn more than others. Many learned and grew from their tragedies. Those who continued to fight their battles at the human level did not. Those who worked on their psychological and spiritual makeup did. It was a question of whether they were in touch with their soul and their life purpose. They might not use those words, but it seemed clear to me that was what was happening.

There is no such thing as joy without pain or happiness without unhappiness. Anymore than there is up without down, dark without light or left without right, or man without woman. These are life's dichotomies. We must accept them. So we must accept that bad things are going to happen in our life as well as good. All things happen for a reason. Those who can come to an understanding as to why their tragedy happened are on their way to a complete and fulfilling life. It doesn't even have to be a serious tragedy. A relatively minor incident can set off frustration, anger, or shame. Then we are forced to deal with these emotions. Isn't that the purpose of our life? To grow? To become the best human being we can be? To get in touch with our higher selves? To find God or meaning and try to understand the Universe? That has certainly become true of my life. It is also true of many of my clients and friends whom I had come to know so well over the years.

Some examples come to mind. First was my client, Scott Morris, discussed earlier in the chapter entitled "The Envelope, Please." He had terrible hand injuries. He was depressed, frustrated, and angry. Slowly, over years of surgery, medical care, and personal growth he began to accept his disability. His relationships improved. He became a much better client. After he received his money, he used it wisely. More importantly, he gained a kind of compassion that I don't think he would have ever had if he hadn't been injured. The injury became part of him. It was who he was. Now some twenty-eight years after his injuries, I see a well-adjusted man in midlife with a loving wife and kids. He enjoys life to the fullest. Scott moved up the learning curve painfully but quickly. I am not sure he would have done this without that terrible injury. He learned and grew from it.

Then there is Sherill Smothers, a young African-American man who worked for the Oakland Tribune as a circulation manager. He has been raised in East Oakland but avoided drug, gangs, and the criminal life of so many of those around him. He came from a hardworking family and worked hard since he was a child. He was twenty-nine years old on November 12, 1988, when he found himself driving his Corvette home from a party. His wife and new baby were with him. He was entirely sober even though it was 2:00 a.m. He was headed east on Highway 80 near Pinole, was driving at about fifty-five miles per hour.

Suddenly, a young, drunken sailor driving eighty miles an hour rear-ended him. Sherill's Corvette careened out of control, off to the side of the road, and rolled over on its roof. Although the car was only going ten to fifteen miles an hour at the time it rolled, the roof on his Corvette collapsed completely. His wife was not seriously hurt. His baby was thrown from the car and luckily, escaped without injury. However, Sherill's neck was broken. He became a quadriplegic.

Sherill's life became very difficult after this. He didn't have good health care and struggled with his injury. He had limited use of his arms and hands. He developed bedsores. He became depressed. He lost weight and his health wasn't good. But he hung in there while we litigated a very tough case against General Motors. We contended that the roof was too weak and should not have crushed, causing his injury.

I don't think there had ever been a verdict against General Motors for a Corvette rollover. They fought the case furiously with one of their top trial lawyers, Richard "Dick" A. Bowman, who frequently defended them in major cases. I wanted Sherill in the courtroom as much as possible. It was difficult for him to get there and his health was not the greatest, but he did the best he could. I wanted the jury to bond with him. It is difficult for the jury to do this when the person is in a wheelchair. Many lawyers feel that spinal cord injury clients should be in the courtroom only for a short time, just while they testify. They feel it adds to the drama of the case. I felt differently about Sherill. About halfway through the case Mr. Bowman approached me.

"Gary," he asked, "Can I talk to you for a minute?"

"Yes," I said as we walked down the hallway outside of the courtroom.

"You know, Gary," he continued, "I'm sure you care about your client but I have a lot of concerns about him."

"Oh," I replied, "What are they?"

"I've tried ten quadriplegic cases with some of the best lawyers in the United States and I have never seen anybody who insisted that their client be in court day after day, as you've done with Sherill. Do you really think you're acting in his best interest to keep dragging him into the courtroom?"

His remarks offended me. I didn't think he gave a damn

about Sherill's well being—he just wanted to win the case. I responded with one question: "Did you win all those cases?"

"Yes," he answered.

"Well, let's see what happens with this one," I said.

After six full days of deliberation, the jury came in with a hard-fought nine to three decision in Sherill's favor in the amount of $6 million. Although the verdict came down in 1992, General Motors appealed it all the way to the United States Supreme Court. General Motors finally paid the sum of $9,182,000 by the end of 1995.

This case was especially satisfying for me. Not only did I win the biggest verdict in Contra Costa County at the time, but I won it against General Motors. It was atonement for the terrible loss that I had taken in the Staples v. General Motors case fifteen years before. Why the difference? I had a better case. I was a better lawyer. I was more experienced and perhaps, even more importantly, I was sober and in touch with my values.

After the verdict, Sherill continued to have serious problems in his life. Not long after his injury, his wife left him. She was a young woman who couldn't deal with her husband being in a wheelchair. Sherill became a single parent and to his credit, a loving and caring father. He raised his son Tony to be an exceptional young man. Later Sherill married a woman who was supportive and understanding about his injuries. When General Motors finally paid, Sherill was fortunate enough to be able to get the kind of care and the handicapped-accessible home that he needed.

I have known Sherill now for almost eighteen years. He is a wise and compassionate man. His injury has helped him grow, develop, and understand what life is really about. Where would he be if the injury hadn't occurred? He would be living a different life and I'm not sure that he would have anywhere near the deep understanding of how unimportant our bodies are compared to our souls. This tragedy, though costly, has made him a better human being. A bad thing happened to a very good man. But that good man grew and developed even more. I believe that all things happen for a reason. I think Sherill understands that reason.

* * *

I represented a couple who had a severely brain-damaged child during the mother's first birth. Little Sarah Freitas had cerebral palsy and was badly handicapped. We brought a lawsuit against Kaiser Foundation Hospital for medical negligence and obtained a settlement. The family was faced with a very tough question: What to do with this young girl who, by the age of eight, only weighed twenty-three pounds and needed to be cared for in a baby crib? Her parents were determined to not put her in a home. They felt that they could love her and care for her as she was. They communicated with her, even though the doctors insisted that Sarah was unable to understand or respond. They had another child who became Sarah's sibling. I am not saying that life was easy for the Freitas family, but they stuck with little Sarah and treated her as a full member of the family. She was still severely disabled and would never walk or speak. However, she was always loved by all.

Some years after the settlement, I received an invitation to Sarah's sixteenth birthday. I went to see her. It was a wonderful birthday party. I tried to talk to Sarah. I don't know if she understood me, but I told her that I was her lawyer and that she was lucky to have parents who loved her. Recently, I received an invitation to her twenty-first birthday. Although I couldn't attend, I wrote her parents, Ray and Ada, telling them to give Sarah my love. For all these years they have kept this girl at home and loved her. They know tragedy but they have overcome it. They love that child and wouldn't change a thing about her upbringing. They have turned tragedy into love. How many people can do that? They understand life and handicapped children in a way that few people do. A terrible thing happened to a good family, but they learned and grew from it. Who is to say they are worse off now? If you ask me, all things happen for a reason.

I previously mentioned Dee Kotla's case. Her case dragged on for eight years before it finally came to resolution. It was never about money for Dee. It was always about fighting for other women and Lab employees who had suffered discrimination and had been wrongfully terminated. Dee is an excellent example of a woman learning from her losses. In many ways, her termination and years of litigation have made Dee a stronger and better person. It is another example of things happening for a reason. Tragedy and loss can lead to strength and growth.

* * *

People will continue to struggle with this question. Why me? Why all of this unfairness and needless pain, and suffering? Why wars? Why premature death? Each of us needs to answer this question for ourselves. This is the human experience. This is why we were put on Earth. We are not meant to fully understand it. We are meant to accept it. We must understand that all things happen for a reason. When tragedy occurs, we are supposed to grow from it. When joy occurs, we can't stop looking for the answers and become complacent. Our life is one of growth: human growth and spiritual growth. How fast can you get up the learning curve? How far can you go? You don't have to wait until you are forty-seven years old and struggle through twenty-five years of alcohol abuse and have two failed marriages. You can do it sooner. I'm no guru. If I am able to understand some of this and come to my own peace with it, then anyone who reads this book can do the same. All things happen for a reason. We must never forget that simple concept. We must live by it.

# CHAPTER 36: UNCONDITIONAL LOVE
## IN THE COURTROOM

It is time to tie together what I have learned on my psycho-spiritual journey. How am I doing with all this and how am I putting it into practice? I'm feeling pretty enlightened nowadays. I have been off alcohol for years and I've been lecturing my fellow lawyers about stress reduction, quality of life issues, and spiritual values. The principles are simple: unconditional love, not being judgmental, letting go of anger and fear, staying emotionally centered, understanding that all things happen for a reason. I've decided it's time to put all these principles to the ultimate test. How do they work in the courtroom? I'm off to a typical day of trial, so I will soon find out.

\* \* \*

It is 10:30 in the morning. We have just started another session of a contentious and difficult jury trial. The defense attorney is objecting to every question I ask and my witness is struggling a bit. The judge, who doesn't seem to know anything about the rules of evidence, is sustaining most of the objections. Another ridiculous objection occurs:

"Hearsay!" The defense attorney stands up and shouts.

"Of course it's not hearsay," I respond reasonably, "It's not offered for the truth of the matter."

"Sustained," the judge rules.

"But your honor. . ." I counter.

"Sustained," the judge repeats. "Move on, counsel."

I'm getting irritated. Now I need to put these principles into practice. I'm going to send some unconditional love to my judge. Of course unconditional means I don't expect anything back but I would appreciate a favorable ruling now and then. And yet he seems so arrogant in his black robes looking down from his bench at me. But then I don't want to judge the judge, do I?

Then I look at the defense counsel, smirking at me again in his self-righteous way. He's been obstreperous and difficult throughout the entire litigation. *Can I see him as a spiritual being and really love him? This is hard. I don't like the bastard, but I'm doing the best I can.*

Now to my witness. *Is this guy stupid or what? I am not trying to be judgmental, but he still doesn't get it. I keep rephrasing the question and he doesn't get it. Like a deer with its eyes caught in the headlights. I smile at him sending unconditional love. I'm trying not to be judgmental, but he still doesn't get it.*

"Let me rephrase the question. . ." I offer helpfully.

*Then I glance over at my jury. I'm getting some stony, cold looks from this bunch. I know some of them think I have a frivolous lawsuit and can't wait to put an X in the "we find for the defendant" box on the verdict form. Still, I'm sending out love as best as I can. But I've got this knot in my stomach. Perspiration is starting to come down the back of my neck. This is _really_ hard. . .*

*Then there's my client. If there's anybody I can love, it's her. I fought long and hard for her case. But I wish she'd quit whining. She seems so needy. The defense doctor says she's got to get on with her life. Maybe he's right. But then of course, I'm her advocate and I've got to love her unconditionally. I certainly can't be judgmental. It's not getting any easier. . . I smile and struggle on.*

By the end of the long session in court, I feel a lot less enlightened than I did before. I need to get in touch with my guides and the Universe about using these principles. *Do I really have to love this judge? And the defense attorney?* But then, I never said I was a guru. I guess it's time to go back to the books.

\* \* \*

Being a trial lawyer nowadays is tough work. The law is a conflict-ridden profession. We are constantly fighting with each other. We are always trying to outdo each other, whether it is in the courtroom, during discovery, or at negotiation. As a plaintiffs' lawyer, I never get anything unless I take it away from somebody. I think it has taken me a long time to learn how difficult this profession really is. But I'm doing better. Experience and sobriety have helped.

*So how do I deal with this situation in the courtroom?* First I have to remember that I am not in control. We can only control ourselves. We have to stay centered and do our best not to let distractions keep us from our goal. It's much easier said than done. Here are some ideas I have found that help:

- **Breathe from your belly.** Breathing is important, not just to stay alive but to stay centered and relaxed. Sometime ago I learned the importance of belly breathing. The principles are quite simple. Many of us were taught as kids that the best way to breathe in was to throw out our chest like a military officer. In truth, if we want to learn how to breathe, we need to watch a baby. A baby breathes by letting its stomach expand on the in-breath and the stomach contracts on the out-breath. When you breathe in, you need to let your stomach out. When you breathe out, you need to force all of the air out by sucking your stomach in. It takes practice, but if you learn this breathing technique you will find it invaluable. So, before I go into the courtroom or start a difficult session of any kind, I try to take a few deep, relaxed breaths. This helps me relax.

- **Remain relaxed.** The courtroom is a tense place. It is easy for our bodies to tense up in stressful situations. This tension is often centered around our shoulders, necks and upper body. It drains our energy. We need to be aware of this tension and make efforts to reduce it. I carry tension in my trapezious muscles by the side of my neck. I find that if I tense those muscles up very strongly, tighten them as tight as I can for fifteen or twenty seconds and then let them go, that makes them more relaxed. I also use Aspercreme® regularly to keep these muscles around my neck and shoulder from tightening up. However, the best advice I can give is simply to be aware of where there is tension in your body when you are in a stressful situation. You must be aware of your body tension. You have to stay loose.

- **Stay centered.** Breathing helps us stay centered. We need to think of the trunk of our body as its center. We need to be aware of our center. This is true whether we are standing in the courtroom, sitting down, or moving around. This is a little bit like what is taught in martial arts. Do not move aimlessly. Move deliberately and stand with your legs spread so as not to be knocked off balance metaphorically. Be aware of your body posture. Stay centered.

**- Let go of fear.** We need to stay in touch with whatever spiritual contact we have, whether that is through meditation, prayer, or reaching out to our guides and higher selves. By putting ourselves into this frame of mind before we get into a trial "battle," we will perform better. It is natural to feel fear. We need to let go of it and turn the case and the outcome over to a higher power. Let go of the fear of losing.

**- Do not react.** It is so easy to turn on the defense attorney and argue after he or she makes an objection. It is particularly difficult not to react if things get personal. Recently, I tried a case where before every objection the defense attorney said, "Mr. Gwilliam is an experienced lawyer and should know better. . ." That was a nice backhanded compliment, and I was tempted to respond in kind. I really had to bite my tongue to try and stay focused. I ignored her and talked only to the judge. I made my objections and arguments to him. If he ruled against me, I just had to move on. By staying focused on what I wanted to accomplish, I wasn't thrown off track by my adversary. Be proactive, not reactive.

**- Maintain concentration.** This is similar to staying focused but you have to keep your mind directly on what you are doing. You can't let your mind wander. Do not think of what is going on at the office, what is happening in your personal life, or even what is going to happen in the next five or ten minutes. Concentrate on exactly what you are doing, bringing your focus back to the task at hand.

- **Stay in the present moment.** This is similar to maintaining concentration, but with a slight difference. Oftentimes lawyers get ahead of themselves and want to start asking questions anticipating what's going to happen in the next minute, or two, or five. This is not good. Stay in the present. Do not worry about the past or fret about the future. This will increase your concentration and listening skills, which will help you be a better advocate.

- **Listen carefully.** Many lawyers get so wrapped up in their own thoughts that they do not hear what the witness or the judge is saying. Listen carefully to what is being said so you can follow the meaning of the words. Remain in the present and do not get ahead of yourself. If you are looking at your notes or thinking about what your next question is going to be, you are not listening. You cannot focus your mind on two things at once, although we oftentimes try to do it by bouncing rapidly from one subject to another. That is the definition of the lack of focus. This gets us in trouble. We need to hear and listen to what is happening now, in the present moment.

- **All things happen for a reason**. I try to keep this as the guiding principle of my life. I need to apply it in the courtroom. Oftentimes, things that seem like losses turn into wins and vice versa. I have to trust the Universe. Once I recognize that I am not in control, I can roll with the punches and go with the flow. Stay in touch with the principle that things are happening for a reason. This keeps us centered in the present moment, so we are relaxed and unafraid. This applies to all things in life.

Many of these suggestions are hard to follow. It is so easy to get caught up in the middle of a trial and lose track of them. After over forty years in the courtroom and doing 175 jury trials, it is still hard. Once again, I am no guru and I am not always able to follow these principles. However, I try to keep them in my mind. Practice makes almost perfect. There is no such thing as perfect!

## CHAPTER 37: FIFTY YEARS LATER

On Saturday evening, October 8, 2005, it rained in Seattle. Pretty typical weather for that city. Lilly and I were dressing for the big party. We were staying at the Sheraton Hotel downtown. Lilly was dressed and had just put on the final touches of her makeup. She looked terrific as usual. Lilly looks like a woman in her prime, more like she is in her early forties, although she is actually twenty years older. People are stunned when they learn her age and frankly, she is pretty proud of it. I guess I didn't look too bad, either, for a guy who is sixty-eight.

I bought a new black cashmere jacket for the party and looked as good as I could. No tie, even though it was a big reunion. I must say that I was a little surprised to be there. I never thought that I would return to Roosevelt High School for my fiftieth high school reunion.

I had a lot of hesitancy about coming. However, I got into the spirit of things and filled out the reunion book with what had to be the strangest quote about what anyone remembered most from high school. It read in part:

*"**Favorite High School Memories:** Selling catnip "joints" to some of the guys for $1.00 a piece; being suspended for smoking on the high school steps on my eighteenth birthday, May 18th, hanging out at the Snow White Café.*

***Highlights Since High School:** I am an unknown alumnus. I know no one from our class and have* *not been in touch with any of our graduates since 1955. My friends were delinquents and gang members and only three of us graduated from high school—one went to prison, the second committed suicide, and I am the third. I wore a duck tail, pegged pants, blue suede shoes, and did not participate in typical high school activities. Mainly, we just partied—a lot of drinking, some drugs, and lots of wild parties (with wild girls.) I am coming back to the reunion not to see old friends, but to make some new ones. I am a former high school gang member returning for a reunion that I never thought would happen. I am certain that I will not know anyone at the reunion and no one will know me. I never did know anybody other than a few of my gang friends and they are long gone. I haven't had any contact with any of the graduates from that class since the day I left in 1955."*

So why did I return? I guess I was proud of the fact that I am arguably one of the most successful members of our class. There may be some other successful professional people— doctors and lawyers—but of the approximately seven-hundred members who graduated from this public high school, I must have had one of the most unusual stories.

The real reason I went was to get closure. I am not that wild, gang-member kid anymore. I am a respected member of my profession and have worked hard to find myself and make changes in my life. I was not there to renew old friendships.

No, I was there to start again. I went to meet some new people who were the same age as I was and who have traveled their own paths for these past fifty years. It was an interesting and strange experience.

I was nervous and excited as Lilly and I walked out the door. We picked up our rental car and drove off to the Shishole Bay Beach Club in Ballard for our big party.

\* \* \*

By a little after eleven o'clock at night, Lilly and I were back in our hotel room. The party had been fun and interesting but it didn't go very late. There were a lot of very old folks there. Those people looked so much older than me! I felt out of place with them until I went to the men's room and looked in the mirror. *Oh my God, I really was one of them!* Although in my mind I think I look a little better than a lot of those old fogies. Still, fifty years is fifty years.

I circulated at the party and tried to meet as many people as I could. John Roger Nowell, a member of our class who had been a deputy city attorney for Seattle until his retirement, said that he had heard of me. I asked him if there were any other lawyers in our class and he pointed out a fellow who he said had gone to Boalt Hall. My God, a Roosevelt graduate had gone to the same law school as me!

I introduced myself and we struck up a conversation. His name was Jack Bernard. He was in an interesting relationship with Marilyn Westerman, a woman he had dated during high school. He and Marilyn had gotten together nine years ago, and were a couple again after all these years. They were a delightful couple and we had a lot in common. We knew several of the same people from Boalt Hall. He had graduated three years after me because he had served in the Marine Corps as a fighter pilot. Instead of practicing law, he became a commercial pilot, so his career path was different than mine. Jack was a popular kid in high school and had a lot of friends who wanted to talk with him that night. In any event, he was very gracious and we struck up a friendship that feels good.

Back in our hotel room, Lilly and talked about the evening. I had gone with her to her fortieth high school reunion, but that was very different. She had been a popular kid and had many friends there. At my reunion I was in a room with a couple of hundred people and literally didn't know anyone nor did anyone know me. But, the get-together satisfied my curiosity.

Actually, it did more than that. It gave me closure. I looked at the picture of that wild eighteen-year-old kid and wondered if it was really me. Would I recognize him today if he walked by me on the street? Am I really the same person? We have the same mother and the same family. We have the same soul inhabiting the same young and old bodies. But it seems like a different life to me. My journey has brought me very far and enabled me to make so many profound life changes.

I have gone from a good little boy to a gang member to a prosecutor. I have gone from a wild hard-drinking fraternity kid to a well-respected trial lawyer. I abused alcohol for twenty-five years and now live in sobriety, and have done so for well over twenty years. I had one bad marriage, a good marriage, and perhaps the most soulfully satisfying relationship that I could ever imagine. I have gone from a poor family background to being better off financially than I could ever have imagined. I spent most of my life struggling with poor male role models and then eventually found not one father, but two. I have been a loser, a winner, a follower, a leader, a lecturer, and a writer. I have gone from being a right wing political ideologue to a socially progressive thinker. I have traveled the path from young to old. I have gone from age eighteen to age sixty-eight in fifty years of a long and interesting life journey.

As Lilly and I reminisced about the reunion and the changes that have taken place in my life, a thought occurred to me. I turned and looked at Lilly.

"I've got an idea!" I exclaimed.

"What's that?" Lilly asked.

"I am going to write a book," I said. "It is going to be a book about my life. I am going to call it *Getting A Winning Verdict In My Personal Life: A Trial Lawyer Finds His Soul.*

"Yes," I added, "That is what I am going to do."

# EPILOGUE

I am standing on a quiet hillside on the foothills of the Wasatch Mountains in southern Ogden, Utah as the sun lights up the lovely fall colors along the mountainside. I can see south towards Salt Lake City and west towards Salt Lake itself. There is a small pine tree a few feet away that will provide shade for those who spend time here. What a peaceful place this is!

There are plots here with a view and shade. That's right. Plots, not lots. I am in the cemetery standing next to the gravesites of four of the most important people in my life. There are four graves lined up next to each other. Buried there are my mother, Marion Anderson Ryan, my sister, Patricia Ryan Johnson, her daughter, Fortune Johnson, and my stepfather, Wayne J. Ryan. They picked out these special plots with a view and shade and each of them spent many hours here until the last of them died. The last was Wayne who died in 2004 at the age of ninety-two.

I don't come here often since it is a long way from California. But when I do, I bring flowers and look down where their bodies are buried. I know this is not where they really are. Only their decaying bodies are here. Their spirits are around me and our souls are in contact. That is especially true of Mom. This place is important. It brings back memories of my immediate family and my long journey as the last survivor.

My mother is proud of me. She wonders how my life has been. She knows I have made mistakes along the way, but she also knows that I am now a well-respected lawyer trying to find my own soul.

So how do I feel? For the most part, I have done quite well. I found my soul mate, have a wonderful family, and my health is great. While I continue to enjoy my work, I spend more time with my grandchildren and frequently travel to interesting places around the world.

So, have I found my soul? As I think back on my life, I have to say that we never "find" our soul. Life is a journey and we continue to grow and develop wisdom. With that wisdom should come a better understanding of who we are, why we are here, and how we are connected to the Universe. So finding my soul is a continuing process.

Have I helped find my soul by telling the story of my interesting and somewhat unusual life? I learned much about myself through this introspective process. The primary theme of this book has to do with my work and being a courtroom lawyer for over forty years. My mission in recent years has been to help other lawyers deal with issues in their personal lives so that they can be better professionals. I hope this book accomplishes that goal.

In a broader sense, I have also written this book to help non-lawyers understand who trial lawyers really are. I have fought for justice throughout my entire career. I have never taken a case I did not believe in. I have fought for the little guy—the average citizen—going up against the biggest, largest, and most powerful entities in our country. There are thousands of lawyers like me who do these same things every day. We are lawyers of conscience. We protect, defend, and fight for our clients against big corporate and government interests. Nothing will deter us from that fight.

My final reflection is as follows: We trial lawyers are often used as scapegoats by the many big interests in this country and their public relations firms. This attack on trial lawyers with so-called tort reform has significantly eroded the rights of the average citizen to obtain justice in this country. That makes me angry! These are my clients. Laws are being proposed and passed every day that continue to limit their right to hold these large interests accountable. We trial lawyers are easy targets. I don't care about that. I know what I do is right and I live by my own conscience. However, it does disturb me that my clients, the people on whose behalf I have fought for over forty years, are losing their rights because of the attacks on my profession.

It is time for a change. This is the information age. People should not be hoodwinked by slick public relations ads, subtle informational campaigns, and marketing efforts by big corporations and others to insulate themselves from responsibility and accountability for their wrongs. People need to understand that there are lawyers who care. Lawyers who do the right thing. Yes, even lawyers who have a soul.

## ACKNOWLEDGMENTS AND AUTHOR'S NOTE

As a long-time courtroom lawyer, I am a better speaker than writer, thus my first book was more work than I expected. Writing my story has taught me a lot. Enlightenment and personal insight have been part of the experience.

The story is mine but the book is a collaboration and team effort of talented publishers, editors, typists, supporters, family, and friends.

The genesis and inspiration for this book belongs to Dr. Ernest Pecci, a well-known psychiatrist and author in his own right. Ernie, as I now call him, is an exceptionally talented therapist and has been my spiritual advisor for many years. He gently encouraged me to write. After my high school reunion in 2005, I felt ready. Ernie immediately offered to assist with his publishing company, Pavior Publishing. Since that time, he and I have worked hand-in-glove in formulating, writing, and publishing this book. His capable and ingenious associate, Robert Sheppie, contributed with technical assistance. Ernie's sister, Marguerite Kelley, was helpful and even typed some of the manuscript.

In the first draft, I laid out the facts like a lawyer but the story lacked drama and didn't read very well. Early on, Ron Kenner helped me with story editing. My wife, Lilly, and Ernie simultaneously recommended an invaluable book, *Your Life as Story: Discovering the "New Autobiography" and Writing Memoir as Literature* by Tristine Rainer. Ms. Rainer teaches autobiography and memoir writing. I do not know her but I highly recommend her book.

By the time I wrote the sixth or seventh draft, I still

needed an editor's help. Jack Russ, then-president of the Mt. Diablo branch of the California Writer's Club, recommended Elisabeth Tuck, who turned out to be just what I needed. She did thorough story and copy edits that added immeasurably to the readability of the book. I owe her a great deal of gratitude for all her hard work. She remained involved and was an objective critic throughout the publication.

I wrote this book the old-fashioned way. I dictated it onto cassette tapes ready for typing. It came out in rough form, which is one of the reasons it needed good editing. Two people were invaluable in translating my rough dictation into a readable manuscript.

First, my thanks go to Althea T. Kippes. Althea is a fine lawyer who has worked with me on a major case. She also teaches writing and once worked as a secretary. She took on the jobs of editing and researching, and even did some of the typing. She gave me continual advice and support, and I very much appreciate her many long hours. Her enthusiasm was invaluable and she deserves great credit for the finished product.

Secondly, there is my long-time secretary, Marilyn Gee-Cartwright. Marilyn did much of the typing and did so with professionalism, efficiency, and without complaint. Her many hours of overtime are much appreciated, as is her friendship and support.

A word of thanks also goes to another first-rate secretary in our office, Nancy Russell, who helped out with some of the typing when Marilyn and Althea were overloaded.

I gave drafts of the book, including a complete galley proof, to many people for comments, advice, and constructive criticism. Many friends were kind enough to read the galley and respond with detailed comments and suggestions. Their input was most valuable in making the book more readable and interesting.

My long-time friend and colleague, Maryanne Murphy, was especially helpful in spending many hours reviewing the early drafts and the final galley. The same is true of my great friend, Ed Caldwell, who has always been there for me. He is one of the unsung heroes of the legal profession and has saved many lives and careers, including my own. My old friend and law partner, Eric Ivary, also gave me some very specific feedback on the book and was supportive as always. My law partners, Steve Cavalli and Steve Brewer, and our office administrator, Jane Gorelick, have all tolerated and supported the many hours of office time that I have spent writing this book.

I have had an overwhelming response from people who have given me testimonials, comments, and endorsements. I have tried to include as many as possible in the review section of the book. Aside from those already mentioned, I am deeply appreciative of and flattered by the wonderful words of the support from Leo Boyle, Arthur Bryant, Dave S. Casey, Jr., Joe Cotchett, Larry Drivon, Jeff Goldberg, Browne Greene, Judge Thelton E. Henderson, Colin King, Stewart L Levine, Peter Perlman, Wesley J. Smith, Fred Sontag, and John Romano, whose spontaneous enthusiasm was especially touching. Colin King's comments were so meaningful and well-written that I have used them on the inside jacket of the book. I also want to thank Will Glennon for his professional support as a friend, publisher, and editor.

Michael (Mike) M. Reyna, the Chief Executive Director of the Consumer Attorneys of California, Jon Haber, the CEO of the American Association for Justice, and Arthur Bryant, the Executive Director of Public Justice, also reviewed the book. Their input is appreciated. All three organizations deserve special credit for the important work they do in bringing about justice in the civil arena everyday in this country.

This is not only a story about me, but a story about the people whose lives touched me and whose lives I have touched. This is true of all of my deceased family, including Wayne, Jack, Pat, Aunt Rose, Aunt Betty, Aunt Vivian, but most of all and always my mother, Marion Anderson Ryan.

Friends and colleagues mentioned in the book are important. I wish I had space to refer to many others who were also significant in my life, but I had to concentrate on the people whose contact was directly involved with the themes of the book.

The clients whose stories I have told are real heroes. I want to especially thank Scott Morris, Dee Kotla, Sherill Smothers, Lana Ambruster, the Adams and the Freitas families, and others mentioned in the book. Unfortunately, I have lost contact with Sandy Staples, but she and the Reno family who were involved in that tragic accident, deserve special credit. Many other clients have had interesting and important cases that have been equally significant in my career; however, there was not space to tell their stories.

This book is dedicated to all the trial lawyers, consumer advocates, and civil rights attorneys who toil day in and day out for justice in this country. It has become an increasingly harder job. Their work is often not appreciated and occasionally vilified or slandered. These champions know who they are and I am proud to call them my brothers and sisters in arms.

Special thanks go to Gene Bambic, who allowed me to tell his story as an example of those few lawyers who get lost along the way.

Last but not least, there is my family. I am fortunate to have an extended family of five wonderful children and seven grandchildren. Although this book emphasizes my career as a trial lawyer, I hope my story will have lasting meaning for all of them.

The last person I want to thank is the most important. I have dedicated this book to her. She has helped change my life and brought me happiness and personal growth in a way that I never imagined possible. She is my soul mate, my life companion, and my wife. She is Lilly.

## BIBLIOGRAPHY

Dyer, Dr. Wayne, *You'll See It When You Believe It: The Way to Your Personal Transformation*, Bookman Press, 1989.

Hendrix, Harville, *Getting the Love You Want: A Guide For Couples*, Harper Perennial; reissue edition, 1990.

Hilton, Hope A., *"Wild Bill" Hickman and the Mormon Frontier*, Signature Books, 1989.

Kübler-Ross, Dr. Elisabeth, M.D., *On Death and Dying*, Scribner; reprint edition, 1997.

Levine, Stephen, *Who Dies? An Investigation of Conscious Living and Conscious Dying*, Gateway; New Ed edition, 2000.

Levine, Steven L., *Getting to Resolution: Turning Conflict Into Collaboration*; Berrett-Koehler Publishers, New Ed edition, 2000.

Levine, Steven L., *The Book of Agreement: 10 Essential Elements for Getting the Results You Want*; Berrett-Koehler Publishers, 1st edition, 2002.

MacLaine, Shirley, *Out On a Limb*, Bantam; reissue edition, 1986.

Nader, Ralph, and Smith, Wesley J., *No Contest: Corporate Lawyers and the Perversion of Justice in America*, Random House, 1998.

O'Donohue, John, *Anam Cara: A Book of Celtic Wisdom*, HarperCollins Canada/Harper Trade, 1998.

Paul, Shale, *The Warrior Within: A Guide To Inner Power*, Delta Group Press, 1983.

Peale, Dr. Norman Vincent, *The Power of Positive Thinking*,

Ballantine Books; reissue edition, 1996.

Pecci, Dr. Ernest F., M.D., *Guidance From Within: You Can Have a Conversation With God*, Pavior Publishing, 2003.

Rainer, Tristine, *Your Life as Story: Discovering the "New Autobiography" and Writing Memoir as Literature*, Tarcher; first trade paperback edition, 1998.

Sells, Benjamin, *The Soul of the Law*, Vega Books, 2002.

Smith, Wesley J., *Commitment to Justice: A History of the Consumer Attorneys of California*, Consumer Attorneys of California, 1999.

Smith, Wesley J., *Fighting For Public Justice: Cases and Trial Lawyers That Made a Difference*, TLPJ Foundation, 2001.

Welwood, John, *Journey of the Heart: The Path of Conscious Love*, Harper Paperbacks; reissue edition, 1996.

Wholey, Dennis, *The Courage to Change: Personal Conversations About Alcoholism with Dennis Wholey*, Warner Books, reissue edition, 1988.

## ASSOCIATIONS

### American Association for Justice (AAJ)
[formerly the Association of Trial Lawyers of America (ATLA)]
1050 31st Street
Washington, D.C.  20007
Telephone: (800) 424-2725 or (202) 965-3500
Website: www.justice.org


### Consumer Attorneys of California (CAOC)
[formerly the California Trial Lawyers Association (CTLA)]
770 L Street, Suite 1200
Sacramento, CA  95814
Telephone: (916) 442-6902
Website: www.caoc.org


### International Alliance of Holistic Lawyers (IAHL)
P.O. Box 371
Milton, DE 19968
Website: www.iahl.org


### Public Justice
[formerly Trial Lawyers for Public Justice (TLPJ)]
*National Headquarters:*

1825 K Street, N.W., Suite 200
Washington, D.C.  20006
Telephone: (202) 797-8600
*West Coast Office:*
555 12th Street, Suite 1620
Oakland, CA  94607
Telephone: (510) 622-8150
Website: www.publicjustice.net


**The Other Bar**
Telephone: (800) 222-0767
Email Assistance: Confidential@OtherBar.Org
Website: www.otherbar.org

## ENDNOTES

[1] The famous Ford Pinto exploding gas tank case came down about a year after my verdict. In that case the gas tank on a very popular model Ford exploded on a low rear-end impact. The case was tried by Mark Robinson, Jr. and made him instantly famous. He later became a good friend of mine. It is also noteworthy that the 1973 General Motors pickup was later found to be defectively and dangerously designed as a result of these gas tanks. This later litigation was no help to my case. However, it is some consolation that my losing this case may have helped other trial lawyers take on General Motors, the largest corporation at that time in the world, and bring them to justice for their failure to design safe vehicles.

[2] My grandmother, Oveda Sturm, was the head of the family. She had the strong pioneering spirit of good Mormon women whose family had come across the Plains. She was a Hickman. Her grandfather, "Wild Bill" Hickman, was the notorious early Mormon who had accompanied Brigham Young across the Plains and was one of his bodyguards. Many Mormon men in that generation didn't raise their families. A man's job was to do the hunting, farming, and protecting. It fell to the women to raise the family.

My grandmother's strong character was proved in a civil case in Oregon in the 1950s. My grandmother only had one son, my Uncle Vincent Anderson, who was two years younger than my mother. Vincent had his own wild streak and had run away from home at the age of fifteen, joined the Navy, and served in World War II. He later married a woman named Anne. However, he always answered to number one: his mother.

It wasn't long before his marriage got into trouble and Vincent began an affair with another woman. My grandmother and Vincent's wife, Anne, never got along. Actually, Anne really hated my grandmother and blamed her for Vincent leaving her and for their subsequent divorce. To say there was bad blood between them is an understatement.

After the divorce proceedings were well under way, Anne retained an attorney and sued my grandmother for alienation of affections. This is an ancient tort involving the intentional and malicious enticing of one spouse to leave the other. Our family went wild over the lawsuit! My grandmother retained an attorney and off they went to trial. Looking back on this case as an experienced lawyer, I could see that my grandmother was a terrible witness. She would have been angry, hostile, and combative. She would have been impossible to control.

This is probably what happened, because when she testified in front of the jury, the jurors found in favor of Anne and convicted my grandmother of alienation of affections. They awarded Anne damages of $5,000, a fairly high sum back then. Fortunately for our family, the case went up on appeal and was reversed. It is one of the few cases in the country dealing with the issue of alienation of affections. See *Anderson v. Sturm*, 209 Or 190, 303 P.2d 509 (1956); Ore. Lexis 265.

[3] Since becoming an adult, I have gone by J. Gary Gwilliam because that is my legal name. It is not meant to be pretentious; it is just one of the side effects of using my middle name as my first name.

[4] I think there was also a woman chosen as a candidate, but in those days, we were not gender sensitive so the award still had the stereotypical male title.

[5] Many of us felt the movie *Animal House* starring John Belushi was patterned after our fraternity.

[6] There is an interesting postscript to our relationship. In 1994, Lilly and I were looking for a house to buy in Contra Costa County. I had a real estate agent who had looked everywhere but couldn't find anything that we liked. I knew that Scott sold real estate, but I thought that he couldn't help us because he didn't handle property in the area we were looking in. His office was in Pleasanton and we were looking in Orinda, which is closer to Oakland. I called Scott to see if he could help us. Scott showed us three houses. The third house was the one we fell in love with and bought. It was the largest sale Scott had ever made, just like his verdict was the largest one that I had ever received at the time. There is something so Karmic about the connection that it is hard to describe.

[7] I remain a Kitaro fan and went to several of his concerts in the late eighties and early nineties. I had the great fortune of meeting

him backstage after a concert in Berkeley, because my then-law partner Jim Chiosso's good friend was their manager. Kitaro was a quiet, slight, and unpretentious man who at the same time exuded a great personal presence and power. I thanked him for making a difference in my life. It was an important and emotional moment for me.

[8] On March 1, 1995, the California Trial Lawyers Association (CTLA) changed its name to the Consumer Attorneys of California (CAOC) as it launched a major public information campaign to turn the spotlight on the anti-consumer goals of the tort reform movement. The campaign showed that the sole purpose of the tort reformers is to allow big business and the insurance industry to avoid responsibility for their acts of corporate crime against individual consumers. However, I will continue to refer to the association as CTLA, the name it had during my involvement.

[9] I wrote Shirley MacLaine a letter about the importance of her book in my life. Lilly and I were fortunate enough to meet her and have dinner together about ten years later at the State of the World Forum that was sponsored by the Gorbachev Foundation. I talked to Ms. MacLaine about my life and how important her book had been, especially in enabling me to find my new relationship with Lilly. She subsequently sent me autographed copies of all of her books and I am still very grateful for her influence in my life.

[10] I have a great picture of Browne turning over the gavel to me. I recently gave him the picture at a special surprise birthday party that was given for him.

[11] This was the settlement allegedly worked out at Frank Fat's restaurant in Sacramento between the trial lawyers and several big corporate interests, with the help of Willie Brown, who was then the Speaker of the California State Assembly.

[12] At the end of 2006, the Association of Trial Lawyers of America (ATLA) changed its name to the American Association for Justice (AAJ.) However, I will continue to refer to it as ATLA, the name it had during my involvement.

[13] I have an audiotape of the eulogy and this is a direct quote.

[14] Anyone who interested in reading the article can contact my office and we will provide you with a copy.

[15] In 2005, the American Bar Association (ABA) interviewed me for an article in their law journal about how lawyers deal with losing cases. The ABA is the largest professional association in the country and The ABA Journal is the flagship magazine of the ABA, with a circulation of over 360,000 lawyers and judges. The ABA Journal published the story in the May 2005 issue. Much to my surprise, they put my picture on the cover of The ABA Journal. This was a rare and unusual honor, and it was all because I had the courage to stick my neck out and talk about what it means to lose a case.

**16** I still have the phone message slip and keep it framed in my office.

**17** As of today, that figure is over fifty percent.

**18** Unfortunately, Lee Sanders died shortly before the publication of this book.

**19** Our law firm handled Kim Norman's case and the trial was scheduled to begin shortly after Dee Kotla was terminated. We were required to settle the case for substantially less than full value because Dee Kotla, our key witness, had been discredited because she had been fired and was under psychiatric care.

**20** Trial Lawyers For Public Justice (TLPJ) and the TLPJ Foundation recently changed its name to Public Justice and the Public Justice Foundation. However, I will continue to refer to it as TLPJ, the name it had during my involvement.

**21** *Cohen v. Brown University* was a precedent-setting Title IX class action lawsuit. TLPJ proved Brown University was guilty of sex discrimination, prevented the University from eliminating successful women's intercollegiate athletic teams, and created new case law that would benefit women athletes and potential athletes nationwide. See *Cohen v. Brown University, 809 F. Supp. 978 (D.R.I. 1992), 991 F.2d 888 (1st Cir. 1993), 879 F.Supp. 185 (D.R.I. 1995), 101 F.3d 155 (1st Cir. 1996), cert denied, 520 U.S. 1186 (1997).*

[22] *"Profiles in Power: The One Hundred Most Influential Lawyers in America," The National Law Journal, June 19, 2006.*

# Index

## A

A.A. (Alcoholics Anonymous)
69, 146, 207, 237
AAJ (American Association for
Justice) 333, 339
ABA, (American Bar Association)
339
ABOTA, (American Board of Trial
Advocates) 121
Academy Awards 156, 270
Adams, Jeanette 272
Adams, Patrick 272, 273
Adams, Stewart C. 97
Adams v. CSAA 270
Africa 225
Alameda County 115, 205, 270
Albuquerque, New Mexico 274
Alcatraz Avenue 113
Alcoholics Anonymous 36, 59, 146
Alexander, Mary E. 250
Alice Doesn't Live Here Anymore 84
All things happen for a reason 10,
166, 289, 290, 304, 310, 316
Ambruster, Lana 264, 268, 329
American Association for Justice
6, 8, 10, 175, 329, 333, 339
American Bar Association 339
American Board of Trial Advocates
121
Anam Cara: A Book Of Celtic
Wisdom 188
Anderson, Anne (wife of Vincent) 336
Anderson, Marion 30
Anderson, Marion (Ryan) 323

Anderson, Vincent 32, 291, 335
Anderson v. Sturm 336
Animal House 337
Ashland, Oregon 274, 276
Ask and you shall receive 165
Association of Trial Law-
yers of America
169, 175, 251, 333, 339
ATLA 169, 274, 275, 284, 285,
286, 333, 339
Atlanta, Georgia 276
Atlantic Monthly 82
Aunt Betty 185, 329
Aunt Rose 185, 329
Aurora Boulevard 48
Australia 225
Avenging Angel 30
Azusa, California 60

## B

Baby Jackson 100, 102
Baldwin Park, California 62
Ballard, Washington 320
Bambic 237, 238, 239, 240, 330
Bambic, Gene
237, 238, 239, 240, 330
Bare ass 73
Baron, Fred 274
Barry Goldwater 98
Bates Advertising Agency 130
Bay Area 110, 111, 113, 241
Benjamin Sells 235
Bennies 49, 54
Benvenue Avenue 113
Berkeley 89, 92, 97, 113, 152,
157, 212, 338
Bernard, Jack 320
Bernard Maybeck 113

"Big Fella" Jones 80
"Big Jay" McNeeley 51
Bill Haley & His Comets 51
Billy Eckstein 76
Biltmore Hotel 177
Black Panther 114
Black, Terri 67
Blue, Lisa 274
Boalt Hall 89, 95, 320, 321
Booger 73
Bowman, Richard A, "Dick" 306
Boyle, Leo 5, 284, 285, 328
Brayton, Al 274
Breathe from your belly 314
Brewer, Robin E. 175, 178
Brewer, Steve
        175, 180, 187, 279, 328
Brigham City 119
Brigham Young 29, 30, 335
British Columbia 227
Brown, Michael 120, 121, 126
Brown University 269, 340
Bryant, Arthur 275, 328, 329

## C

Cadillac 59, 60
Caldwell, Edwin Train 5, 143,
        207, 233, 235, 237, 239,
        246, 328
California Bar Exam 208
California Casualty Insurance Com-
        pany 264
California State Assembly 339
California State Automobile Associa-
        tion 270
California Supreme Court 96, 273
California Trial Lawyers Association
        13, 162, 333, 338

Campbell, Joe 120, 126, 127, 128
Canadian Rockies 227
CAOC 162, 333, 338
Cartwright, Sr, Robert (Bob) 250
Casey, Jr., David S.
        6, 175, 179, 328
Catnip 50, 318
Cavalli, Steve 127, 149, 152,
        153, 279, 280, 328
Central Avenue 77
Chevrolet 52
Chicago 89, 169, 222, 274
Chief trial deputy 111
Child abuse 100, 102, 112
China Pheasant 51, 52
Chiosso, Jim & Judy 127, 128,
        272, 279, 280, 289, 338
Christmas 128, 288
Chubby Checker 51
Citrus Junior College
        60, 68, 69, 72, 146, 292
Claremont Hotel 157
Clark Hall 75
Cohen v. Brown University 340
Coit, Lee 199, 201
Colin Kelly Junior High School 41
Colorado 196, 287
Commitment Ceremony 20, 221
Condon Grade School 38
Consumer Attorneys of California
        6, 7, 162, 285, 329, 332,
        333, 338
Contra Costa County 307, 337
Cook County Circuit Court 169
Cornell, Liz 119
Cornell, Roger 282
Cornell, Roger 282
Corvette 305, 306

343

Cotchett, Joseph W. Jr. 6, 328
Country Club Malt Liquor 67
Courage to Change 146, 332
Covina 62
Critchfield, Burke M. 143
CSAA 270, 271
CTLA, (California Trial Lawyers As-
    sociation) 162, 168,
    174, 175, 180, 186, 198,
    205, 231, 237, 238, 240,
    250, 333, 338
Curry, Richard L. 169

**D**

Dalkon Shield 170
Dallas Cowboys 129
Dallas, Texas 274
Daughters of the American Revolu-
    tion 92
Deam, Woodruff "Woody" 99
Dean Prosser 95
Deitzler, Harry 274
Demerol 56
Dempsey, Thomas M. 274
Department of Energy 267
Digardi, Ed
    111, 116, 126, 127, 156
Do not react 315
Drivon, Larry E.
    6, 175, 179, 240, 328
Drivon, Laurence "Larry"
    6, 175, 179, 240, 328
Duck embryo 109, 110
Ducktail 49, 53, 67
Dunes 146, 194, 200
Dyer, Wayne, PhD 164, 331

**E**

"Earth Angel (Will You Be Mine)" 51
East Bay 112
East Oakland 114, 305
Egypt 193, 215
Elegant Farmer 135
Elvis Presley 50, 76
Esquina, Leonard "Lenny" 175, 178
Eugene, Oregon 31, 32, 36, 38,
    39, 40, 41, 44, 61

**F**

Fats Domino 51
Fighting For Public Justice 270, 332
Fiji 225
Finer Filter Products 149
First Street, Seattle Washington 49
Foote 276
Foote, Jeff 276
Foothill Boulevard, Glendora,CA 60
Ford Phaeton 41
Ford Pinto 170, 335
Fort Jones 292
Frankfurt, Germany 138
Fraternity 14, 28, 72, 73, 75, 76,
    77, 82, 88, 97, 121, 130,
    140, 141, 243, 246, 253,
    274, 321, 337
Frayne, Bobbie 206
Freitas, Ada 308, 329
Freitas, Ray 309, 329
Freitas, Sarah 308
Freud 34
Fuller Brush Company 39
Furry 84

# G

Gee-Cartwright, Marilyn  327
Gene Bambic
    237, 238, 239, 240, 330
Gene Morgan  116, 126
General Motors  25, 26, 27, 71,
    106, 117, 122, 132, 148,
    158, 186, 187, 306, 307,
    335
Georgia Laflin  89
Gerson Smoger  274
Getting the Love You Want: A Guide
    For Couples  200, 331
Gibbs, Bill
116, 120, 126, 128, 140, 143
GI Bill  68
Glacier National Park  227
Glendora, California
    59, 60, 62, 64, 292
GM  27
God  14, 141, 165, 202,
    213, 231, 256, 290, 303,
    304, 320, 332
Goldberg, Jeffery (Jeff)
    7, 274, 277, 328
Golden Gloves  83
Golden State Warriors  135
Good driver initiative  174
Good Earth Restaurant  215
Gorbachev Foundation  338
Gordon, Marilyn  193, 194, 195
Gorelick  328
Gorelick, Jane  328
"Grab", see Dr. Steven Kobayashi  80
Greene, Browne  7, 154, 162, 163,
    168, 169, 172, 179, 262,
    263, 328
Gwilliam, Helen (Stepmother)
    59, 60, 69, 292

GWILLIAM & IVARY  20, 126
Gwilliam, Ivary, Chiosso, Cavalli &
    Brewer  279
Gwilliam, John "Jack" (Father)
    30, 31, 32, 36, 37, 38, 59,
    69, 90, 126, 146, 291,
    292 - 298, 301, 329
Gwilliam, Lillly  3, 208, 209, 210,
    211- 232, 244, 245, 265,
    279, 282, 285, 286, 289,
    291- 295, 318, 320, 321,
    322, 326, 330, 337, 338
Gwilliam, Liz  118, 130, 133,
    134, 136-139,
    141-144,
    159, 185, 192, 194, 196,
    197, 198, 199, 200, 202,
    204, 205, 207, 220, 223,
    281, 282, 283, 289, 292

# H

Haber, Jon  8, 329
Habiby, Armand  97
Harper, James, MD  81, 331, 332
Harvard University  89
Harvey Mudd College  72
Hatchwell, Michael  198, 199
Hawaii
    84, 120, 145, 221, 224, 301
Hayward Field  39
Heatherly, Kay  214
Hegenberger Road  143
Henderson, Judge Thelton E.  8, 328
Heroin  49, 56
Herzog, Ian (Buddy)  179, 205, 206
Highway 101  107
Hinton, Peter  162
Hobler  246
Holistic Lawyer  260

Holocaust 101
Horn 46, 52, 57
Horsemeat 75
House of Un-American Activities
    Committee 97
Huey Newton 114
"Humper", see Dr. Harper 81

**I**

"I Can't Help Myself (Sugar Pie
    Honey Bunch)" 135
I. Magnin 128
International Alliance of Holistic
    Lawyers 261, 333
Intervention
    15, 144, 146, 207, 233, 283
"In The Midnight Hour" 135
Irwindale, California 62
Ivary, Eric 9, 126, 127, 128, 216,
    245, 279, 328

**J**

Jack London Square 135
Jackson, Karen 100, 101, 102
Janis Joplin 83
Japan 159
Jasper, British Columbia 227
Jeanette Adams v. City of Fremont
    272
jelly jacket 77
Jerry Lee Lewis 51
Joaquin Miller Road, Oakland 136
John Belushi 337
Johnny Cash 83, 84
Johnson, Fortune 323
John Wayne 206
Jones, Ward "Big Fella" 73, 80, 343

Journey of The Heart: The Path of
    Conscious Love 213

**K**

Kaiser Foundation Hospital 308
Kappa Delta 140, 246
Karma 165, 221
KD
    73, 80, 81, 82, 84, 88, 89, 274
Kelley, Marguerite 326
Kelly Employment Services 118
Kelly Girl 118
King, Colin 328
King Henry VI, Part II 173
Kippes, Althea T. 327
Kitaro 159, 167, 196, 337, 338
Kline, Justice Anthony J. 273
Kobayashi, Steven, MD 80
Korean War Vets 68
Kotla, Dee
    266, 268, 309, 329, 340
Kris Kristofferson 82
"Kritter," 82
Kübler-Ross, Elisabeth, MD
    288, 331

**L**

Lafayette, California 226
Laflin 89
Laflin, Georgia 89
Laguna Nigel, California 74
Lake Merritt 203, 211, 224
Lake Tahoe 126, 227, 231, 239
Las Vegas, Nevada 140
Lawrence, Bruce
    138, 223, 266, 267
Lawrence Livermore Lab 266, 267

Leftwing liberals 98
Let go of fear 315
Levine, Harvey 179
Levine, Steve 288, 331
Levine, Stewart 9, 328
Lewis, Barbara 51, 83, 199, 201
Lexington, Kentucky 274
"Light My Fire" 135
Listen carefully 316
Live in the present 165, 195
Liz 120
London 135, 295, 296
Los Angeles, California 46, 59, 62,
    99, 104, 107, 129, 140, 154,
    162, 177, 178, 208, 262, 274
Luau Mai Tai 74
Lynds, Tony "Furry" 84

# M

MacLaine, Shirley 164, 331, 338
Maintain concentration 315
MAN MOST LIKELY TO SUCCEED
    59
Man's Award 75, 76
Marijuana 49, 50, 140, 287
Marion 30, 323, 329
Maui 224
Mayan 196
Maybeck, Bernard 113
McCabe, Michael "Mike" 246
McGeorge School of Law 241
McNichols, Jr, Stephen (Steve) "Nip-
    per" 84, 246
"Me and Bobby McGee." 83
Mercedes 350SL 136
Mexico 50, 196, 274
Mickle, Kay 96
Mills, Peter 168

Mitnick, Mordechai 189, 247
Montclair, California 77
Monterey Bay 146
Montgomery, James 81
Morgan 111, 116, 126
Morgan, Gene 111, 116, 126
Morris, Scott 149, 155, 156,
    157, 158, 284, 304, 329
Mount Baldy 74
Mt. Fuji 159
Murphy, Maryanne 9, 328

# N

Napkin settlement 172
Nashville, Tennessee 83
Newark, California 115
New York 222, 223, 224, 284
New Zealand 225
Nichols, Jesse 111, 112, 116,
    118, 126, 157, 245
Nichols, Williams, Morgan & Di-
    gardi 111
Nipper (dog) 64
Nipper, Stephen (Steve) "Nipper",
    Jr. 84
Norman, Kim 266, 340
Norman Vincent Peale 45, 184
North Carolina 274
Northern California
112, 222, 270, 271, 282, 293
Norton Hall 72

# O

Oakland Raiders 123, 141
Oakland Tribune 305
O'Donohue, John 188, 331
Oedipus complex 34, 299

Ogden, Utah 29, 30, 31, 32, 37, 99, 119, 139, 181, 299, 323
"Oh, Pretty Woman" 226
On Death and Dying 288, 331
Order of the Coif 96
Oregon 31, 32, 36, 39, 227, 274, 276, 335
Oregon Trial Lawyers Association 276
Orens, Nobby 77, 81
Orinda, California 337
Out on a Limb 164
Oxford University 83

**P**

Pachucos 46
Paul, Gary M. 179
Paul, Shale 196
Pecci, Ernest, MD 16, 326, 332
Perlman, Peter 10, 274, 328
Perry Mason 170
Pete Wilson 97
Phalen (Phelan), Lilly 209
Phelan, Liz 224
Phi Beta Kappa 95
Phi Delta Phi 97
Pingel, Steve 207, 209
Pinole, California 305
Pleasanton, California 126
Pleasanton Fire Department 115
Plymouth 47
Pomona College 12, 72, 73, 77, 89, 140, 246, 274
Power of Positive Thinking 45, 184, 331
Proposition 51 161, 163, 168, 172, 179
Proposition 103 174, 179

Proposition 106 172, 173, 177, 178
Public Justice 7, 10, 269, 270, 3 29, 332, 333, 340

**Q**

Quadruplets 105

**R**

Rabies 19, 107
Ralph Nader 11, 174
Randick, Robert (Bob) "Crab" 84
Rankin, Rich 203
Rastus, see Dr. Robert White 73, 80
Regnier, Richard (Dick) 97, 99
Reibe, Debbie 180, 191
Remain relaxed 314
Remcho, Joe 172
Republicans 92, 97
Reyna, Michael M. 10, 329
Rhodes Scholar 83
Robinson, Mark 335
Robinson, Sandra 274
"Rock Around the Clock." 51
Roger Staubach 129
Rolaids 128, 129
Romano, John F. 11, 328
Ronald Reagan 98
Roosevelt High School 45, 50, 86, 318
Rosemead Nursery 62
Rosenfield, Harvey J. 174
Ross, James Montgomery "Turkey" 73, 77, 78, 79, 81, 140, 141
Roth, Danny 52
Round Hill Country Club 226

Roy Orbison 226
Russell, Nancy 327
Ryan, Gary 36, 38
Ryan, Jack 329
Ryan, Marion Anderson (Mother)
    28 -36, 45, 47, 54, 56, 58,
    59, 69, 70, 86, 130, 139,
    140, 157, 181-191, 195,
    218, 288, 289, 296, 297,
    323, 329
Ryan, Patricia Johnson 323
Ryan, Wayne J. (Stepfather) 32- 40,
    45, 55, 56, 126, 157, 181,
    183, 185, 287, 291, 294, 2
    96, 297, 298, 299, 300,
    301, 323, 329, 331

## S

Sacramento, California
    168, 171, 241, 333, 339
Sacramento County Superior Court
    171
Saint Vitus Dance 110
Saladoff, Susan 274
Sally Rand 64
Salt Lake City 323
Sanders, Lee 246, 340
San Francisco Bay Area 110, 111
San Jose, California 265
San Luis Obispo 223
Santa Clara County Superior Court
    265
Sarah Lawrence College 223
Scottsdale, Arizona 181, 184
Screen Actors Guild 130
Sea Ranch 126
Seattle, Washington 44, 45, 46,
    50, 51, 53, 57, 59, 60,
    69, 86, 92, 223, 274, 318, 320

Semansky, Michael P. 246
September 11, 2001 283, 284
Shakespeare 173
Sheppie, Robert (Edward) 326
Shishole Bay Beach Club 320
S. Hobler 246
Simons, Rick 175, 179
Skyline High School 194
Smith, Clyde 39
Smith, Wesley J.
    11, 270, 328, 331, 332
Smith, William (Bill) 246
Smoger 274
Smoger, Gerson 274
Smothers, Sherill 305, 329
Snead, Bill 274
Sontag, Fred 12, 88, 243, 328
Sontag, Fred 88, 243, 328
South America 225
Southern California 59, 61, 62,
    76, 93, 176, 198, 199, 222
Spain 200
S.P.C.A. [Society of Prevention of
    Cruelty to Animals] 108
S.S. Monterey 120
Stanford University 76
Stanley Home Products
    39, 86, 183, 185
Stanley parties 54, 86
Staples, Sandy 26, 329
Staples vs General Motors
    71, 106, 307
State of the World Forum 338
Stay centered 314, 315
Stritmatter, Paul L. 274, 275, 277
Stuart, Dr. Susan 198, 213, 218
Sturm, Oveda 59, 93, 335, 336
"Sunday Morning Coming Down."
    83

Supreme Court of Palestine 97
Switchblade 49, 53

**T**

Taber. Jacqueline 205
Tattoo 46, 47, 53, 60, 70
Thanksgiving
        210, 211, 215, 224, 301
The ABA Journal 339
"The Art of Losing" 191
The Beach Boys 76
The Coasters 51
The Doors 135
The Drifters 51
The Four Tops 135
Theodore Roosevelt 188
The Other Bar 5, 233, 334
The Penguins 51
The Platters 51
There are no coincidences 166
The Righteous Brothers 226
The Scripps Research Institute 282
The Soul of the Law 235, 332
The Warrior Within: A Guide to In-
        ner Power 196
Title IX 269, 340
TLPJ 269, 270, 272, 273, 274,
        275, 276, 278, 287, 332,
        333, 340
TLPJ Foundation
        275, 287, 332, 340
Tort reform 13, 117, 161, 163,
        257, 278, 325, 338
Trattler, Larry 287
Traveler's Insurance Company 127
"Trial Lawyer of the Year" 270
Trial Lawyers for Public Justice
        269, 333

Trial Lawyers for Public Justice
        (TLPJ) 269, 333
Trial Lawyers That Care 285, 286
Tuck, Elizabeth 327
Tupperware 39
Turks 46, 49, 55, 56, 73, 80
Tyler Medical Clinic 104

**U**

U.C.L.A 104, 107
"Unchained Melody" 226
Uncle Vincent 185, 335
United States Military Academy at
        West Point 83
United States Supreme Court 307
Universe 148, 149, 164, 165, 190,
        194, 195, 204, 208, 216,
        256, 304, 313, 316, 324
University of California
        89, 104, 151, 267
University of California at Berkeley
        89, 151
University of California at Los Ange-
        les 104
University of Chicago 89
University of Oregon 39
University of the Pacific 241

**V**

Ventura, California 99, 100, 105,
        106, 110, 111, 112, 113, 140
Ventura County
        99, 100, 105, 111, 112
Ventura County District Attorney's
        Office 99
Vince Lombardi 188

**W**